Psychopathologies of the Living

Psychopathologies of the Living makes the work of the French psychoanalyst Pierre Fédida (1934–2002) available in English for the first time.

Patrick ffrench and Nigel Saint present key essays selected from Fédida's extensive œuvre. The book directs attention to two salient dimensions of Fédida's writing: his attention to the pathologies of the body, considered as both a psychic and somatic entity, and his insistence on the relevance of psychoanalytic thought to the sciences of life. The chapters included in this collection detail Fédida's creative use of aesthetic sources in his psychoanalytic work, his distinctive and creative manipulation and revision of central psychoanalytic concepts and his precise attention to the texts of Freud, Ferenczi and Winnicott, among others. This selection of Fédida's essays also shows his avoidance of thematisation or explicit theorisation; for Fédida the *theory* of psychoanalysis must arise out of the specific interplay of language and the 'space of the session'.

Psychopathologies of the Living will be of great interest to psychoanalysts in practice and in training and to academics and scholars of philosophy, aesthetics and literary studies.

Patrick ffrench is Professor of French at King's College London where he teaches 20th-century French literature, philosophy and cinema, critical theory and psychoanalysis.

Nigel Saint is Associate Professor of French at the University of Leeds, where he teaches literature, culture and critical theory, and works on contemporary artists and art theory.

The International Psychoanalytical Association Psychoanalytic Ideas and Applications Series

Series Editor: Silvia Flechner

IPA Publications Committee
Natacha Delgado, Nergis Güleç, Thomas Marcacci, Carlos Moguillansky,
Rafael Mondrzak, Angela M. Vuotto, Gabriela Legorreta (consultant)

Recent titles in the Series include

The Freudian Matrix of André Green
Towards a Psychoanalysis for the 21st Century
Edited by Howard B. Levine

Desire, Pain and Thought
Primal Masochism and Psychoanalytic Theory
Marilia Aisenstein

Trauma and Pain Without a Subject
Disruptive Marks in the Psyche, Resignified
Juan-Eduardo Tesone

Outsider Art and Psychoanalytic Psychiatry
The 'Nativity of Fools' at the Cogoleto Psychiatric Hospital
Cosimo Schinaia

The Astonishing Adolescent Upheaval in Psychoanalysis
Edited by Roosevelt Cassorla and Silvia Flechner

Psychoanalytic Studies of Change
An Integrative Perspective
Siri Erika Gullestad, Erik Stänicke & Marianne Leuzinger-Bohleber

Psychopathologies of the Living
Selected Essays of Pierre Fédida
Edited by Patrick ffrench and Nigel Saint

Psychopathologies of the Living

Selected Essays of Pierre Fédida

Edited by
Patrick ffrench and Nigel Saint

Routledge
Taylor & Francis Group

LONDON AND NEW YORK

Designed cover image: Pascal Convert, *Crystallised Book, Fragment of a Library*, 2015. Crystallisation of lost book, optic glass, in-8, OCAT collection, Beijing. Photo ©Pascal Convert.

First published 2025
by Routledge
4 Park Square, Milton Park, Abingdon, Oxon OX14 4RN

and by Routledge
605 Third Avenue, New York, NY 10158

Routledge is an imprint of the Taylor & Francis Group, an informa business

Pierre Fédida, 'Le Site de l'étranger' in Le Site de l'étranger, pp. 53–69 © Presses Universitaires de France/Humensis, 2009

Pierre Fédida, 'L'Interlocuteur' in Le Site de l'étranger, pp. 121–86 © Presses Universitaires de France/Humensis, 2009

Pierre Fédida, 'La Régression' in Le Site de l'étranger, pp. 221–44 © Presses Universitaires de France/Humensis, 2009

Pierre Fédida, 'Le Souffle indistinct de l'image' in Le Site de l'étranger, pp. 187–220 © Presses Universitaires de France/Humensis, 2009

Pierre Fédida, 'Restes diurnes. Restes de vie' in Crise et contre-transfert, pp. 45–66 © Presses Universitaires de France/Humensis, 2009

Pierre Fédida, 'Par où commence le corps humain?' in Par où commence le corps humain. Retour sur la régression, pp. 29–43 © Presses Universitaires de France/Humensis, 2000, 2015

Pierre Fédida, 'Du primitif' in Par où commence le corps humain. Retour sur la régression, pp. 45–60 © Presses Universitaires de France/Humensis, 2000, 2015

British Library Cataloguing-in-Publication Data
A catalogue record for this book is available from the British Library

ISBN: 978-1-032-63759-4 (hbk)
ISBN: 978-1-032-63758-7 (pbk)
ISBN: 978-1-032-63760-0 (ebk)

DOI: 10.4324/9781032637600

Typeset in Palatino
by Taylor & Francis Books

Contents

Acknowledgements

The editors would like to thank Anne-Marie Smith-Di Biasio and Timothy Mathews for their translations of 'Day's Residues, Life's Residues' and 'On the Primitive' respectively, as well as for their advice about other aspects of these translations. Thank you to Pascal Convert for generously providing the artwork for the cover image. We would also like to thank Naomi Segal and Nicola Luckhurst, who provided expert and decisive commentary on some of the essays. Tom Derose at the Freud Museum London was instrumental in the early genesis of the project by hosting the first part of the 'Situating/Translating Pierre Fédida' symposium in June 2022. The second part of that event was supported by funding from King's College London and the School of Languages, Cultures and Societies at the University of Leeds. We would also like to thank the participants in that symposium, Monique David-Ménard, Anne-Marie Smith-Di Biasio, Ana Minozzo, François Villa, Steven Jaron and Dany Nobus and, last but by no means least, Mareike Wolf-Fédida, whose generous support and enthusiasm have sustained this endeavour. Matt ffytche's interest in our project led to the translation of a separate essay, with commentaries from Raluca Soreanu and Dany Nobus, in *Psychoanalysis and History* 25: 1 (April 2023). Thank you as well to Silvia Flechner and Rhoda Bawdekar of the International Psychoanalytical Association and to Nick Craggs, Susannah Frearson, Saloni Singhania and Patricia Teasdale of the Routledge team for all of their support. Patrick ffrench would like to thank all of his colleagues and interlocutors at King's College London's Department of Languages, Literatures and Cultures, as well as Tom Baldwin, Céline Lefève, Roger Lippin, Sinan Richards, Andrea Romaní Lopez, Céline Surprenant, Neil Vickers and François Villa. Nigel Saint thanks the British Academy for a Small Research Grant that funded a visit to the Bibliothèque nationale de France in Paris, as well as colleagues and friends in Leeds and beyond: Adrienn Almásy-Martin, Marie-Claire Barnet, Terry Bradford, Martine Convert, Dirk Dehouk, Georges Didi-Huberman, Helen Finch, Stephen Grosz, Sameh Hanna, Richard Hibbitt, Lucien Massaert, Richard Parkinson, Elizabeth Pender, Andy Stafford, Emma Wagstaff and Magdalena Zolkos.

Series Editor's Foreword

The Publications Committee of the International Psychoanalytical Association continues with the present volume in the series 'Psychoanalytic Ideas and Applications'.

The aim of the series is to focus on the scientific production of significant authors whose works are outstanding contributions to the development of the psychoanalytic fields and to set out relevant ideas and themes generated during the history of psychoanalysis, that deserve to be known and discussed by psychoanalysts.

The Publications Committee's goal is to share these ideas with the psychoanalytic community and with professionals in other related disciplines, to expand their knowledge and generate a productive interchange between the text and the reader.

The IPA Publications Committee is honoured to publish *Psychopathologies of the Living: Selected Essays of Pierre Fédida*, edited and translated by Patrick ffrench and Nigel Saint, with Anne-Marie Smith-Di Biasio and Timothy Mathews.

This volume makes available to an anglophone readership – for the first time – the work of the French psychoanalyst Pierre Fédida (1934–2002), through translations of key essays selected from Fédida's extensive œuvre.

The editors of this valuable effort visualise this as a first major step in the long-overdue dissemination of Fédida's important work. They seek to highlight two prominent dimensions of Fédida's writing; his attention to the pathologies of the body, considered as both a psychic and somatic entity, and his insistence on the relevance of psychoanalytic thought to the sciences of life.

It is from its basis in phenomenology and psychopathology that Fédida's work includes substantial attention to the pathologies of the body, to the somatic; his grounding in phenomenological psychopathology and clinical practice makes Fédida's work amongst the most consequential investigations of psychoanalysis as a theory and practice within the human and life sciences.

Taking up the words of the editors, Fédida's influence on subsequent generations of psychoanalysts cannot be underestimated. He had a founding role in the establishment of psychoanalysis as a university discipline and was a gifted and generous teacher and interlocutor. The mobility and generosity of his thought also enabled him to move between the French and British schools; like others of his generation, but perhaps to an even greater extent, his writing draws in references to and commentary on Winnicott, Klein, Searles, as well as Freud, Lacan, Ferenczi and many others.

The editors' selection from Fédida's writing ranges widely across his work and aims to introduce readers to the most distinctive elements of his thought, while also enabling in-depth analyses of specific concepts and instances. Just as they suggest, Fédida's writing demands much of his readers, but the work is rewarding, through the gains it affords not only in terms of knowledge and insight, but also in terms of awareness of the contingencies of expression and the corresponding importance of a precise use of language.

I agree with the editors who propose that this is a challenge for its translators, as are Fédida's sophisticated and wide references across multiple disciplines and his meticulous attention to the letter of Freud's texts, as well as to the contingencies of specific cases.

This impressive work carried out by these distinguished colleagues allows us to learn more about an author who has undoubtedly left an indelible mark in relation to his contributions to psychoanalysis and the understanding of the human being. These invaluable contributions are a gift to the psychoanalytic community and to a more general readership.

Silvia Flechner
Series Editor
Chair, IPA Publications Committee

Introduction

Patrick ffrench and Nigel Saint

The purpose of this volume is to introduce the work of the French psychoanalyst Pierre Fédida (1934–2002) to a broad Anglophone readership for the first time. The venture is overdue. Despite sporadic instances principally attributable to the efforts of Anne-Marie Smith Di-Biasio, who has herself contributed to this volume, and Michael Stone-Richards, Fédida's work has not enjoyed the same degree of attention in the Anglophone world as other French psychoanalysts of his generation, such as André Green, Jean Laplanche or Didier Anzieu, and the translation of his work into English is belated.[1] We believe that the reasons for this are entirely contingent and that this selection of his essays will remedy the situation, leading, we hope, to greater currency for Fédida's work and to further translations.

Readers acquainted with the work of Jacques Lacan, Green, Anzieu, Laplanche, Jean-Bertrand Pontalis or Julia Kristeva will be familiar with the idiom of French psychoanalytic writing of the late 20th and early 21st centuries, which features a high degree of rhetorical reflexivity, draws heavily on the Continental tradition in philosophy, moves fluidly between theoretical reflection and case studies, and tends towards polemics. It also often features close attention to the texts of Freud, either in their original German or in the various available translations into French, along with regular recourse to French and European literary and aesthetic history. Fédida's writing is no exception to all of these characteristics. If it may be differentiated from that of Lacan through the absence of the latter's idiosyncratic terminological codifications (*Symbolic, Imaginary, Real, objet a*, etc), it shares the same sense of a derivation from seminars; many of Fédida's published works draw on his seminars at the University of Paris VII, where he worked for the larger part of his career and where, in 1987, he founded the Laboratory of Psychoanalysis and Psychopathology.

While Lacan's 'return to Freud' is mediated through structuralist linguistics and Alexandre Kojève's reading of Hegel, among other factors, Fédida may be said to stick closer to the matter of Freud's texts, while drawing out the connections to other points of reference in philosophy, most notably to the phenomenological tradition in which he trained and

DOI: 10.4324/9781032637600-1

to the discipline and practice of psychopathology – the work of Ludwig Binswanger in particular –, as we will see further on in this Introduction. The attention to the letter of Freud's texts and the commentary upon them, often accompanied by a keen attention to issues of translation from the German, the dynamics of Fédida's discussion of polemical questions, or issues of doctrine, within psychoanalytic theory and practice (around transference and countertransference in particular – see Chapter 2, 'The Interlocutor' in this volume), and the recourse to the history of philosophy from Heraclitus to Deleuze through Plato, Aristotle and Husserl and Heidegger, as well as the recurrent parallels with and lessons on poetry and art, all make Fédida's texts a challenge, but also a pleasure, to translate. These factors, as we have said, will be familiar to those acquainted with the idiom of post-war French psychoanalytic writing.

Readers more comfortable with the language of the post-WWII schools of British psychoanalysis will also find much that is familiar, since Fédida was a keen reader of Melanie Klein, Donald Winnicott, Harold Searles, Masud Khan, John Forrester and other significant figures in the diverse psychoanalytic contexts of post-war Britain. While his work in no way sits easily within the field of object-relations, Fédida is extremely attentive to the dynamics of the object and, with the notion of the *objeu*,[2] proposes his own distinctive entry into that terrain in the context of the fraught and already-mentioned issues of transference and countertransference, and to the experiential elements of the clinical session – gesture, posture, air, breath, absence, speech, interval – in ways which we consider to be potentially refreshing and distinct from the excesses in theory of which the French are often accused, and for which they are sometimes caricatured.

Fédida's written work is substantial. The *Œuvres complètes*, published by MJW Fédition, now amount to 11 volumes, and there are more to come. Proceeding chronologically, volume 11 covers the years 1996–1998. In addition to the independent essays collected in these volumes, Fédida published seven single-authored books in his lifetime. We list them in the bibliography and here, with our provisional propositions for their translation: *Le Concept et la violence* [Concept and Violence] (1977), *Corps du vide et espace de séance* [The Body of Emptiness and the Space of the Session] (1977); *L'Absence* [Absence] (1978), *Crise et contre-transfert* [Crisis and Countertransference] (1992), *Le Site de l'étranger* [The Site of the Stranger] (1995), *Par où commence le corps humain: retour sur la régression* [Where the Human Body Begins: Reconsidering Regression] (2000) and *Des Bienfaits de la dépression: Éloge de la psychothérapie* [On the Merits of Depression: In Praise of Psychotherapy] (2001). A posthumous volume, *Humain/déshumain* [Human/Unhuman] (2007) comprises the text of Fédida's final seminar of 2001–2002, alongside critical reflections from several interlocutors and participants in the seminar. Each of these books, save for the final seminar volume, includes articles revised from material previously published in journals – a typical recourse in French psychoanalysis – as well as new essays written specifically for the book. While this suggests a degree of contingency, the titles of the volumes do function to highlight the unity of each volume, which we might here signal with a series of keywords that themselves give a good sense of the insistence across Fédida's work of certain concepts and affects: *violence; body; absence; countertransference; strangeness; depression; regression*. We must add to this bibliography, however, the numerous articles not collected in the books (included in the *Œuvres complètes*), among them regular contributions to the *Nouvelle revue de psychanalyse* which, under the direction of its general editor Jean-Bertrand Pontalis, was a significant vector of intersection between the French and the British schools and traditions in psychoanalysis.

Fédida's institutional activity was a substantial element of his life and work. After completing analysis with Georges Favez, in 1969 he participated in the creation of the Department of Clinical Human Sciences (*Sciences humaines cliniques*) at the University of Paris VII alongside Jean Laplanche, having previously been recruited by Juliette Favez-Boutonnier to a University post in psychoanalytic psychology at the Sorbonne (Paris IV). He was a member of the Association psychoanalytique de Paris and from 1988–1990 its President, and thus was also a member of the International Psychoanalytical Association. He was the co-founder and co-editor, with the philosopher Dominique Lecourt, of the series 'Forum Diderot' at the Presses Universitaires de France, which published the proceedings of interdisciplinary discussions on questions relating to the human in all its dimensions (e.g. *Qu'est-ce qui guérit dans la psychanalyse?* [What is that heals in psychoanalysis?], *La Dépression est-elle passée de mode?* [Is Depression now unfashionable?], *La Fin de la vie, qui en décide?* [Who decides on the end of life?]).[3] In 1993 he founded the Centre d'études du vivant, an interdisciplinary research centre which remains active today, and whose title may be translated as Centre for Studies of the Living.[4] With Daniel Widlöcher, he also founded the interdisciplinary *Revue internationale de psychopathologie* in 1990, and just before his death in 2002 he created the Institute of Contemporary Thought with Julia Kristeva, Dominique Lecourt and François Jullien.[5] These initiatives are testimony to the remarkable interdisciplinary energy which Fédida embodied and which he mobilised, in which psychoanalytic theory and practice became porous to work in neuroscience, evolutionary biology, psychopathology, philosophy, literary studies and aesthetics, a porousness much in evidence in the essays translated for this volume, in which Darwin rubs shoulders with Georges Bataille, and Freud with Paul Klee.

It is from its basis in phenomenology and psychopathology that Fédida's work includes substantial attention to pathologies of the body, to the somatic. Fédida suspends recourse to thematisation or explicit theorisation; for Fédida the *theory* of psychoanalysis must arise out of the specific interplay of language and the somatic, experiential content in the session. Psychotherapeutic practice works only on condition that the analyst is open to the *surprise of the encounter* in the session itself, in which a word, a gesture or a non-verbal instance punctures the representational content of the discourse of either party. Fédida's early philosophical training and familiarity with the work of Binswanger is significant here: in his introduction to the French translation (1970) of the latter's work *Existential Analysis and Freudian Psychoanalysis*, Fédida describes the sustained friendship between Freud and Binswanger against the background of their epistemological disagreements – Freud was reticent with regard to Binswanger's 'metaphysical' tendencies, while Binswanger resisted psychoanalytic doctrine, and what he saw as a potential 'naturalism' in Freud.[6] Fédida hypothesises that Freud's connection to Binswanger was motivated by the hope that Binswanger would in some way act as a 'mediator', 'calling on psychiatry to put itself into question' and calling on psychoanalysis to recognise 'the phenomenology inherent to any psychiatric clinic worthy of that name'.[7] For Fédida, then, the importance of Binswanger's work and of his critique of Freud lies in the way that it opened up psychoanalysis to the dimensions of a 'phenomenological anthropology' (Fédida citing here the words of Henri Maldiney).[8] In less austere terms this means recognising in the writing of Freud and of Binswanger that 'the concepts that are set to work are constantly re-formed and revised in the concrete (existential) dialectic of acts of comprehension and acts of experience'.[9] It also entails a resistance to thematisation and theorisation; Fédida writes: 'The phenomenological project, Binswanger tells us, involves first of all the will to renounce "what Flaubert calls the 'rage to want to conclude'"'.[10] It insists that one 'allow the thing to come to speech itself' [*laisser la chose elle-même venir à la parole*].[11] This insistence on *non-thematisation* is a fitting description of Fédida's own method and mode; it implies a resistance to the logos – to the impulse toward scientific categorisation and epistemological closure, and a concomitant fidelity to the project of *comprehension* as the 'foundational phenomenological act intimately linked to the questions of *meaning*, of (human) being and of presence'.[12]

The fidelity to comprehension and the resistance to conclusion and to closure support the sense in which theoretical ideas and moments of interpretation emerge through the process of Fédida's writing and through dynamic attention to the 'space of the session', to use his own locution. We might describe this as a concerted attention to the *pathos* of the human; Fédida's 'fundamental psychopathology' is thus not a *psychology* – a theory of the psychic – but an experiential and dynamic questioning of the relation between the dimension of suffering and the passions (*pathos*) and their always problematic and incomplete articulation in speech (*logos*). Along with Maldiney, Fédida emphasised the importance of the *pathei mathos* (quoted from Aeschylus' *Agamemnon*), the wisdom that comes from suffering.[13] The conjunction of these two elements – *pathos, logos* – in *patho-logy* refers back to the broader objectives of Fédida's project: to mobilise all the resources, including those of science, philosophy, poetry and art, which can draw from the representation of suffering an understanding of the experience of the other, and a sense of their possible treatment, without however closing it as a system or doctrine.

As Fédida's reference to Aeschylus makes clear, poetry is a profound means of accessing the tragic dimension of language, in which humans suffer from their divided, separate, indeterminate and open condition. Across his voluminous body of work, Fédida draws on poetry and aesthetics to propose a powerful and conceptually stimulating reconfiguration of the relationship between language, image and the dynamics of the presence/absence of the body, which is ultimately part of the fundamentally strange (as he sees it) phenomenon of psychoanalytic transference. So it is worth underlining at this point that the kind of comprehension at stake in Fédida's work is not that of an intersubjective communication in the Habermasian sense. The transference, and the comprehension it supports, is not a face-to-face dialogue or an interpersonal relationship (see Chapters 1 and 2: 'The Site of the Stranger' and 'The Interlocutor'). It involves, rather, a kind of displaced and never fully manifest encounter with the archaic depths of the human being, and it makes it possible, especially through dreams, to bring to light the fact of language, the silent and communal background to which speech and words bear witness as if in negative. In this way, the image evoked or manifested in the dream or in the poetic text is always at play, as a mobile form moving against an uncertain and indeterminate background – echoing perhaps what Maurice Blanchot says about the troubling ontology of the image, which is never in its place.[14] This kind of insight also informs Fédida's attention, in 'The Indistinct Breath of the Image' (Chapter 8), to Plato's commentary on the necessary indeterminacy and indistinction of the colour white (and blank space) in *Theaetetus* and the notion of the hard-to-define *chora* (space understood as the receptacle of life and birth of thought) in *Timaeus*, as well as to the way in which, in the work of artists like Cézanne or Giacometti as commented on by the French poet André du Bouchet, the object is never simply represented but always emergent, coming into presence. Fédida's writing thus plays between, across and through the spoken word (the voice), the text and the image, between the page and the air, breaking the self-enclosed silence of images, words and names.

This emphasis on betweenness is pronounced in a brief essay on Fédida's book *L'Absence* by the philosopher Gilles Deleuze from 1978, originally published in *Le Monde*. Deleuze writes that the unifying theme of Fédida's work is to make of psychoanalysis a theory and a practice of *intersubjectivity* (but again without the Habermasian stress on discursive communication): 'to construct a structure of intersubjectivity which would be something like the condition of possibility of psychoanalysis'.[15] Pointing to Fédida's background in phenomenology and existential analysis, and naming not only Husserl but also Binswanger and Maldiney, Deleuze thus identifies Fédida's major contribution to psychoanalytic theory and practice as his effort to establish intersubjectivity as a transcendental, 'original' and 'primary' field, informing what passes *between*, between the analyst and the patient, between present and past, between dream and consciousness, voice and writing, between the living and the dead and between times and places.[16] For Deleuze, Fédida's *objeu* works precisely to underline this 'prior intersubjectivity'.[17] Presented in this light, Fédida's work, in parallel to that of Lacan, but also somewhat aslant it, positions the transcendental field of intersubjectivity as the terrain in which a whole set of concepts and techniques in psychoanalysis have to be revised, while all the time referring back to the work of Freud as their foundational origin. The relation of the individual subject to their own body must thus be re-thought in terms of intersubjective relationality, and specifically, but not only, in relation to the intersubjective field of language. Deleuze thus identifies the 'complaint' as a salient feature of Fédida's concerns and as a species of a 'disturbance' [*trouble*] of intersubjectivity, delineating three major forms of such complaints: the *melancholic*, the *hypochondriachal* and the *depressive*; such 'psychosomatic' disturbances function to pivot the whole of psychoanalysis away from the model of neurosis.[18]

The emphasis in Fédida's writing on betweenness, the indistinct and the asymmetry of interlocution also aligns with what we might call the para-discursive aspects of the therapeutic encounter, with the respiratory and gestural accents of and in the session. These are neatly encapsulated in the title of a work devoted to Fédida – *Gestes d'air et de pierre* [Gestures of Air and of Stone] by the French visual theorist Georges Didi-Huberman, in homage to the friendship and intellectual proximity between the two writers in the later period of Fédida's life and work.[19] Having drawn on Fédida's work in several books, including his study of art historiography and of Aby Warburg and the interpretation of culture, Didi-Huberman explores the betweenness of the dream image and of the analyst in this study.[20] In his view, Fédida's insistence on the muteness of images, the obscurities of dream accounts and the need to resist their over-hasty conversion into words emphasises the importance of non-verbal indistinct expression, which he also heard in his patients' manner of breathing, leading him to bring these ideas together: 'The breath of the image is indistinct when it is held back during the struggle to insert it into a narrative'.[21] In his reflections on images, including dream images, Fédida resisted their confinement and reduction to familiar philosophical, semiotic or aesthetic modes of interpretation, instead celebrating indistinctness and the absence of discursive authority. As he put it elsewhere, the analyst must also avoid taking control: '*To appropriate the place of analysis in any way is to make both the place and the session impossible.* Metapsychological writing is authorless since *neither* party has mastery over the language used'.[22]

The renewed attention to the body and dreams, discussed by Fédida in 'The Dream's Hypochondria' (Chapter 6) and in 'The Relic and the Work of Mourning', informs Didi-Huberman's thinking, viewing and feeling body on heightened alert in front of artworks.[23] Next, Fédida's search for precision about cases and his revision of concepts involves experimentation with the writing up of problems and the development therein of his ideas.[24] For both writers, habitual ways of responding to art and of using language are tested by 'the surprise of the encounter' with their subjects.[25] Didi-Huberman also coopted Fédida's work on memory and transmission in dreams for his own transhistorical studies of cultural forms and gestures, particularly inspired by Warburg, but also inflected by Fédida's writing about the temporality and genealogy of ancestors in relation to the complexities of transference.[26] His characteristic manoeuvre of reopening questions included his reconsideration of memory and trauma since, as Didi-Huberman has noted on many occasions across his own work – and continuing to underline this point more than 20 years after Fédida's death – the ambition to combine what Fédida calls a reminiscent present with an anachronic past poses an ongoing challenge to the adequacy of our language, but also offers a potential source for our capacity to witness in spite of trauma: 'Our present is obligated to, subject to, alienated from memory'.[27] In Didi-Huberman's view, historians in all disciplines needed to listen to Fédida's emphasis on anxiety about the past, which would contribute in turn to their reading, for example, of Freud's 'delayed action' [*Nachträglichkeit*] and Warburg's areas of research.[28] At the same time Fédida's essays in psychoanalysis and adjacent fields underline how analysis enables acts of transmission in images and above all, for him, language. Such work protects us from excessive melancholy: 'Perhaps *mourning's great enigma* is the way that over time the living can dream about death while they sleep and thus be protected from the violence that afflicts sufferers from melancholia'.[29]

We have noted how Fédida's explorations of psychoanalytic concepts often engage with aesthetic or literary works, as if these latter media were also manifestations of the emergence of the indistinct, the ancestral or the 'glacial' into the form of speech or image, in parallel to the dream. This exploration is also in some sense extended in the work of the Brazilian artist Lygia Clark, who undertook an analysis with Fédida, and whose practice, especially what she referred to as her 'relational objects', evolved in intimate proximity to Fédida's work and the wider psychoanalytic field. In the chapter 'Substance informe' of *Par où commence le corps humain*, Fédida remarks that the exploration of the roles and 'aspects' of clinical work can lend themselves to a degree of abstraction.[30] This is aligned with the notion of the *informe* which derived from the work of Georges Bataille (see Chapters 4 and 5 in this volume), and Fédida proposes that Clark's work is a 'putting to work' (*mise en œuvre*) of the *informe*, that works on the other side of words (*l'envers des mots*).[31] Here it is as if Fédida's concern with the 'indistinct' and non-formal aspects of therapeutic practice join with a 'de-objectified' aesthetic practice which itself becomes therapeutic.[32]

Our selection from Fédida's writing ranges widely across his work and aims to introduce readers to the most distinctive elements of his thought, while also enabling in-depth analyses of specific concepts and instances. The chapters 'The Site of the Stranger' and 'The Interlocutor' (both from the volume *Le Site de l'étranger*, 1995) concern the inter-locutory dynamics of the transferential situation, with an emphasis as noted above on the necessary mobility of the analyst's receptivity, and an awareness of the modalities of the countertransference. 'Regression' and 'Where Does the Human Body Begin?' showcase Fédida's dis-tinctive attention to the interface of Freudian thought with the theory of evolution, drawing also on the work of Ferenczi and, with the essay 'On the Primitive', extending into the domain of art and aesthetics. These texts derive from *Le Site de l'étranger* and the later volume *Par où commence le corps humain*. With 'The Dream's Hypochondria' (from the *Nouvelle revue de psychanalyse* (1972) and then the earlier volume *Corps du vide, espace de séance*, 1977) we engage with Fédida's complex and creative consideration of the hypochondriac's *complaint*, in its relation to the sites of the body, the space of the dream, and the tissue of lan-guage, while 'Residues of the Day and of Life' (from *Crise et contre-transfert*, 1992) represents the most concerted manifestation of Fédida's persistent interrogation of the temporality of the 'remainder' or the relic. The final essay of the volume, 'The Indistinct Breath of the Image' (from *Le Site de l'étranger*), represents Fédida's acute awareness of the importance of the respiratory body both in the analytic session and in the work of art; this is perhaps the most manifest dimension in which his thought extends beyond psychoanalytic theory and practice to affirm their pertinence for the understanding of the conditions of life and art as such, although it must be said that this is a feature of all his work.

Fédida's writing demands much of his readers, but the work is rewarding, through the gains it affords not only in terms of knowledge and insight, but also in terms of awareness of the modes of expression and the corresponding importance of a precise use of language. This is a chal-lenge for its translators, as are Fédida's sophisticated and wide references across multiple disciplines and his meticulous attention to the letter of Freud's texts, as well as to the contingencies of specific cases. We believe that we have met these challenges in the translations for this volume, and that the versions which result preserve and communicate the singular idiom of Fédida's voice. We have tried to strike the right balance between the demand to translate what is on the page, and the desire to move the material towards an Anglophone readership, and we believe this effort has also influenced Anne-Marie Smith-Di Biasio and Timothy Mathews, who have translated two of the pieces in the volume. This has produced certain aporia and tensions, particularly as concerns reference to Freud: our recourse to the *Standard Edition* is sometimes out of joint with the translations into French to which Fédida often refers or when he provides his own translations. The derivation of Fédida's written texts from seminars, and the quality of orality, also occasion a degree of flexibility in Fédida's referential apparatus; sometimes quotations are given without reference, in which case we have sought to provide it in the footnotes. We hope that our strategies have resulted in a translation which retains something of the vitality and presence of Fédida's teaching, and his attention to the processes through which experience comes into words.

Notes

1 Anne-Marie Smith, 'In Memoriam: Pierre Fédida, or That Singular Insistence on the Dream', *Paragraph* 27: 3 (November 2004), pp. 113–20; Anne-Marie Smith-Di Biasio, 'Emerging Phantom-Like from Some Other Reality: Thinking Back and the Apparition of the Feminine' in *Paragraph* 32: 2 (July 2009), pp. 214–25; Michael Stone-Richards and Ming Tiampo, 'To Introduce Pierre Fédida' in *Qui Parle* 10:1 (Fall/Winter 1996), pp. 43–48; Michael Stone-Richards, 'Pierre Fédida 1934–2002: a mémoire' in *Journal of Visual Culture* 2:1 (2003), pp. 69–72; 'Depression and the logic of separation: situating Pierre Fédida's "La Relique et le travail du deuil"' in *Journal of Visual Culture* 2:1 (2003), pp. 51–61. Existing translations of Fédida into English, some of them attached to the aforementioned articles, include, by Anne-Marie Smith: 'Constructing Place: The Supervision of a Psychoanalytic Cure. Psychoanalysis and Psychotherapy' in *The Bulletin of the European Psychoanalytical Federation* 56 (2002), pp. 17–28, and 'The Body of Emptiness' in *Pages/Paysages* 9 (Birkhäuser, Autumn 2002), 'Embodied: Figures in a Landscape', pp. 78–83; and by Michael Stone-Richards: 'The Movement of the Informe' in *Qui Parle* 10: 1 (Fall/Winter 1996), pp. 17–28, and 'The Relic and the Work of Mourning' in *Journal of Visual Culture*, 2:1 (2003), pp. 62–68. There is also, translator unknown, 'Depressive Doing and Acting: A Phenomenological Contribution to the Psychoanalytic Theory of Depression' in *The Human Being in Action: The Irreducible Element in Man, Vol II: Investigations at the Intersection of Philosophy and Psychiatry*, ed. by Anna-Teresa Tymieniecka (Dordrecht, Holland; Boston, USA: D. Reidel Publishing Company, 1978), pp. 81–92. Patrick ffrench and Nigel Saint have contributed a translation of 'Anxiety in the Eyes', to *Psychoanalysis and History* 25:1, pp. 83–94 (April 2023), with an introduction (pp. 79–82) and 'responses' from Dany Nobus and Raluca Soreanu (pp. 95–100). For readers of French, the volume *Autour de Pierre Fédida: regards, savoirs, pratiques* (Paris: PUF, 2007) includes a series of critical essays and recollections from contemporary philosophers and psychoanalysts including Monique David-Ménard, Julia Kristeva, François Villa, Dominique Lecourt, Catherine Cyssau and Georges Didi-Huberman. See further on, and the Bibliography, for other critical work concerning Fédida.

2 A neologism Fédida draws from the work of the French poet Francis Ponge, *objeu* conflates *objet* (object) and *jeu* (play); it can be tentatively translated as *play-object*, evidently losing the condensation Fédida seeks to effect. See Pierre Fédida, 'L'"objeu". Objet, jeu et enfance. L'espace thérapeutique' in *L'Absence* (Paris: Gallimard, 1978), pp. 97–195. This substantial essay, originally Fédida's seminar in 1976 and then published in successive issues of the review *Psychanalyse à l'Université* (1–5), was significantly extended for its publication in *L'Absence*. Its thoroughgoing engagement with Winnicott's accounts of play and transitional space, with Freud's *fort-da*, and with case studies make it a

suitable candidate for translation. However, it is not included in this volume due to its extreme length.

3 See https://www.puf.com/forums-diderot for further details.

4 The Centre is currently under the umbrella of the Université Paris-Cîté and is directed by Derek Humphreys. See https://centre-detudes-du-vivant.u-paris. fr/presentation/.

5 The impetus behind the *Revue internationale de psychopathologie* was to confront the challenge to psychotherapeutic theory and practice instigated by the scientific reification of pathological categories, on the one hand, and the benefits of pharmacological advances in psychotropic medications, on the other. In a late essay, 'De l'importance de la psychopathologie pour la psychothérapie' included in *Des Bienfaits de la dépression* (2001, pp. 217–42), Fédida argues for a pluridisciplinary psychopathology, and for a redefinition of the field and of its object, thus a fundamental psychopathology, insisting on the radical strangeness of the symptom and on its singularity. This describes the project of the *Revue internationale de psychopathologie*, the aim of which was to articulate psychoanalysis with perspectives from other scientific horizons, including neuropsychology, phenomenology, cognitive science, linguistics, cybernetics and evolutionary biology. The review had 24 issues between 1990 and 1997.

6 Pierre Fédida, 'Binswanger et l'impossibilité de conclure' [Binswanger and the Impossibility of Concluding]' in Ludwig Binswanger, *Analyse existentielle et psychanalyse freudienne. Discours, parcours, et Freud* (Paris: Gallimard, 1970), pp. 9–37, p. 13, p. 15. See Jacob Needleman (ed. and trans.), *Selected Papers of Ludwig Binswanger: Being in the World* (New York: Basic Books, 1963) for translations into English of some of the essays included in the French volume. Aside from this volume, and Michel Foucault's well-known introduction to Binswanger's *Dream and Existence*, trans. by Keith Hoeller (New Jersey: Humanities Press, 1993), Binswanger's work has not benefited from extensive translation into English. The significant correspondence between Freud and Binswanger has however been translated: *The Sigmund Freud-Ludwig Binswanger Correspondence 1908–1938*, ed. by Gerhard Fichtner, trans. by Arnold J. Pomerans (New York and London: Other Press, 2003).

7 Fédida, 'Binswanger et l'impossibilité de conclure', p. 14.

8 Fédida, 'Binswanger et l'impossibilité de conclure', p. 18.

9 Fédida, 'Binswanger et l'impossibilité de conclure', p.19.

10 Fédida, 'Binswanger et l'impossibilité de conclure', p. 25.

11 Fédida, 'Binswanger et l'impossibilité de conclure', p. 25.

12 Fédida, 'Binswanger et l'impossibilité de conclure', p. 25.

13 See Fédida's essay 'Tradition tragique du psychopathologique: à propos du *pathei mathos* de l'*Agamemnon*' [The Tragic Tradition of the Psychopathological: On the *pathei mathos* in *Agamemnon*] in *Crise et contre-transfert* (Paris: PUF, 1992), pp. 20–36. In her excellent translation of the play Anne Carson renders this: 'Zeus put mortals on the road to wisdom/when he laid down this law/*By suffering we learn*'; *An Oresteia*, trans. by Anne Carson (New York: Faber and Faber, 2009), p. 16.

14 Maurice Blanchot, 'Two Versions of the Imaginary' in *The Space of Literature* (Lincoln; London: University of Nebraska Press, 1982), pp. 254–63.

15 Gilles Deleuze, 'The Complaint and the Body' in *Two Regimes of Madness: Texts and Interviews 1975–1995*, ed. by David Lapoujade, trans. by Ames Hodges and Mike Taormina (New York: Semiotexte, 2006), pp. 164–65, p. 164.

16 Deleuze, 'The Complaint and the Body', p. 165.

17 Deleuze, 'The Complaint and the Body', p. 165.

18 Deleuze, 'The Complaint and the Body', p. 165.

19 Georges Didi-Huberman, *Gestes d'air et de pierre: corps, parole, souffle, image* (Paris: Minuit, 2005).

20 Georges Didi-Huberman, *Confronting Images: Questioning the Ends of a Certain History of Art*, trans. by John Goodman (University Park, PA: Pennsylvania State University Press, 2005); *The Surviving Image: Phantoms of Time and Time of Phantoms*, trans. by Harvey Mendelsohn (University Park, PA: Pennsylvania State University Press, 2017); and *Gestes d'air et de pierre*. Fédida provided an introduction to a combined reprint in 1984 of Charcot and Richer's *Démoniaques dans l'art* (1887) and Charcot's *La Foi qui guérit* (1897) (Paris: Macula), for which Didi-Huberman wrote an Afterword.

21 Pierre Fédida, 'The Indistinct Breath of the Image' in *Le Site de l'étranger* [The Site of the Stranger] (1995), p. 220; see Chapter 8.

22 Pierre Fédida, 'Théorie des lieux' [Theory of Places] in *Le Site de l'étranger* [The Site of the Stranger] (1995), p. 285.

23 Pierre Fédida, 'L'Hypocondrie du rêve' [The Dream's Hypochondria] in *Nouvelle revue de psychanalyse* 5 'L'Espace du rêve' (1972), pp. 225–38; Pierre Fédida, 'The Relic and the Work of Mourning' in *Journal of Visual Culture*, 2:1 (2003), pp. 62–68 ['La Relique et le travail du deuil', *L'Absence* (Paris: Gallimard, 1978), pp. 53–59]; Didi-Huberman, *Gestes d'air et de pierre*, pp. 20–29.

24 Compare with Nicola Luckhurst's comment in her 'Translator's Preface' to Sigmund Freud and Josef Breuer, *Studies in Hysteria*, trans. by Nicola Luckhurst with an introduction by Rachel Bowlby (London: Penguin, 2004), p. xxxvii: '[Freud is] often working and thinking aloud – making the reader party to his intellectual processes'.

25 Pierre Fédida, *Crise et contre-transfert* (Paris: PUF, 1992), pp. 124, 229; Georges Didi-Huberman, *The Man Who Walked in Color*, trans. Drew S. Burk (Minneapolis: Univocal, 2017), p. 81.

26 Pierre Fédida, 'L'Ombre du reflet. L'Émanation des ancêtres' in *La Part de l'œil* 19 (2003–2004), pp. 195–201. See 'Regression' (Chapter 3); and Didi-Huberman, *Gestes d'air et de pierre*, p.78.

27 Didi-Huberman, *Confronting Images*, p. 85 and n. 1; Georges Didi-Huberman, *La Fabrique des émotions disjointes: Faits d'affects, 2* (Paris: Minuit, 2024), p. 120. On both occasions Didi-Huberman references Pierre Fédida, 'Passé anachronique et présent réminiscent: Épos et puissance mémoriale du langage' in *L'Écrit du temps* 10 (1985), pp. 23–45, reprinted in *Ouvrir la parole*, ed. by Riccardo Galiani (Paris: MJW Fédition, 2014), pp. 87–109. Galiani's careful selection of 19 essays, which was published in French and Italian, has a particular focus on shorter essays about the analytical session, including an earlier version of one essay in our volume.

28 Sigmund Freud, 'Project for a Scientific Psychology' in *The Standard Edition of the Complete Psychological Works of Sigmund Freud Volume I: Pre-Psycho-Analytical Publications and Unpublished Drafts*, trans. by James Strachey et al (London, UK: The Hogarth Press, 1966), pp. 283–397, p. 356; Didi-Huberman, *The Surviving Image*, pp. 213–15.

29 Pierre Fédida, 'La grande énigme du deuil. Dépression et mélancolie. Le beau objet' in *L'Absence*, p. 78.

30 Pierre Fédida, 'Substance informe' in *Par où commence le corps humain* (Paris: PUF, 2000), pp. 105–19, p. 113.

31 Fédida, 'Substance informe', p. 114.

32 Fédida, 'Substance informe', p. 113. See also Ana Carolina Minozzo, 'Chaos and the Speaking Body: Spitting on Hegel with Lygia Clark and the Limits of Language in Psychoanalysis' in *Excursions* 10: 1 (2020), pp. 123–40; Cornelia H. Butler and Luis Pérez-Oramas (eds.), *Lygia Clark: The Abandonment of Art, 1948–1988* (New York: Museum of Modern Art, 2014).

1 The Site of the Stranger

In an aside concerning the *ideal aim* of psychoanalytic treatment Freud expresses the wish that the analyst become again the *stranger* that they were, and, once love has been freed from the egoism of transference, that they carefully help the patient from that point on to become the clear-sighted agent of their own object-choices and thereby available to pursue the associations made possible by these choices. The remark occurs at the end of the 'commentary' that accompanies Freud's reading of Jensen's *Gradiva: 'Der Artzt ist ein Fremder gewesen und muss trachten nach der Heilung wieder ein Fremder zu werden'.*[1] So, from the stranger they cannot fail to have been, the analyst must strive, once the treatment is done, to 'become a *stranger* once more'.

As tautological as this statement may seem, even appearing to state the patently obvious, what's surprising is the kind of *doubling* of the stranger that occurs here, as if it were a case of restoring *strangeness* back to a previous *state of the stranger*. Alternatively, it is as if being the *neutral stranger* required by the treatment – thus the *origin of the strangeness* that drives the transference – would not in itself guarantee that the analyst *become a stranger*, in other words, a *distanced other*, having that estranged identity characteristic of the social person. What is certain is that the expression Freud proposes to account for the ideal aim and for the end of the treatment makes the *aim* of strangeness coincide with an awakened *exteriority*; in Hegelian terms the exteriority that requires interiority, or for Husserl what can be called intersubjective objectivity.

Freud's expression can be clarified, nevertheless, if primarily understood as the incompletion of the amorous effects set in motion by the transference; this incompletion then introduces the stranger *asymptotically* (as Freud says in a letter to Fliess[2]) by virtue of the *gap* – even of the 'horizon' – that keeps the unknowability of this incompletion possible, in a sense maintaining the *endless* nature of the analysis. The diabolical idea of the notorious 'negative therapeutic reaction' is of course what is at stake here.[3] It makes it fully evident that the patient, glimpsing the promised separation of the cure, can 'prefer' to take refuge in a reinforcement of the symptom with which they are familiar. And while a psychoanalytic

DOI: 10.4324/9781032637600-2

treatment can be considered to be definitively over when the transference is 'liquidated', doesn't that make such a liquidation inherently *problematic*? Since the criteria of the cure remain uncertain, due to its symptomatic dependence on the person of the analyst, and thus on the positive trans-ferential actuality of the image of this person, can this liquidation be any-thing other than problematic? The ideal end of restoring a foreign exteriority to the person of the analyst certainly conceives such a liquida-tion of the transference as its neurotic un-fixation – its *de-solidification*, and in this sense the production of a *fluid circulation* of affects restored from then on to the resonating power of words in language. Doesn't the ideal of such an end, opening onto an endless analysis, confirmed however by the practice of treatment, therefore have the power to estrange the person of the analyst? More generally does it not seem that beyond the end of the sessions the person of the analyst remains psychically intimate to such a degree that for a long time the affective resonances of relations to others can only move through the analyst and that the interlocutory address to the person of the analyst thus persists, within language?

If accorded to the *person*, isn't the qualification *'stranger'* reinforced, moreover, by ambivalence, such that it could well constitute the *aporia* of the *end of analysis*? The separation of mourning accomplishes, Freud tells us, the animist operation of the unconscious, since the corpse of this other self – a foreign power of hostility – is decomposed at the same time that the reflection of the person, which is none other than the very person of the self, is immortalised through the belief in the soul (the belief in the *psychic*). The neutralisation of this *hostile force* by the psychic is one of the benefits of the 'work of mourning' as protector of the person themselves [*la personne propre*]. Transference would thus have inherited so to speak something from mourning and the belief in immortality: *the murder would be frozen in this glacial formation*, and analysis – in other words, language – would come to awaken the *hostile force* and make it so that death would not preserve the possibility of a murder which can no longer take place. It is precisely this issue which is at stake in the ideal movement prescribed for the treatment and restoration of the stranger: *to make the stranger come forth belongs to language as a signified and unaccomplished murder*; perhaps then the only certainty that the *stranger* can be at the same time behind and in front – in advance, that they can be the presence of a person and the presence of no-one [*présence d'une personne et présence de personne*], resolutely becoming an absence. That the stranger finally can become the *other*. Only murderousness [*la meurtralité*] can recognise the other.

It is quite possible that the doctrinal idea whereby the liquidation of the transference is brought about through the patient's expression of their aggressivity has been diminished. Ferenczi openly reproached Freud for having left his analysis unfinished due to the analyst's defiance when faced with the aggressive impulses of the transference. The analysis could go as deep as possible and right to the end if the analyst could only allow the aggressive impulses directed against them to arise when they do, and if they did not seek to close the work in advance out of an incapacity to tolerate the patient's aggressivity. This lesson has been formally accepted by psychoanalytic training institutes, a fact proved by the oft-posed question of whether analysts can or cannot bear the aggressivity of their patients toward them. But has the lesson really been accepted? What has this aggressivity in analysis become, in reality? The concept of aggressivity generally serves as a disguise for hostility and works to stifle the hatred in the transference. We should understand this to mean that the concept of aggressivity is a kind of funerary rationalisation of the irrationality of murder, and that it freezes the paradoxical injunction to attack the image of the father in the person of the analyst without putting this image to death, and even while maintaining the recourse to this person. The relatively common assimilation of analytic work to the work of mourning follows the same path, provided it is preserved in the psychic. And to realise this effect it appeals to an aggressivity deprived of any power other than that of neutralising the hostility of the dead. If, as Freud reminds us, 'when all is said and done, it is impossible to destroy anyone *in absentia* and *in effigie*', the stranger risks remaining imprisoned in the *person* of the analyst, and so never able to escape from the intimacy of the transference.[4]

'The doctor has been a stranger, and must endeavour to become a stranger once more after the cure'. We know that no treatment is possible if the analyst is a close relative. The facility of this familial proximity would put them in the position of a *third person* and would remove from them the unknown absence that distance affords them. To be the *stranger* therefore really means for the patient that they can confidently take the time they need to express their recollections and thus be reassured that they are speaking about their own memories, avoiding any confusion or risk of separation from their own past due to their relative's preferred perspective. Being the *stranger* is also what gives the analyst the freedom to hear and to interpret. More radically, it is a negation which installs neutrality. For Ferenczi 'to have been analysed' is the second fundamental rule of analysis – in this instance for the sake of its practice – and, we should add, it is essential to remain conscious of this training in the presence of the patient, given that the latter will so often seek to normalise their analyst, as someone *not yet analysed*! The negation which installs neutrality is first of all a work of silence, which is the act in language of the de-institution of the third person; in person, the analyst signifies by their non-response that the fact of their presence does not make them responsible for the *question* addressed to them by the patient's demand, nor that they have to respond to them in person. Nevertheless, this still requires the analyst to be genuinely open to the question, *in language* – something which Freud initially thought had to be the unspoken or explicit insistence of *questioning* ('Ask questions, go on then, ask questions!'). The negation of the neutral is held in this *Versagung* of speech – which we may translate as 'frustration', 'renunciation', even 'abstinence' – which is the analytic *decision* of the movement that returns speech to its silence, that is to say to the words opened up to their polysemy in language. The neutral is reflected by negation so as to oppose [*faire face*] its neutralisation by the inertia of effects of massification. The massification of the neutral annuls negation and draws language to its disappearance. What threatens to disappear with it in an auto-conserving death is the *murder* which is constitutive of its existence. The *stranger* is thus the neutral which installs transference: the analyst is radically estranged from this body which, at first, arrives *facing you [en face]*. This body carries in its architectural outline the geology of its construction. In the same way the analyst is no less a stranger to the dialect of the dreams of the analysand, or of their obsessions – as Freud let it be understood of the symptom as of the dream, whose *Bildersprache* (language of images) is withdrawn from anyone's comprehension, including that of the subject themselves. The language of images is of no use in socialised person-to-person communication. It is a *strange situation* when the dreamer or the ill person wants to share with someone the hallucinatory intimacy of their *belief* in their condition, when the person supposed to recognise themselves in these confidences disappears during their articulation. The communication of a dream doesn't restore language to speech: it obscures the obscurity of visual images. Speaking of the dialect of the obsessional symptom Freud underlines that the situation it engenders is all the more strange in that, distinct from the hysterical symptom and from the dream, which are designed in some sense to impose their strange vision on the observer, this dialect provokes in us the disconcerting illusion of a familiar *thought*:

> The language of an obsessional neurosis – the means by which it expresses its secret thoughts – is, as it were, only a dialect of the language of hysteria; but it is a dialect in which we ought to be able to find our way about more easily, since it is more nearly related to the forms of expression adopted by our conscious thought than is the language of hysteria. Above all, it does not involve the leap from a mental process to a somatic innervation – hysterical conversion – which can never be fully comprehensible to us.[5]

Analysis will not fail to count the cost of this illusion of familiarity in thought if it does not translate the dialect of consciousness into that of the dream. This dialect will then affect the analyst more deeply because it will feel strange rather than familiar.

The *paradigm of the dream* is thus in many respects constitutive and exemplary of the *stranger* status of the analyst. It is strange in the sense that Freud designates it as a *shibboleth* (analysts recognise each other by means of the reference accorded to the interpretation of dreams) – but also because *to hear* and *to listen* in psychoanalysis are in some way to make the dream the 'prism' of words, which absorb its visuality and diffract its figures. Freud refers to Greisinger in support of this emphasis: the patient must be seen and observed *in the same way* as one listens to a dream. The character of 'the most asocial psychic production' ruins any pretention to comprehension in advance and introduces an asynchronous temporality by virtue of the fragmentation of images by associations (no direct interpretation of the dream is possible), and by virtue of the gap between the moment when the analyst could interpret and the moment when the patient could hear this interpretation. If the theory of the transference is *formed* from the metapsychology of the dream, it is because nothing of it would be comprehensible without keeping in view the *value* of the *person* that the dream confers: aren't people seen in the night-time dream projections of the dreamer themselves [*la personne propre*]? Elucidating all the consequences of such a constantly reiterated position in itself justifies calling the analyst a stranger. We have already underlined the specifically dialectal form of the *Bildersprache*, this language of images which is close to an ideogrammatic writing; we have suggested that, like hysteria, the patient's dream is such that their body undoes the usual perceptual schemas of other bodies (in the paradigm a body's expressions are *seen* as a structured configuration) and that this strange *sight* is accentuated by the respective positions of couch and armchair. This kind of power of figurability engenders – just like a text – the support-surface of the *identifications* of the analyst, since these proceed in the analysis from the figuring of imaginary situations. Isn't *to identify* to read the outline of what is given as an image? And ultimately if the familiar is, against all the odds, an obstacle to identifications, the stranger is at that place where the most intimate part of intimacy is to be found – the infantile sexuality of a speech which does not itself know what such an intimacy means for it. This speech does not know it, but we could say that it recognises it, in wanting to preserve – through the person of the stranger – *the refusal of the familiar*. In his text on 'Constructions in Analysis' Freud is very explicit:

> What we are in search of is a picture of the patient's forgotten years that shall be alike, trustworthy and in all essential respects complete. But at this point, we are reminded that the work of analysis consists of two quite different portions, that it is carried on in two separate localities, that involves two people to each of whom a distinct task is assigned. It may, for a moment, seem strange that such a fundamental fact should not have been pointed out long ago, but it will immediately be perceived that there was nothing being kept back in this [...] We all know that the person who is being analysed has to be induced to remember something that has been experienced by him and repressed, and the dynamic determinants of this process are so interesting that the other portion of the work, the task performed by the

analyst, has been pushed into the background. The analyst has neither experienced nor repressed any of the material under consideration. His task cannot be to remember anything. What then is his task? His task is to make out what has been forgotten from the traces which it has left behind, or more correctly to *construct* it.[6]

Remembering and reliving, on the patient's side, belong to the intimate memory of the hallucinatory regression of the transference. The separation of the two scenes, reminiscent of the theatre of classical tragedy, excludes any kind of symmetry of one with the other, and the specific role of the speech of the 'analysed' in analysis is to appropriate the voice of the half-sleep (Aeschylus) of consciousness while the dream that it shelters comes to encounter its figures – in the place where language has the task of collecting these tonalities and of constructing, in another place, its memory.

If we communicate to a patient some idea which he has at one time repressed but which we have discovered in him, our telling him makes at first no change in his mental condition. [*We could even add that such an interpretation can, depending on the associations of the moment and the temporality of the analyst's understanding, modify the status of the psychic reality of the representation, by crediting it with a kind of external objective reality.*][7] Above all, it does not remove the repression nor undo its effects, as might perhaps be expected from the fact that the previously unconscious idea has now become conscious. [*The 'cognitive' act of 'making conscious' engenders the hope of a suppression of the unconscious reality which is active here. But as we know (see the paper 'Disavowal'), 'intellectual' knowledge of the repressed does not lift the repression. Indeed, strictly speaking, can repression be lifted?*] On the contrary, all that we shall achieve at first will be a fresh rejection of the repressed idea. But now the patient has in actual fact the same idea in two forms in different places in his mental apparatus: first, he has the conscious memory of the auditory trace of the idea, conveyed in what we told him; and secondly, he also has, as we know for certain, the unconscious memory of his experience as it was in its earlier form. Actually there is no lifting of the repression until the conscious idea, after the resistances have been overcome, has entered into connection with the unconscious memory-trace. It is only through the making conscious of the latter itself that success is achieved. On superficial consideration this would seem to show that conscious and unconscious ideas are distinct registrations, topographically separated, of the same content. But a moment's reflection shows that the identity of the information given to the patient with his repressed memory is only apparent. *To have heard something and to have experienced something are in their psychological nature two quite different things, even though the content of both is the same.*[8]

We have cited this passage at length firstly because it clearly expresses the connected problematics of the theory of repression and the weaknesses of inscription, of inscription-re-inscription (*Einschrift-Niederschrift*), of translation – problematics which concern the 'unconscious mnesic traces' and the status of *memory* as a function of language afforded by speech. Moreover, interpretation isn't summarily defined here as the conscious expression of an unconscious meaning or desire, but as the restitution by the *hearing* of a *word* of a representational content which (as with the case of memory) relates to a lived past. Now, 'to have heard something and to have experienced something are [...] two quite different things'. The *phonic acoustics* of a spoken word (which can also refer to a patient at the moment they are speaking) enters into the language of interpretation as arising from the intimate strangeness of the same spoken word. At the distance – in the temporal gap – in which they are (re-)pronounced, these words are re-endowed with a sonorous material, and it is precisely *this* factor which makes it possible to reach the unconscious *thing*. It is clear that at the *conscious level*, supported by a phenomenal structure of the symptom (like the manifest content of the dream), there is a 'wish' to lead the analyst to a conscious familiarisation with the things represented: if the analyst finds themselves under the grip of such conscious representations (and this does not fail to arise constantly in the dynamic of a cure – notably in favour of dramatic expressions of the suffering of the patient in the events of their personal life), such a reinforcement of the *level of consciousness* makes them leave the position of the intimate stranger, to the supposed benefit of so-called empathetic understanding.

To 'become a stranger again'; in view of what has just been proposed, the question whether the possibility of such an outcome is linked to the 'resolution of transference' definitely arises here. The dialectic of becoming in analysis, which concerns the changes arising in a treatment (as much for the patient as for the analyst), supposes that, *ideally*, a new object relation (which is truly *inter*-subjective, even *inter*-personal) comes after the sessions, between analyst and analysand, between the *analysed*. It is on the basis of such an ideal, among others, that the hope of an *analytic community* depends, notably in the framework of analytic groups and societies. This is not our immediate concern here, but the observation of interpersonal relations in such a framework would provide many occasions to doubt this! If we keep only to the consideration of the *termination* of an analytic treatment, it is certainly not the role that would be accorded *in fine* to 'aggressivity in the transference' that could serve as our criteria. It would certainly be more just to say that the stranger cannot 'become' the *stranger* of the end if the *stranger* of the beginning is not set up in the first place. In other words, if the *stranger* in analysis does not include the function of the strangeness of the unconscious and of the *translation* of language in the hesitancy proper to speech and the restitution of words in their materiality, the analyst's (re-)becoming a stranger would only be a strategic element in an 'amicable' ending to the analysis.

We have already described the *aspect* of the *constitution of the neutrality* of the non-person of the analyst in their very existence as a person. Not only did we find indicated the metapsychological continuity of the hysterical symptom with the dream and of the dream with the transference, but we were also reminded of the obstinate hostile force that Freud included in the myth of the *Urmensch* – the 'original man', the ancestor of the unconscious. Isn't the *hostile force* the abrupt relation that anxiety knows and recognises when faced with the *stranger-other* (the meaning given by Freud to that which is *fremd*, that is, to the otherness this side of the animist attitude of the analogical inference of potential identification). And if anxiety has its 'seat' in the ego, if it is understood in its nature as an archaic affect as *being in the ego as a foreign body*, that is because it is effectively the *apprehension* (in all the senses of the word) of the *other existence* [*existence autre*], without the least possibility of identification, thus this side of any condition of figurability. The *hostile* is thus the sketch of a perception of the *other* 'as other', the virtual bearer of *murderousness*. Isn't it hostility which, *primitively*, affords sight of the other living being, and which is the basis of an analytic of observation – even before, one could say, any figures of the other can be formed, from which identifications are generated. Insisting too much on the empathetic capacities of the analyst in relation to their patient, and notably with regard to the commencement of the treatment, means wilfully neglecting what relates back to *anxiety* and to the *hostile* as the necessary condition of the *estrangement* of the patient, which enables the analysis. The banalisation of meetings and sessions, the becoming-anonymous of 'encounters', prey upon any analytic practice which can no longer be re-awakened each time by the unknown other. Of course one could rightly say that *this* anxiety and *this* hostility are no longer directly recognisable as anxiety and hostility, that the analysis of the analyst does something else with them and has metabolised or metaphorised such affects. But the attention we are drawing here to anxiety and hostility, as the affective conditions of the awakening of perception and of language in the analysis, appears to us crucial to pose the problem of the analyst's so-called 'countertransferential' knowledge of their own strangeness for the patient. After Ferenczi but before Searles, it is surely Winnicott who has taken furthest the exploration of the place of 'negative feelings' – notably of 'hate in the countertransference', that of the analyst in the presence of their patient: however it is not certain that *hate* accounts exactly for the function of strangeness in anxiety and hostility and, for that reason, for their analytic potential. One gains nothing perhaps by making of hatred the operation of intrasubjective knowledge in the service of intersubjectivity. Analytically, it is certainly more exact to position oneself at the level of a metapsychology of anxiety in the activity of analysis in the treatment. Since it falls to such an anxiety – to 'listen with *the* anxiety' as Georges Favez might have said – to allow the analyst to be in contact with the thoughts and affects that they were not expecting, the better to discern what belongs to the anxiety of the patient and what this becomes in the metaphor of their own anxiety.

So, from the stranger he had been, the analyst becomes a stranger again if 'anxiety is there at the meeting' (Favez) and, with it, that *unconscious hostility* which is the legacy of opposition – the *counter* of the *encounter* (in the German word *Begegnung* the *counter* – *gegen* – is heard more explicitly). The full measure of this unconscious hostility does not even have to be experienced (as would be the case with the paranoiac) but rather recognised by the analyst as entering into the *decision of the analytic act*. This act is abolished by any marking up of the 'attitudes' of positive understanding. From this point of view the structuration of the analytic situation by language has no other aim than to maintain the *stranger* as a potential for *hostility*, whatever 'positive' expressions might be taken on by transference and countertransference. *To become a stranger again* – the very process of the treatment becomes responsible for this, one could say. This process – if it is indeed a process – does not need the provocation of conscious aggressivity, but nevertheless it is the path towards the discernment of the other – perhaps to what one calls their *distinction*. Doesn't language allow this point of view, and doesn't the discernment it permits give an exact perception of the distance from which the other can hear? While the word 'love' ensures a kind of popular synthesis of various effects that are often distinct from each other (tenderness, sexuality, but also friendship, solicitude, as well as all the qualifying categorisations: maternal love, etc), isn't it precisely the word which discerns the least what the other is made of? And isn't its use often justified by the hope for a renunciation of hostility? Here again the love of the transference would serve perhaps to make audible the intolerable annihilation that the 'recognition of the unconscious' carries with it – in effect, to hear the hostile power.

As a function of the radical stranger-ness of the unconscious constitutive of its reality – and perhaps of reality *itself* – Freud did not draw out the consequences that this strangeness would imply as regards the designation of the site of the analytic situation. As solid as his technical recommendations to analysts are (notably concerning neutrality and the mastery of countertransference), the normativity of these recommendations can seem weak with respect to the demand for a 'recognition (*Agnoszierung*) of the unconscious'. What does this mean? If the unconscious is 'constituted' by thing-representations entering as *material* into the phonic nature of words, then not only can mnesic traces be determined as the *inscription* of events by language (because of repression after the event or 'true repression'), but above all we would deny any speech the status of an interpretation if it does not include, when expressed, the sensorial imagination of words and their affinity with the attractive mnesic traces. The interpretation must in some way be regulated at the same time by the preconscious of words insofar as they carry the representation in their becoming-conscious and by the phonic existence of the trace which can be acoustically re-invested. In this way interpretation is only possible if it is engendered by construction, thus on the basis of *infantile memory*.

The relation of interpretation to construction is weakened by the comparative idea of the content of constructions (in the sense of the reconstitution of the past) and the content of interpretations (supposed to bear specifically on meaning). One of the strengths of Freud's argument consists in putting into perspective the paradigm of the dream (the onto-phylogenetic past), delirium (its truth) and construction. Construction is thus topically – and aoristically – equivalent to language insofar as it arranges the site of the stranger. This is where language is. We have said that the site of the stranger cannot be occupied by the person of the analyst: it is the activity of construction in analysis which *theoretically* determines its *topos*. As a consequence one could *write* [*écrire*], rather than *describe* [*décrire*], the analytic situation of the *chora* in the Platonic sense, as the place receiving all forms but retaining none and not assimilable to any of them.

We know that the concept of technique in psychoanalysis is hardly easy to think about descriptively, which is to say that it is withdrawn from the metapsychological reference to the unconscious. Moreover, when we undertake to characterise actions with reference to a metaphorical or analogical model (for example that of the dream) we inevitably devalue the designation of the situation of its site through a familiar (anthropological) re-personalisation of the 'attitudes' of the psychoanalyst 'in their relation' with the patient. This is why to try to explain the technical expressions of the installation of the analytic situation is to inevitably compartmentalise the strangeness of the analyst and thus misrecognise that the latter does not occupy the place of the unconscious any more than it is 'fundamentally' the site of the atemporality of the processes at work. This kind of misrecognition generally results in a simplified understanding of both the 'stranger to oneself' and, indeed, of the foreign-sounding language that restores the specific qualities [*le propre*] of the so-called maternal language. *The site of the stranger calls for the only community possible* – our shared language – *whose a-communicational state can only be altered through our understanding of language in general*. Language is to be understood here as a site where sound and meaning are one. Describing the 'work of language', specifically the task of poetic language, with Francis Ponge as his example, Henri Maldiney rightly argues that 'poetic transformation is a transformation of language itself, to the extent – which is its *raison d'être* – that poetry actualises in language the trans-possibility of the word [...] So poetry is the only one of all modes of speaking which is, in its full measure and its full sense, the phonic articulation of reality'.[9] So the site of the stranger, which cannot be the object of a psychological or linguistic localisation, is indeed the invisible foundation of a site of the visuality of things in the phonic material of the figurable: it would be indicated rather as a 'passage' (in Benjamin's sense), or more exactly as the *trans* of translation, transcription and transference. The fact that a site arises from an invisible foundation and has recourse to no other support than speech and its specific sight of reality [*son voir-réalité*] makes the site of the stranger imprescriptible. To define it as the 'place of operations' for transformations would introduce a function of knowledge (or of 'cognition') external to language itself. The stranger cannot be a referential instance decided by a site. Thinking about the site of the stranger as a passage is definitely productive because it avoids giving it any topos or dynamics other than those related to the reality of the unconscious. So one could say that it's the *analytic situation* that is 'structured' like a language rather than the unconscious, whatever the inconvenience caused here by the notion of *structure* and also whatever the inconvenience of its advantage.

At the start of his public lecture on Hölderlin (1970), André du Bouchet refuses to impute to his own deficient competence in German the strangeness that arises in his encounter with Hölderlin's words: 'But neither can I identify myself entirely with the speech which I am now in the process of uttering in French: this is also, I observe, partly foreign to me'.[10] The stranger is not here the feeling of strangeness provoked by the speech of one's *own* language: it is in fact the obstacle of the appropriation of the familiar and this threshold of discouragement or cowardice on which the familiar language can be toppled if, instantaneously, it does not have the *courage* to accept the insurrection of words. André du Bouchet continues: 'Along a fracture, inherent to the act of speaking – and which each of us can sense in his own language, in the language which I should emphasize is ours by pure chance (...) – along a fracture it is sometimes given to us to glimpse, close up, something which every word one grasps, beginning with those of the language which we assume we know, seeks to obliterate'.[11]

This 'fracture' or 'breach', as Freud would have put it, allowing a glimpse of the unconscious through the retina of language – is described by the poet as 'inherent' to the 'ownness' of one's own language in the *upstream* opening [*ouverture amont*] (as René Char would say) which is drawn by the genealogical memory of words and which the speech of language is always prompt to receive.[12] The *optical dispositif* of the analytic situation dependent on the *frame* – both visual and linguistic – would not be akin to the perspective of the *drawing* [*dessin*] but to its anamorphosis, which deconstructs any perspective. Drawing, like naming, brings forward the projection on an *instant of the surface*. Depth cannot be imagined, any more than the *background* can, even if they are the fantasy of the 'analytic space', as the anteriority of the past of childhood: the *image* is that instant of the surface which is formed from the *phonic air of the word*. The phonic air is the only support of the visual image – of its 'day' [*jour*] as Du Bouchet would say – which is undone as soon as it is produced.[13] Giacometti gives us this intuition in his drawings: the lines of projection come from outside, on an empty instant of the surface, and *blank space* [*le blanc*] is the very abyss of construction.

Drawing is a work of listening, just as the tracing of invisible lines engenders the surface of the visible [*la surface du voir*].

To look at things requires the distance arranged *within* language for their naming. Familiarity makes us lose the intimacy of words – the intimacy at the *fracture* of the stranger.

So things can begin to be spoken. They are not spoken in the excess of a speech that wants to say it all: they are spoken when speech hesitates, or when it is suspended at the moment when the name is formed, through the sonorous return of the word. Someone who becomes familiar with the things they speak of no longer sees the name they are made of – they no longer hear the name in which these things see each other. Claudel would no doubt say that they copy them 'according to the feeling they have of them'.[14] To *imitate* them and thus give them *logic* and *energy*, one must place oneself on the *vertical of the stranger* – a rupture of level, a *background* [*arrière*] reversing the passion of time. The *site of the stranger* is nothing but the *movement of this vertical* which engenders in speech the memory of language – *the unconscious*: the thing of the words that they are heard to name.

The mimetic process of identifying the *stranger* gives to the thing the gesture which will make it singularly present. If this gesture does not belong to the initiative of the thing and instead proceeds only from the know-how of the observer, they will only wish for the success of its effect, and anonymise the thing in a familiar representation. It will be a copy, and the copy – as Claudel understands it – withdraws the thing from its name, through the abstraction of the name alone. When drawing ceases to be the *writing* of things in language, it can represent them, but it is no longer the essential act of naming. The hope for a hieroglyphic writing of the dream clearly belongs to this *writing of the drawing* which may be the *mimesis* of the dream relative to the *Dingvorstellungen (thing-representations)* of the unconscious.

Drawing and writing are one and the same if they proceed from the stranger, if they are engendered by the *site* of language where the name is formed.

Ort – even before the common noun indicates the *place* [*lieu*] in its generality – the *site* originally signifies, according to Heidegger, 'the point of the spear'.[15] Indicating this *point*, in fact, the word solicits the acuity of height and also the *exteriority* of the *views* which are synthesised in a *point* situated *ahead* – nothing other than a point of *views*. The site carries the *virtuality* of the places that it collects together without taking any of them as a 'point of view', since what is proper to it is the *engendering* of just as many *points of view* as *inactual localities*, whose actualisation can only occur at the same time as the formation of the site.

The site is not the place of perspective – such is the melancholy to be attributed to perspective henceforth, involving a projection that espouses a timeless mastery of space and entails immobilised vision fixed on the axis of a future of the past as well as a past of the future. On the contrary, as *the place of places*, the site would confer to sight the movement of its passages and traversals *in the present* of its temporal potential.

The site is not closed in on itself as a space, and if its *foundation* still gives it a designated area it is from this event of foundation and not from the space thus materialised that it gets its *definition*. In myth such a foundation may be the act of a founder issued from the earth or a stranger to it, a hunter-warrior, a sage or a prophet, but it can also emerge from the collective culture of human beings, from the practice of their arts and their gods, from their *language*, which ensures them the transmission of the *already same*, thus absorbing in the founding act the tradition of a foreign alterity which watches over the invisible tracing of the limit. In recalling that the *Same*, the *Already There* and the *Other* are three terms 're-activated by Plato and his old man in sketching out the ideal colony of Crete', Marcel Detienne observes that these are barely categories but rather half-categories, which cannot assure the place or date of a foundation, either anthropologically or philosophically.[16] Charles Malamoud has also shown this very clearly in relation to Vedic India: Isn't the beginning a time of atemporal anteriority *in act* in the present of signs? *Wouldn't the act of founding a site be an ancestral act of beginning which is unassignable outside acts of recommencement?*[17]

Indeed, the analysis undertaken by Freud in *Moses and Monotheism* speaks of foundation, but in this case the foundation arises from an act of *murder*, a murder which, as Marie Moscovici points out, is a *gesture* that the text reproduces by desacralising it. She calls it 'the Murder of a murder' in her Preface to the new French translation of Freud's book.[18] This should be understood as the foundation of a religion, as the engendering of the bond between sons, and the desacralisation of murder which defines the *psychoanalytic act*, liberating this murder from its mythic immutability and thus awakening the dream in it, which will always continue to realise it, and which from that point *returns* in language, since only language can henceforth bear witness to the fact that there has been a murder and that this desacralised murder of the father is at the same time both the *absence* of the father and the *existence of language*. One could put it differently: the *transposition* (*Umsetzung*) that Freud effects in the passage from the murder to its desacralisation is the analytic operation which makes the *absence* of the father both radical and absolute, turning this *absence* into *language*, whose existence bears witness to the *murder and the murder of this murder*.

For the father, in a sense, monotheism consecrates a *site* he must occupy, and a site that he occupies all the more insofar as the nostalgia of human beings accords him a *hauteur*, a 'grandeur', which despite the feeling of *guilt* it induces should not lead us to forget that it allows an omnipresent and penetrating sight. Doubtless, indeed, as we shall see, at the masochistic centre of the transference there lies this relation between *showing* and *being seen*, which requests of the *person* of the analyst that they occupy the whole site. In this the transference is certainly of a monotheistic and religious nature, but precisely, if it cannot be otherwise, the *analytic act of murder* and the recognition of its becoming intervene as the installation of a *situation* in which everything will seem to be protected from the murder and its guilt (the compulsion to repeat will preserve the murder in order to stop it) and nothing will be ceded from the rigorous demand of language, holding the tragedy of murder to have taken place, since language exists and is unfinished as long as language is covered by the words spoken to a person. This *situation is psychoanalytic* insofar it is *founded* by an analytic act, but one can only describe it thus on condition that one understands that the founding act absorbs the amnesiac memory of the murder and *decides* (Wladimir Granoff) that murder will take *place* as language demands. That the *situation is structured like a language* – which entails the *necessary absence of the father* – means that the installation of language establishes both the *presence of a person* and the *signifying of their absence*. This person will be a non-person. *Jemand wird Niemand*.[19]

If one can say of the analytic situation that it is the very thing to which human illness consents and that it is also the very thing which language *sets up for work* about and through *this* illness, it would be philosophical hubris to want language to be the foundation or installation of this situation. Of course one cannot say either that the foundation of this situation derives from the rules – and certainly not from a supposedly single fundamental rule – since that would imply that the pronunciation of such a foundation was the preserve of the analyst in person. Can the rule, which would be that of naming as the condition of speech, be articulated or even pronounced by someone whose manifestation would be the initial disavowal of the murder? Must we seek the foundation of the analytic situation in the *theory* which makes it possible? After all is it legitimate to take the same self-reflexive route borrowed by the hermeneutics of the site to describe not only a foundational murder but also the act of language which desacralises this murder and installs a specific *negativity* in the designation of *absence*?

Translated by Patrick ffrench and Nigel Saint

Notes

1 ['The doctor has been a stranger and must endeavour to become a stranger once more after the cure', 'Delusions and Dreams in Jensen's *Gradiva*' in *The Standard Edition of the Complete Psychological Works of Sigmund Freud*, Vol. IX, trans. by James Strachey et al. (London: Hogarth Press, 1959) [1906], pp. 1–95, p. 90. Footnotes in square brackets are additions by the translators.]
2 [Fédida may be alluding to Freud's letter to Wilhelm Fliess of April 16th 1900, in which Freud remarks that: 'I am beginning to understand that the apparent endlessness of the treatment is something that occurs regularly and is connected with the transference [...] The asymptotic conclusion of the treatment basically makes no difference to me, but is yet one more disappointment to outsiders'. *The*

Complete Letters of Sigmund Freud to Wilhelm Fliess 1887–1904, trans. by Jeffrey Moussaief Masson (Cambridge, MA: Harvard University Press, 1985), p. 109.]

3 [See, for example, 'New Introductory Lectures on Psychoanalysis' in *The Standard Edition of the Complete Psychological Works of Sigmund Freud Vol. XXII*, trans. by James Strachey et al (London: The Hogarth Press, 1964) [1932], pp. 3–184, p. 109].

4 ['The Dynamics of Transference' in *The Standard Edition of the Complete Psychological Works of Sigmund* Freud Vol XII, trans. by James Strachey et al (London: Hogarth Press, 1958) [1912], pp. 97–108, p. 108.]

5 Sigmund Freud, 'Notes upon a Case of Obsessional Neurosis' in *The Standard Edition of the Complete Psychological Works of Sigmund Freud Vol. X*, trans. by James Strachey et al (London: The Hogarth Press and The Institute of Psychoanalysis, 1955) [1909], pp. 153–518, p. 157.

6 Sigmund Freud, 'Constructions in Analysis' in *The Standard Edition of the Complete Psychological Works of Sigmund* Freud Vol. XXIII, trans. by James Strachey et al (London: The Hogarth Press, 1964) [1937], pp. 255–69, pp. 258–59.

7 [In this long indented quotation from 'The Unconscious' the words both in italics and in square parentheses are Fédida's comments. In the passage at the end Fédida is underlining Freud.]

8 Sigmund Freud, 'The Unconscious' in *The Standard Edition of the Complete Psychological Works of Sigmund Freud Vol. XIV*, trans. by James Strachey et al (London: The Hogarth Press, 1957) [1915], pp. 157–215, pp. 175–76.

9 Henri Maldiney, *Francis Ponge, Colloque de Cérisy*, 1975, Ed. Bourgois (Paris: Union Générale d'Editions, 1977).

10 [André du Bouchet, 'Hölderlin Today', trans. by Beatrice Cameron with the assistance of Madeleine Hage, in *SubStance* 4:10 (Autumn 1974), pp. 5–15, p. 5, translation modified].

11 [Du Bouchet, 'Hölderlin Today', p. 5, translation modified].

12 [Fédida alludes to a collection of poems by René Char, *Retour amont* (Paris: Gallimard, 1966), translated by Gustaf Sobin in *The Brittle Age* and *Returning Upland* (Denver, Colorado: Counterpath, 2009).]

13 [Fédida mainly alludes to André du Bouchet's collection of poetry, *Air*, suivi de *Défets, 1950–1953* (Fontfroide-le-Haut: Fata Morgana, 1986). English translations of a number of the poems that Fédida has in mind are available in these two volumes: A. Du Bouchet, *Openwork: Poetry and Prose*, selected, translated and presented by Paul Auster and Hoyt Rogers (New Haven and London: Yale University Press, 2014); and A. Du Bouchet, *Outside: Poetry and Prose*, selected, translated and presented by Eric Fishman and Hoyt Rogers (Fayetteville, NY: Bitter Oleander Press, 2020). See also Chapter 8 in this volume, where Fédida discusses the work of Du Bouchet more extensively, notably in relation to Giacometti and Cézanne.]

14 [Paul Claudel, 'Ça et là' in *Connaissance de l'Est* (Paris: Editions Larousse, 1920) [1900], p. 133. English translation: P. Claudel, 'Here and There' in *Knowing the East*, translated by James Lawler (Princeton, NJ.: Princeton University Press, 2004), p. 74.]

15 [Fédida alludes to Martin Heidegger, 'Language in the Poem' in *On the Way to Language*, trans. by Peter D. Hertz (New York: Harper and Row, 1971), pp. 159–98. Unfortunately this translation into English misses Heidegger's point that the German word for site – *Ort* – also means the 'point of a spear', 'die Spitze des Speers'. See Martin Heidegger, 'Die Sprache im Gedicht. Eine Erörterung von Georg Trakls Gedicht' (1952) in *Unterwegs zur Sprache* (Frankfurt: Vittorio Klostermann, 1959), pp. 31–78, p. 31.]

16 M. Detienne, 'Qu'est-ce qu'un site?' in *Critique* 503 (1989), pp. 211–27. [Detienne refers to the unnamed Athenian in Plato's *Laws*.]

17 Charles Malamoud, 'Sans lieu ni date. Note sur l'absence de fondation dans l'Inde védique' in F. Lévy and M. Ségaud, *Anthropologie de l'espace* (Paris: Éditions du Centre Pompidou, 1983). (I refer also to a lecture given by Charles Malamoud in the context of the *Psychoanalytic Dialogues* of the Association psychanalytique de France, in 1992, on 'Beginnings'.)

18 Sigmund Freud, *L'Homme Moïse et la religion monothéiste*, new translation (Paris: Gallimard, 1986). See also the important preface by Marie Moscovici.

19 [Fédida draws on Celan's distinction between *Jemand* (somebody) and *Niemand* (nobody) as it is developed in various texts such as 'Conversation in the Mountains', *The Meridian* and 'The No-One's-Rose': see P. Celan, *Selected Poems and Prose*, trans. by John Felstiner (New York, London: W.W. Norton, 2001).]

2   The Interlocutor

While transference is no longer the phenomenon which Freud described, in a letter to Pfister, as our 'cross',[1] and if it therefore doesn't merit the mistrust from which the doctrine of countertransference[2] has largely drawn its inspiration, one cannot nevertheless fail to be struck by the relative inertia of the metapsychological theory which supports it.

Transference has become a rather weak speculative resource for analysts, who are nevertheless quite ready to invoke it systematically in their clinical texts.

On the other hand, the latter can explain the former: isn't the domestication of the phenomenon of transference by means of formalised categories responsible for its conceptual banality as a theory of inter-relationality? On rare occasions Freud invited analysts to master their countertransference. Has this mastery not instead been shifted onto transference, leading to attitudes which are professional and ideological instead of specific to the 'technical' craft of the psychoanalyst? On the other hand, these technical attitudes are certainly not foreign to the doctrinisation of countertransference, the sole preoccupation of the training Institutes, which reinforce their control of the teaching of psychoanalysis to the detriment of its transmission. Doesn't the training or formation required for the transmission of psychoanalysis need instead to point us toward the enigmatic resource of transference?

In becoming a doctrine in the professional training of psychoanalysts, countertransference has been definitively deprived of an analytic theory drawn from the metapsychology of transference: notably in regulating the ethics of the practice of supervisions (controls), it deprives young analysts in return of any curiosity about transference and the incomprehensible and unpredictable elements it holds; this doctrinisation inhibits the imagination and the language of the treatment. We could put it differently: isn't the personal analysis that analysts undergo in some way responsible for the idea-logical formation of countertransference *during their own treatment*, through identification with defensive attitudes and even with a resistance to psychoanalysis? This can't be proven. But could one nevertheless consider that such an idea-logical formation (pertaining to the ideal ego), mimetic in

DOI: 10.4324/9781032637600-3

nature, corresponds to a locking-down of the concept of the person? If this is the case – with the (legitimate) institutions of psychoanalysis contributing to this locking-down – the transmission of psychoanalysis would come up against what Freud had already called a 'paternal complex', which from this point of view amounts to nothing other than a persistent belief that the father has been killed, that this act can in no way be repeated, and all that there is left to do is to mourn. In this respect the concept of counter-transference would be the inheritance of the belief of the sons in their own immortality, while their identification with the dead father would eliminate the event of the murder. In this case the banalisation of transference accompanying the inhibition of imaginative speculation could be taken as equivalent to an auto-sterilisation, the libidinal counterpart of the immortality assured by the incorporation of the dead father.[3] The relation between Freud and Ferenczi is exemplary in this respect: as Monique Schneider has argued in her book, their paradoxical filiation involved on Ferenczi's side the necessity of interiorising the same transferential hostility which Freud avoided through internal mastery.[4] If we owe a lot to Ferenczi, it is because he was the first to offer a technical elaboration of countertransference (through a transference in process) and because he gave a theoretical sketch of supervision (notably in the fruitful yet fantastical notion of mutual analysis). But Ferenczi's importance lies mainly in the discovery that no analysis can be held to be over if it has not involved the rediscovery, through transference, of the primitive *hostility* of which it is the phylogenetic memory. Displacement onto the person of the analyst, and the distorting function of attachment, protect against the desperate horror of the murder of the father. We can better understand in this light how counter-transference might appear to function as an *immortalisation* of the analyst, who mimetically borrows the defensive attitudes of the father, faced with what he senses to be the *murderousness* [*meurtralité*] of the transference. This account has the benefit of proposing the *disavowal of the murder* of the father by the son, and the *retroactive elimination of the act* through the (cannibalistic) incorporation of the dead man into the species of death. Isn't 'the dummy' [*faire le mort*] the expression Lacan uses to indicate the 'place' of the analyst?[5] It is a serious matter to have inserted into the principle of a 'place' and its occupation a mimetic attitude that would condemn the analyst to neutralise the anxiety inevitably provoked by the unsettling strangeness [*l'inquiétante étrangeté*] of transference.[6]

However – and perhaps it is already appropriate to say this – psychoanalytic scholasticism with respect to transference has responded quite adequately to the degradation of the epic hero stigmatised by Freud in the form of normative justifications of suffering and the experience of pathos. Isn't the degradation of the epic hero the negligent and cowardly insouciance of someone who flouts danger? Like Anzengruber's Stone Chopper John, he says to himself and even explicitly to others that 'Nothing can happen to *me*'.[7] Countertransference – turned into a kind of strategic psychological malice in the face of death – would be the expression of the buffoonery of the epic hero and a derision of the *epos*. The *epos* demands a tectonic disruption of language and thus of this relation to death. At the same time as it testifies to it, the concept of transference might then be defined as a disavowal of the murder.

As Émil Staiger has shown, what is at stake is precisely the fact that in Homer's epic poem the encounter between two men, especially when it's a question of engaging hostilities in a duel, invariably entails the reciprocal interrogation of the name and of its origins:

> When two men ready themselves for combat with each other they ask for name and origin, and the man questioned relates the history of his clan back to the oldest forefathers, even to the god that founded the family. When Agamemnon takes hold of the sceptre, we hear its whole history, who made it, who carried it, how it went from Zeus to Hermes, from Hermes to Pelops, and finally came into Agamemnon's hands.[8]

Someone like Glaucos, belonging to a matriarchal people, who says 'why ask about my birth? Like the generations of leaves, the lives of mortal men [...] as one generation comes to life, another dies away',[9] flees from the *memory* ordained by the 'epic commemoration' of the reciprocal interrogation by means of language – what is demanded of language is that it *names*. Since in naming language claims filiation in a lineage. This 'epic commemoration' (*das epische Gedenken*, used here in the Heideggerian sense of *Gedächtnis*) [memory] accords precisely to the language that names the power to arrest the negligent flight of men, who speak to forget their origins and thus the dead of their lineage. Like Glaucos, matriarchal men are prone to treat generations like 'generations of leaves' and thus to discourage in advance any consideration of the order of their genealogy. If they make common use of language to devote themselves to an exclusive bond with the mother – who denies genealogy – isn't it because, for them, *entering into the nomination process of language* means entering into the terror of the distance from the place from which the question arises? The place from which the question arises belongs to language itself, which speech fears to approach. Staiger continues:

> Thus I can only ask 'From where' if a fixed 'here' exists; likewise, the position of 'here' can only be determined by knowing 'from where'. The answer to the question anchors in a solid base all that is in question. This base is in the past, which, being something complete, stands still and can no longer change. Whoever asks the question 'from where' must take up a position in relation to this past. Thus opposite sides are created: the position of the person asking the question as well as the position of the object of the question are fixed.[10]

If the one who is questioned is tempted for a long time by the *passion of time* and by a speech that bears memory – *Er-innerung* marks at once the emergence of the deepest inside and the appropriation of interiority – such a passion roots itself in the past and knows no limit. The only limit it can encounter is that of the memory of the language that names. *This memory does not belong to someone, but only to the language spoken by someone.* The temporality of this memory does not arise out of the past but from the distance of the words of speech inclined towards the complaint: the *epos* of this memory, both in and against the encounter with the duration of memory, names what words pronounce. The anachronic memory of the *epos* is the *naming of the name*. The act of naming makes the name come to memory.

Of course, one can take as read any account of the *transferential passion* for the name and its origins. But perhaps not, especially when a question like the following arises: if transference is reminiscent speech, suffering from the impossibility of recalling a fleeting past that haunts it, how can we speak of *the* transference, rediscovering in this word the occult and strange aspects it gestures towards – the ungraspable movement that displaces any site, its plural aspect, its constantly mobile play of masks, its uncertain affects? In this respect isn't countertransference a discursive consciousness which tends precisely, so that the analyst can refer to the transference of his patient, to *relationise* the patient's experiences (the well-known invocation of the 'transferential relation') and *intentionalise* its objects (maternal or paternal) or modes (positive or negative)? In the clinical expositions of psychoanalysis the description of transference proceeds most often through a sort of discourse of relational legalism which is supposed to preserve, by means of disjunction, the property and identity of persons by doubling their reality (physical person and psychical person). The countertransferential consciousness according to which, in the context of the sessions, the patient *addresses themselves to me* as if *I* could respond maternally to their elemental need for tenderness and affective warmth – while all the time demanding that nothing about *my person* should be a cause for illusion and that *I* remain *the one* who proves and guarantees the rigour and stability of the *frame* against their *own* impulsions to transgress it: this is a quite ordinary observation which, expressed as closely as possible in relation to what is perceived, can either remain at the level of factual observation or (bearing in mind what I know of the patient's relation to their mother and to an absent father) form an explanatory discourse out of implicit parental imagos. The operation of disjunction is the perceptual function of the countertransference. The move to explication – if based on the patient's associations – can of course also lead us to differentiate the imagos (and allow the integration of other figures, ultimately substitutes from childhood: uncle, aunt, brother or sister...) and to more finely qualify the affective movements associated with them. But this will remain a relational discourse that will set itself in place on the basis of *an understanding of countertransference as a meta-communicative function*. It is as if this technically strategic function sought to *isolate* the projective dynamics of an imaginary formation provoked by the *presence of the analyst in person* by outlining the object of the intended addressee. Amongst those who currently seek to formalise, on the basis of the institutional practice of supervision, the complex discursive processes of transference as a meta-communicative model, the theoretical work of Robert Langs is the most ideologically exemplary.[11] However one cannot fail to be struck by the legalistic character of the reasoning that the discursive explanation of transference leads to. Jean Laplanche – rightly suspicious of such definitions – discerns the risks of this kind of legalism:

> Transference is thus a transport of something from… to… The *transport itself* is the ultimate point: it is what we are trying to focus on, while we cannot approach it directly (…) So I prefer to stick with the *from… to…*. The *to*, as we will see later, is *to* the analyst: what is the person of the analyst, what situation and what personality must be there for there to be transference?[12]

Laplanche underlines the ambiguities of the expression 'transference *from* [de]', noting the grammatical doubling at stake here ('transfer *of* [de] merchandise *from* [de] Paris'):

> With an ambiguity of meaning, because one can wonder to what extent the place from whence one transports and what is transported are not related? Does one not transport the point of departure, in transporting something from this point of departure? I will explain: we speak of paternal transference, maternal transference, and so on; of course, this means that something has been transported from the father; but if there was, let's say, a pure and simple transport of the father, as such, onto someone else, it would evidently be a question of a delirious transference.[13]

We cannot fault Laplanche for exploring these grammatical ambiguities and their syntactic consequences, arising from the question: *what is transferred from and to?* We can see that under these conditions the term 'transference' implies logical and causal representations of and about the point of origin and destination, as well as questions about the nature of the object that is transported. But does *transference* imply specifically *this* linguistic formation, or is that imposed solely by the word itself? Freud's discovery of the phenomenon of transference submits it of course, and we will return to this, to the self-representation of the role played by the *presence of the analyst in person*, but it doesn't steer it away from the a-temporality and hallucinatory aspect of the unconscious:

The unconscious impulses do not want to be remembered in the way the treatment desires them to be, but endeavour to reproduce themselves in accordance with the timelessness of the unconscious and its capacity for hallucination. Just as happens in dreams, the patient regards the products of the awakening of his unconscious impulses as contemporaneous and real; he seeks to put his passions into action without taking any account of the real situation. The doctor tries to compel him to fit these emotional impulses into the nexus of the treatment and of his life-history, to submit them to intellectual consideration and to understand them in the light of their psychical value. This struggle between the doctor and the patient, between intellect and instinctual life, between understanding and seeking to act, is played out almost exclusively in the phenomena of transference. It is on that field that the victory must be won, the victory whose expression is the permanent cure of the neurosis. It cannot be disputed that controlling the phenomena of transference presents the psychoanalyst with the greatest difficulties. But it should not be forgotten that it is precisely they that do us the inestimable service of making the patient's hidden and forgotten erotic impulses immediate and manifest. For when all is said and done, it is impossible to destroy anyone *in absentia* or *in effigie*.[14]

This text unambivalently situates the phenomenon of transference *in continuity with the dream*: we find the same notion of the *real present* that in the dreamer's image gives credence to what he is living in the dream. With the slight difference, however, that in this case the nocturnal dreamer appears in the waking state, and also that this waking appearance creates a baroque and unsettling strangeness, since the analyst immediately credits the hallucinatory image to his own real presence using this presence (like the dream) as a diurnal residue. In this sense – as Freud doesn't stop recommending on other occasions – analysts *should* listen to the transference just as they listen to dreams. How is it then that the analyst is *attracted* by the hallucinatory content of the transference to the extent of having to represent himself as distinct from his own person through a quasi-conscious disjunction and doubling of himself? Finally, and especially, speaking of 'hidden or forgotten' 'amorous impulses', Freud concludes with the formula: 'it is impossible to destroy anyone *in absentia* or *in effigie*': the Latin locution 'in effigie' designates the putting to death of the criminal and their change of *aspect* (Patrick Lacoste). What is played upon the present person of the analyst – which in the transference can pass as amorous capture – *puts the image to death*. Isn't the hallucinatory image the clearest manifestation of the function of a visual credence in the presence of the present and of anachronic memory sealed by *forgetting*? At the same time the necessarily violent aspect of the phenomenon of transference arises from the fact that in its insistence transference tends to put the image to death as if to effect an elusive murder. In this light we can understand that the expression 'transfer onto the person of the analyst' is ultimately misleading, since it arises – for supposedly technical reasons – from the analyst themselves, in part through their hypnotic identification with the *lure* of the transferential address.

We have used the term *legalism* to describe a tendency in the (clinical) explication of psychoanalytic discourse. We can qualify this legalism as mannerist, recalling that for a writer such as Baltasar Gracian, one of the particularities of baroque mannerism is the production of a rhetoric of exhaustive explication, inverting, as in a mirror, the temporal schemas of the perception of the other. At the centre of this operation, making identification and projection play against one another and providing the driving force of this dynamic, is the *person* who is the author of this play. In the end, the only rhetorical question one can ask concerning transference is this: *who* is the *author* of the transference? This question is partially implied in this well-known proposition from Freud:

> But the productive powers of the neurosis are by no means extinguished; they are occupied in the creation of a special class of mental structures, for the most part unconscious, to which the name of 'transferences' may be given. What are transferences? They are new editions or facsimiles of the impulses and phantasies which are aroused and made conscious during the progress of the analysis; but they have this peculiarity, which is characteristic for their species, that they replace some earlier person by the person of the physician. To put it another way: a whole series of psychological experiences are revived, not as belonging to the past, but as applying to the person of the physician at the present moment.[15]

The conception of transference that Freud expresses here is not far from the one he drew in 1888 from Bernheim's thesis: the transfer of sensitivity from one part of the body to the corresponding part on the other side is a phenomenon which is reproducible by means of suggestion, and the introduction of the *person* of the hypnotiser doesn't only produce the phenomenon but *intensifies* it. The idea obviously depends on the associationism current at the time, notably in neurology. But it also belongs – precisely through the light thrown on it by Hume – to the evolution of the Latin term *translatio*.

Moreover, if when he uses the word for the first time Freud does so in French ('*transfert*' and not *Ubertragung*), this is because he wanted to underline its Latin origin.[16] And today – whatever specificity the term transference has in psychoanalysis – we can hardly keep this term apart from those other words that perceptibly carry the same meaning: *transport, transmission, translation, traduction*, especially in light of the attention these terms have merited from Walter Benjamin, Martin Heidegger, Hannah

Arendt, and closer to us, Antoine Berman.[17] It certainly behoves us to inter-rogate, as others have,[18] the question of the internal correspondences in Freud and in psychoanalysis between the words and concepts of transference, translation, transmission, transcription and reinscription – such words raising the difficult and considerable problems of memory, speech and writing. Not conflating these words and working with the distinctions between them would perceptibly enrich the semantic capacities of the word 'transference' in psychoanalysis. For the moment let it suffice that we outline the horizons of the word, precisely at that point where the difficulty that concerns us is met: *the critical rejection, by the word itself, of an explanatory discursivity, given that the word wants to maintain the link to anachronic memory, as well as to its non-com-municative and non-relational aspects.* This amounts to saying that there is no meta-language for transference. And if for analysts what matters is to com-municate to others the testimony of an experience drawn from treatment, they cannot do this in a valid way without restoring to their sources the *figures of language* arising as echoes from spoken words. An analytic process is *trans-mitted* more effectively if it is communicated under certain conditions, in restoring certain words to a *moment* that keeps their associative silence alive, in the analyst themselves. An exhaustive account of the treatment (telling all) would certainly not do justice to the *process*. It should thus suffice to speak only a few words at the nodal points of the associative tissue for these words, heard again when they are pronounced, to indicate the sites of transference. What's at stake here is nothing less than knowing *under what conditions* (where, with whom, at what point and to what end) an analyst can give an account of the work they have done or are doing with the patient. Evidently, as we'll see, this brings up the question of the *situation of supervision*, under-stood both in the narrow and broader sense.

Language would thus be made such that it does not – without distor-tion – incorporate the capacity to *give an account* of what is transported from one person to another when what is transported is not materialised in the semiotic form of a message. We refer here to 'language': it would be more apt to say that it is language insofar as it concerns certain languages that lexically and syntactically privilege the *content* of the *communication* at the expense of place, distance and time. Since Aristotle we in fact know that the corporeal – physical – place of interlocutors pertains to the act of enunciation. This place is imposed in the encounter as that of an epoch and the memory of an epoch in relation to the interlocutor and with the intention of telling and speaking. This disposition of the spoken text is inherent to the poetics of tragedy: bodies are held at a certain distance that evolves in the course of the 'exchange' and the meaning of what will be spoken and pronounced depends on this distance which each *must* recog-nise in relation to their own memory. In this light everything then becomes very important, because it takes the slightest carelessness with respect to distance and misunderstanding of the memory of the ages to result in mad violence – madness or murder – in which a human being loses their identity and errs through a betrayal of themselves. The sites of human speech – places of transport or transference – are obscured or illuminated as soon as the functions of signification or communication in language or speech are over-privileged. In different ways this is what J. Lohman and Walter Benjamin understood so well. If it is a question of rediscovering the truly 'spiritual' function of speech, then signification and communication belong to words alone, insofar as they point to local positions, which bear witness to the 'relation' of those speaking to each other.

Once we agree that transference does not mean either a 'relation' (in the discursive sense of the term) or an affective-representational intention (in the 'cognitive' sense), the language that bears witness to it should not 'hetero-genise' its nature as a transport of places. The Freudian notion of *Entstellung* supports this consideration. This concept implies that any change of place not only transforms its agent but also modifies the place itself. In another context this idea was remarkably expressed by Walter Benjamin in relation to the archaeological metaphor of memory: it is not only what is exhumed (*Ausgraben*) that matters but the changes to the soil that this exhumation involves (see Georges Didi-Huberman's book *Ce que nous voyons, ce qui nous regarde* [What We See Looks At Us]). At a certain point the metaphor of archaeology brings geology into play. *Entstellung* is precisely that: the place is not fixed, or, at the least, it is *delocalised* by the very fact of a change of place. In analysis, what is first thought is not the same when that thought returns. The movements that displace places (and perhaps lines too![19]), and which mean that each place is transported by its displacement to become another place, these are transferential movements. In other words the specificity of transference is a physical *translatio*. On this account, *transference* in psycho-analysis receives – at least in the idea of the word – the still Aristotelean and even Thomist determinations according to which translation is the dynamic of a movement or physical passage that affects language (the same words are modified each time they are spoken) and cannot on its own do justice to the *action of transport* that itself does the work of *traductio*, that is *the engendering of form*. Following the crucial description offered by Antoine Berman:

> The term *traduction* appears in the Middle Ages in theological writings in the wake of Aristotle (Saint-Thomas, Averroes). We still find it, in the sense it had for these thinkers, in Leibniz's *Theodicy*, in which the context is not at all the activity of translation. *Traductio* is used in the framework of speculations on form and matter. (…) Translation [*traduction*] is the transfer or transmission of a form. In the *Theodicy* Leibniz gives as an example the 'translation of souls', 'as if the souls of children were engendered (*per traducem*) from the soul or the souls of those from which their body is engendered' (§ 86). Because the soul is a form, form being, Leibniz says, 'a principle of action, found in the one who acts' (§ 87).
>
> *Traductio* is thus the active transmission of a form, form being itself the active principle of a being.[20]

The 'translation of souls' is a *transfer of souls*. This of course means the passage of one generation to another through engenderment but also, keeping as close as possible to Freud's Leibnizian filiation, passing through Fechner, the transfer of souls also implies that the *Seele* (soul), in being translated, genealogically transmits the former soul – which can be described as the soul of the ancestor. Under these conditions the transfer of souls links two words: if the soul is the ancestral form specific to the genealogy of the individual and to the memory of a species, it is not straightforwardly 'translated' from parent to child. The child – and on this account also what Freud refers to as 'childhood' or 'infancy' – is the one whose sexual embodiment on the verge of language gives the most intense and fugitive eligibility to the *form* which is by definition 'fossil'. Wouldn't transference – in its psychoanalytic sense – thus involve the two meanings of *translatio* (a dynamic movement) and *traductio* (the engendering by the soul of a form of the soul which is the *reproduction* – the copy – of the ancestral soul)? The copy of the ancestral soul can thus be said to be the fossil-form of the ancestor.

In this light the importance accorded by Freud to language in the concept of a recapitulation (this time of a metapsychological order) of phylogenesis within ontogenesis belongs to the Leibnizian tradition of the unconscious. Languages function as the deposit of inheritance and it is through the relation to language that the transfer of souls takes place. As such it makes sense to reconstitute – exactly on the model of the memory of the dream – the metapsychological meaning of what one refers to as regression – that is, a *present* which remembers an anachronised past, the *time* of which is an *Erinnerung* (the reappropriation of a background), a passionate *Erinnerung* of the soul insofar as the soul is the absent ancestor. Perhaps, through approaching such a genealogical idea of transference, a formulation like this should speak of the reappropriation of the souls of ancestors through transference, but we will see further on what it might be appropriate to think about such a proposition.

What is implied by this argument is not only that any discourse on communication and relation (any metadiscourse) is radically inadequate when it comes to describing transference. We must also preserve, in analytic transference, the unsettling power of the memory of the soul which is at work in the *copies* of *imagos* for which the *person of the analyst* is the *screen*, in the two senses of the word. It is on this that we must focus our attention concerning the meaning that transference gives to the *person* and moreover to the *presence of the analyst in person*. Because rather than asking ourselves about 'transference onto the person' what makes sense is to wonder why *such a person*, under conditions we all know, *increases* the regressive intensity of the memory of the soul of the ancestor.

The Transferential *Imago*

The interest presented by Jung's use of the term imago has definitely been drastically reduced either through joining him by privileging through it the notion of the archetype, imbued with cultural phylogeneticism, or in sticking closer to Freud with the notion of the 'unconscious complex'. However, the perspective deliberately adopted by Jung, in *The Psychology of Dementia Praecox* and especially in *The Metamorphosis of the Soul and its Symbols*, concerned the intention to give credence to a metaphysical-theological concept drawn from the Middle Ages, describing the mirror of the soul, giving access to the knowledge of its genealogy and through it to a knowledge of the ancestor. The reproaches subsequently addressed to Jung for having recourse to mediaeval psychology would not have surprised him, since the deliberate choice of the word *imago* corresponded in fact to a project to restore the presence of an organisational 'image' unknown to consciousness in the actual present of an encounter or a relation. Moreover Jung did not forget what his interest in the *imago* and its animation owed to the reading of Daniel Paul Schreber's *Memories of my Nervous Illness* – in which the destiny of souls is a major preoccupation.

However, following here some suggestions from Georges Didi-Huberman, the Roman meaning of *imago* involves a quasi-juridical reality pertaining to the practice of mourning. Patrician families have the duty and privilege of possessing an *atrium* inside their house, a closed room with a series of heads or busts constituting *casts* of the living or rather of the dead with the features of the living. These images of ancestors are made of wax. They are enclosed in small cupboards. The atrium is a room which is kept closed, which in some sense delineates the genealogy of the master of the house. The images have an extraordinary indexical resemblance.[21] In certain circumstances (*pompa funebris*) an operation is carried out which consists in 'opening the images' (*imagines aperire*): this involves opening the cupboards of the atrium and making the images move in procession. So the ritual of showing the *imagines* (the dead family) in the presence of the living family (in the broad sense of *familia*) is not only about celebrating the dead but, through the procession of images, it is also about transmitting and edifying. According to a text by Polybius (*Histories*, Book 6, 53) the image in question is a mask with an extraordinary resemblance as much through its shape as through its colour:

> On public holidays, they open up the shrines and carefully decorate the icons, and whenever a notable family member dies, they take them out for the funeral procession and put them on those who seem to bear the closest resemblance to the dead men, in height and general appearance.[22]

These men are extras (*figurants*). They wear the colours of the deceased's toga. This figuration accompanying the images as well as their insignia is itself exposed to the speech of an orator, who speaks about the dead man. Epic immortality is thus constructed by this relating of images, accompanied by a processional figuration, to other images – those borne by the words describing the virtues of the deceased. The 'young people' present at the spectacle are impressed in their souls by images (masks with 'the closest resemblance') and by the *living figuration* of the latter. The *imitation* made possible by the *procession* depends in some way on the *intensification* engendered by the opening of the images. Such an opening under these conditions is destined towards a *heroic reproduction* – thanks to the casts – of that which is contained and conserved by the *imago*.

These suggestions are interesting in more than one respect, due to the very semantic ambivalence held by the *imago*. The *imagines* – which are masks taken immediately from the dead and which have 'the closest resemblance' to them – refer of course to what one can describe as the *imago* of the dead ancestor; and this is all the more true insofar as the *imagines* are kept in the house in a place which represents a specific location genealogically unifying the lineage of the deceased. The procession of images is fact a *process* of reanimation through transport. The *imago* is at the same time one of these images and *the* immortalised image which transcends them all. From the perspective that interests us here, we credit Jung with having made of the image (notably but not only the paternal image) the mirror of the genealogical soul, which transferential regression seeks to revive in each of us so we can take possession of our own psychic life. So through the manoeuvre of the funeral rites the Romans in fact aimed as we've said to produce a transference which transmits and reproduces it in an augmented way. That the *transferential imago* hides the image of a dead ancestor, even of the genealogical lineages of the dead – this can point in the direction of the idea that we have begun to develop, that according to which *transference* involves the exhumation of a death and a process consisting in making it alive again for the psyche. In summary, transference would be at the same time the putting back to work of mourning and the 'work' of forgetting. In the same way that dream images attempt to give a psychic sepulchre to our dead, the transferential imago could be said to involve this passion for the soul of the ancestor. But on the other hand, one can consider that the *imagines* which are masks of *faces* with 'the closest resemblance' to the dead are *already* cast on the basis of the *appearance* of the living. We believe we can uncover that such casts have the capacity to *reveal* the transference of the dead to the living, those who visually *appear*. Would it not then be the specific property of the cosmetics of the masks obtained by means of such casts in wax to call in some way for the *appearance* of a *figure* with the indexical power to embody the soul of the dead for sight? In which case the images obtained (engendered or produced) through the transference would be 'copies' of an original that would not allow itself to be directly recognised. Those who, in the Roman ceremony, augment resemblance by doubling it, – the 'extras' – have the function of immortalising death by means of living memory at the same time as they have the function of visual *allusion* through the *imago*. The opening of the images is the transferential *process* itself. The role of epic speech on the part of the orator is no less equivalent to the intervention of images in the voicing of words, with the aim not only to impress young souls but also to avoid the image materialised or embodied by the mask and the extra (*figurant*) being fixed as an idol: this speech and its voice give a psychic sepulchre to the imago before the latter returns to the atrium, within the house. It is only under these conditions that one could then suppose that the *imagos* – that the living will become – can be transferred (and therefore be also transferential) for the one who seeks the memory of the soul of the ancestor, in order to appropriate their own soul for themselves.

In the text of the essay on *Gradiva*, even if they are not masks made of wax, we are also in fact dealing with *casts*. While this isn't the right moment to follow the commentary that Freud devotes to Jensen's 'Pompeiian fantasy' step by step, we can note that the archaeologist's dream of the burial of Gradiva consigns to his delirium the care – under the direction of Zöe Bertgang – of following the regressive path of the 'sick man' towards the deliverance and the reappropriation of his living love object, held captive up to that point in the bronze or stone casts. The *process(ion)*, in this case *the movement towards*, if we heed the role played by the walking steps and the always slightly suspended posture of Gradiva, is literally indicated as a transferential *Entstellung*, a change of place and a modification of the place through this change. Beyond the exemplary and ideal 'cure through love', we should retain precisely the point that the *cast*, restoring with closest resemblance the *aspectual* form (the aspect of time) of the living form of the dead person, works as an unwritten writing (a reimpression) of the most fundamental corporeal elements of the incorporeal (the voice, the gestures, the face); the cast is thus an *imprint of the soul* which only manifests the most readable form of the image that is seen. If the transferential *imago* is a *mask*, its appearance is such that its features are the *signs of language* which resemble the features of the face but cannot be taken for them. In this sense, the *mask of the imago* pertains exactly to the *memory* which Freud tells us is so evanescent that it seems the only thing that 'can trace (*einzeichnen*) the old features (*die alten Züge*) in the new picture (*in das neue Bild*)'.[23] How in fact could it be otherwise when it comes to giving life back to the inanimate? Does animism operate any differently? The famous 'inference of identification' of which Freud speaks[24] to indicate the essence of the animist process cannot be explained solely through the term projection. Unless we turn things round and say that *projection*, the secret of which is made intelligible through the dream itself, is the mode of perception through the image, the element of what it has seen that it remembers.

But perhaps it is from this point on that we should focus our attention on the recurrent expression in Freud, '*the person themselves*', and, as concerns the dynamics of transference, on the 'person of the physician'.

The Person

Freud's 1915 text 'The Unconscious' will be our point of reference here for a moment. His reasoning depends on the inference of an identification, – '*per analogiam*' – which enables us to believe, on the basis of our conscious awareness of 'our own mental states', that *another* human also has a consciousness as we do; this in order to make the other's behaviour understandable 'by analogy from their observable utterances and actions'.[25] Such an attitude is certainly not foreign to the need to defend ourselves against the hostile strangeness of the *other* and is the base of communication, which substitutes identificatory exchanges for hostility:

> This inference (or this identification) was formerly extended by the ego to other human beings, to animals, plants, inanimate objects and to the world at large, and proved serviceable so long as their similarity to the individual ego was overwhelmingly great; but it became more untrustworthy in proportion as the difference between the ego and these 'others' widened. Today, our critical judgement is already in doubt on the question of the consciousness in animals; we refuse to admit it in plants and we regard the assumption of its existence in inanimate matter as mysticism.[26]

The appeal in this instance to the *animist conception*, which is a psychic theory of life and of the living being, recognises the 'original inclination to identification', 'where the original inclination to identification has withstood criticism – that is, when the "others" are our fellow men'.[27] And the 'psychoanalytic assumption of unconscious mental activity' is nothing other than a 'further expansion of the primitive animism which caused us to see copies of our own consciousness all around us'.[28] Except that, after the 'Kantian correction':

> We must say: all the acts and manifestations which I notice in myself and do not know how to link up with the rest of my mental life must be judged as if they belonged to someone else; they are to be explained by a mental life ascribed to this other person. Furthermore, experience shows that we understand very well how to interpret in other people (that is, how to fit into their chain of mental events) the same acts which we refuse to acknowledge as being mental in ourselves.[29]

The denial of the unconscious, that is of the psychic processes belonging to the individual person [*la personne propre*] takes the route of a double operation: the impossibility of recognising them as belonging to us and their attribution to the other as a conscious activity.[30] Reasoning through inference and identification – undertaken in the abstract – leads to the hypothesis of a 'second consciousness'. Psychoanalysis teaches us to modify this inference:

> Analytic investigation reveals some of these latent processes [*which enjoy a high degree of mutual independence, as though they had no connection with one another, and knew nothing of one another*] as having characteristics and peculiarities which seem alien to us, or even incredible, and which run directly counter to the attributes of consciousness with which we are familiar.[31]

We know that thus is clarified the behaviour of the paranoiac who refuses 'the category of the accidental [...] as far as the psychical manifestations of other people are concerned':

> How does he reach this position? Probably here as in so many similar cases he projects onto the mental life of other people what is unconsciously present in his own. In paranoia many sorts of things force their way through to consciousness whose presence in the unconscious of normal and neurotic people we can demonstrate only through psychoanalysis.[32]

The capacity to 'see more clearly' with which paranoia endows the individual consists notably in recognising the unconscious hostility which escapes normal consciousness.[33]

We know that Freud was not preoccupied in the slightest by the phenomenological philosophy of intersubjectivity, at a time however when the question was so to speak the order of the day for philosophers and clinical psychiatrists such as Ludwig Binswanger. Isn't the originally animist belief in the 'original inclination to identification' enough to account for the particular case of inference *par analogiam* which accords to the other the same capacity to recognise oneself as oneself? The repression of hostile movements which characterise the *Urmensch* (the 'original man') and which lead them immediately to consider the other as a foreign enemy corresponds to a cultural development involving the origin of psychology: communication between human beings depends on the same kind of repression – that is, a *refrigeration* of the psychic. And, inversely, the paranoiac is endowed with a consciousness and a memory supposed not to miss any aspect of the perception of the other as a hostile other. Paranoia, accordingly, is incontestably a vestige of the original human. The importance that the paranoiac accords to the integrity of their own body as well as the vigilant consciousness they have of their *ego* positions them at the installation of the ethics of the person as the juridical expression of the *property* of the person, and of the person as a property. And if the paranoiac is not especially predisposed towards *transference*, this is specifically because they can see that it entails the risk of alteration represented by giving oneself over to the power of another. This informs the whole issue of transference for Schreber. But it is the so to speak metapsychological character [*personnage*] of the paranoiac that interests us here, because of the counterpoint it can provide in the clarification of what Freud seems to have in mind as concerns the *original man*. As long as the latter is faced with the *other* as a stranger-enemy, death retains its meaning as an immediate or deferred suppression of life. We've seen that the cultural evolution of man with respect to death entails a distancing of the *other* [*autre*] into the other person [*autrui*] – a distancing which is equivalent to the negation of death as a 'power of disappearance'. The original man tends to endow the souls of those others that they love with immortality, a guarantee – contemporary with the discovery of mourning – that death will not mean their disappearance. The *person* is then the projection onto the loved other of what constitutes the consciousness of the *own person* [*la personne propre*]. The point of doubling the word 'person' with the reflective qualification 'own' is obviously to secure the *psychological content* of the word, without which it would remain as crystalline as the optical formation of the eye.

It is nevertheless important to consider that the word *person*, fortuitously playing on the sense of *someone* (*Jemand*) and *no-one* (*Niemand*),[34] engages us with the strangeness of the transference. It is not enough to say in fact that the person signifies the mask, we have to recognise that it relates to the invisibility of the other and the transparent double of the self. In this sense, the person always has the potential for unsettling strangeness when, as in Freud's words, what should remain hidden becomes manifest. Freud was interested, after Rank, in the motif of the 'double', as one of the motifs that 'provoked the feeling of the uncanny':

> These themes are all concerned with the phenomenon of the 'double', which appears in every shape and in every degree of development. Thus we have characters who are to be considered identical because they look alike. This relation is accentuated by mental processes leaping from one of these characters to another – by what we should call telepathy –, so that the one possesses knowledge, feelings and experience in common with the other. Or it is marked by the fact that the subject identifies himself with someone else, so that he is in doubt as to which his self is or substitutes the extraneous self for his own. In other words, there is a doubling, dividing, and interchanging of the self. And finally, there is the constant recurrence of the same thing – the repetition of the same features or character-traits or vicissitudes, of the same crimes, or even the same names through several consecutive generations.[35]

Rank had already considered the theme of the double in relation to reflections in mirrors, to guardian spirits, to the belief in the soul and to the fear of death ... Freud confirms that 'probably the "immortal" soul was the first "double of the body"'.[36] He adds: 'This invention of doubling as a preservation against extinction has its counterpart in the language of dreams, which is fond of representing castration by a doubling or multiplication of a genital symbol. The same desire led the Ancient Egyptians to develop *the art of making images of the dead in lasting materials'*.[37]

W. Granoff and J.M. Rey have already explored the correspondences between telepathy and transference, notably with respect to the *Uber-tragungsgedanken* (transference thoughts – transference of thoughts).[38] What attracts our attention here is precisely this *question*: how can the *person* be the *place* of the manifestation of *what it is* – that is, a stranger with respect to its own intimacy? In other words, doesn't the unsettling strangeness of the person appear – as we can note with certain patients – as a *projection of the same* in the waking state, and isn't it this projection which constitutes, *intrapsychically*, the experience at the basis of obsessional doubt?

> In a first interview with a view to starting analysis Charlotte describes the intolerable sensation that she now feels every day (notably since the birth of her son, now 3 years old) of *forgetting what she has done between one gesture and another*. Just after her labour she felt an intense panic and a deep despair at the thought that she could never look after her child if she couldn't immediately find her mother again, her mother having disappeared more than fifteen years ago. During the first months after the birth of the child Charlotte finds every activity more and more difficult: in her house, where she is alone in bringing up the child, she accomplishes the same gesture several times in order to assure herself that she has completed it, but this does not bring her any certainty and completely exhausts her. It's mainly when it comes to 'changing the baby' that she is overcome with doubt. She explains this idea by stopping a long time in front of the mirror, trying to persuade herself that she 'is not changing'. She had hoped that pregnancy would cure her of doubt about her continuity as a person, but it was not to be, and the refusal of the man – already married, moreover – to acknowledge the child that he did not want put her in a state of disarray which was quickly substituted by the relief of only having to look after the child. In the most difficult moments of her doubt she has to struggle against the phobia of an impulse to suffocate the child, an impulse that takes hold of her when she realises that she has not experienced what she thought would be the benefit of pregnancy. She reproaches her mother, who despite her appeals has still not appeared, for having brought her up to the age of fifteen in complete ignorance of her father (who she has never seen) or any family. She hopes that analysis will rid her of the 'responsibility for her person'

and relieve her of the exhausting consciousness of always having to remember what she is doing. The fact that her mother hasn't responded to her appeals is 'perhaps not as bad as all that': nothing is less certain, she thinks, than the idea that she could come to know her past thanks to her and at her side.

In this observation – limited only to the first session – we find condensed the specific qualities of the doubt provoked in the subject by the anxiety surrounding their own sense of themselves as a person, *in the waking state*: nothing can in itself assure this young woman that she stays the same person between one gesture and another, all the more so insofar as the presence of the child diffuses her perception of her own body which she nevertheless tries to put back together – but in vain – through extended periods in front of her mirror.

The interest we have here in obsessional doubt is that provoked by the *person themselves*. While in the dream – as Freud reminds us – projection has the specific quality of producing in some way the *sameness of the person* [*le même de la personne*], as masked or disguised in other figures who, in reality, are *the person of the dreamer* themselves it is as if the experience of obsessional (and paranoid) doubt only had the capacity of this recourse in the mode of waking consciousness, through transferentially soliciting the analyst to dream in some way what the patient is unable to dream in their own sleep.[39] The comparison between the dream and the joke affords Freud the opportunity to underline the *value of the person themselves* – as the *person of the dream* – since the transgression of which it is the object is constitutive of the *belief in the present of the image*; in this case the *person* does not provoke the unsettling strangeness of the same in the form of the double and the endopsychic functioning of the dream's projection paradoxically guarantees the dreamer's own self by means of belief in the alterity of the figures [*personnages*] *seen* in the dream. In the joke (*Witz*) the function of alterity finds its mobility thanks to the circularity of the third, inherent to the transport in the *Witz*:

> A dream is a completely asocial mental product; it has nothing to communicate to anyone else; it arises within the subject as a compromise between the mental forces struggling in him, it remains unintelligible to the subject himself and is for that reason totally uninteresting to other people.[40]

The 'nullity' of the dream is aligned with the solipsism of the person. We are reminded, in the 'Metapsychological Supplement to the Theory of Dreams' that:

> we know that dreams are completely egoistic and that the person who plays the chief part in their scenes is always to be recognized as the dreamer themselves [*la personne propre*].[41]

The egoism of the person of the dreamer in their dream is in some way 'responsible' for the *incomprehensibility* of the dream to the person and its *incommunicability* to others: two characteristics that can be understood precisely as indicating the *transference of which the dream is made* and on the model of which the symptom is conceived.[42]

It is on this point that the dream in fact constitutes the paradigm of transference in the treatment. And, one must add, no interpretation of the transference can proceed from anything other than the dream, since it is the dream that forms the language of this interpretation. In other words, any interpretation of the transference which would tend to focus explicitly on the person of the analyst, forgetting that they are only the present shadow (*figurant*) of the person of the analyst, makes its language inadequate for interpretation.

But it is appropriate now to understand *transference in the treatment* as at the time making use of a projective mechanism analogous to that of the dream (the disguising of the person of the dreamer in figures in which they do not recognise themselves) yet nevertheless different insofar as the presence of the person of the analyst obliges the projection to come back into words, as the speculative sites of the person themselves [*la personne propre*]. In this sense the regression inherent in transference in the treatment is made possible by the personal presence of the analyst insofar as this presence inhibits the oneiric mechanism of projection (it involves the appresentation of an *other*) and this *person* figures the enigmatic point of memory in regression. While delirium, in the psychotherapy of a psychotic, offers the analyst the means to appresent themselves in person under the mask of the protagonists of the delirium, in delirious transferences, the person of the analyst becomes the focus of the provocation of the unsettling strangeness of the person's double.

The technical complexity of work with patients prone to delirious transferences has been well illustrated by studies like those of M. Little and H. Searles.[43] In a contribution on psychotic states, Harold Searles writes:

> I emphatically do not mean that, in order to function effectively as a therapist for the schizophrenic person, one needs to become crazy, or partially crazy, along with him. What I mean is that, while keeping in touch with one's own individual identity, one must become able to experience within oneself, in manageable increments, the intense and discoordinate emotions the patient is having unconsciously to defend against with his craziness. This process provides the necessary therapeutic context for the patient's coming to explore and understand the meanings of his psychosis, his psychosis which is being projected upon the therapist as the transference personification of the crazinesses in the parents. It provides the foundation, also, for the patient's coming to accept and integrate [their] own human emotions, partially

through identification with the therapist whose humanness has been able to cope with and integrate this projected schizophrenic onslaught.[44]

In the light of the importance accorded by this psychoanalytic literature to the problematic of the *identity of the psychoanalyst*, we can certainly better understand the conditions under which such a problematic emerges; the theory of psychotic transference – even the theory of the psychotic dimensions of transference – in fact necessitates an intersubjective conception of countertransference, that is of the means found in the latter to accept the 'parental projections of madness' by the patient onto the person of the analyst, and to operate a subjective disjunction, allowing them to maintain their own identity. But we know that such a conception – arising from a pragmatic phenomenology – tends precisely to ignore, in the transference of the treatment, everything that relates at once to the *optical structure of the person themselves* (in the sense that we have brought out from the dream and from the feeling of the uncanny), which 'functions' in the framework, which is itself optical, of the *analytic situation*, and, on the other hand, to the pulsional function accorded conjointly to the active/ passive alternative and to the couples of voyeurism/exhibitionism and masochism/sadism.

In *Instincts and their Vicissitudes*, even if not referring to transference, Freud speaks of a 'turning round [...] upon the subject's own self':

> The turning round of an instinct upon the subject's own self is made plausible by the reflection that masochism is actually sadism turned round upon the subject's own ego, and that exhibitionism includes looking at his own body. Analytic observation, indeed, leaves us in no doubt that the masochist shares in the enjoyment of the assault upon himself, and that the exhibitionist shares in the enjoyment of [the sight of] his exposure. The essence of the process is thus the change of the object, while the aim remains unchanged.[45]

In fact, the pairs of opposites, *masochism/sadism, exhibitionism/voyeurism, passive/active* – which distinguish the changes of the object of the drive, 'while the aim remains unchanged'[46] – with respect to the *person* (ego-body), and through the articulations between them, structure the *polarity of the phantasm*, in such a way that the transference makes the latter intelligible. Thus, first of all, the passivity induced by the analytic situation, which would make of masochism a fantasy specific to the transference. The autoerotic investment of the ego is reactivated in this instance so as to avoid annihilation by the presence of another person, offering to this other the sexual power of being a guardian assuring the possession of the body and the inhibition of acting out. Finally this enables, from the sensations of the body-organ, active figurations (as is the case with autoeroticism) of an other who is always the potential source of diverse experiences of one's own body. In other words, the economy of the masochistic fantasy of transference can be understood mainly as the 'negative' condition of the restitution of primary auto-eroticism and the constitution of one's own self [*la personne propre*]. But such a masochism certainly affords a prevalent function to the marking of *seeing* and *being seen*. The conditions that we know to be the case with *the analytic situation* join up here with the proper nature of the look beneath its perverse actualisations (in the exhibition-ism/voyeurism pair) since the look, returning here to its function as the *anamorphic mirror*, abandons the visual object itself – in this instance the corporeal illusion of the evidence of the other person – to the benefit of regressive deformations. The whole logic of fantasy developed by Freud on the subject of the vicissitudes of the drives could thus support the understanding given by transference of the person establishing the optical register of their psychological *indeterminacy*. Such a point of view brings up, one suspects, as much the question of the status of projection as that of perceptual appresentations, representations and identifications. What the term *transference* thus restores is less a necessary disjunction between the 'psychic person' and the 'physical person' or even between an 'imaginary representation of the person' and the 'psychological identity of the person themselves' [*la personne propre*] as the *projective structure of the person*, as if the latter had no reality outside the specular function of the ego in the presence of the other.

This indeterminacy around the conceptual content of the person, which takes account of the dynamic of transference in terms of the mobility of affects, the indeterminacy of identifications and the impossibility of representing their object, is certainly necessary to conserve, in the idea of the *person*, its value as a reflection, with which the theological representa-tion of man as a fragment of the mirror of God has traditionally endowed it. The person is the *resemblance* thanks to which something of it can be the *mirror of its appearance* [*miroir de la semblance*]. In a crucial work on the mirror and thought, Agnès Minazzoli notes the following in particular:

> Resemblance is in the eye that sees and the true mirror is of the inside, look, vision, thought, first image of an unknown king, living mirror: this object that I see, this face, its reflection is always deviated and doubled by a model which is 'in the head': thought searches for it and pursues it, it reaches it sometimes and finds it perhaps where it was not looking. Then between the visible model and that of the mental image glimpsed with eyes closed there arises a coincidence which puts into question any opposition between the sensible and the intelligible as an undue return to a frozen Platonism.[47]

While Agnès Minazzoli is of course dealing here with the mirror in the self-portrait (Dürer), the precious insights she offers are singularly echoed in the project that concerns us here to designate the coincidence of the person and transference. At the beginning of her book, the author under-lines that 'the eye cannot see itself and only finds its image in a look dif-ferent from its own, because the eye is a mirror, but not of itself. The mirror brings closer and keeps the distance' – this mirror, which bears within itself the dialectical transparency of the same and the other, accords to the other the sameness of a look through which the ego identifies with the person – a person of which one cannot decide if it is oneself [*soi*].

> By wanting to circumscribe the mirror too much as the space of the recognition of oneself we forget perhaps that it is often the place of disorientation and disarray, at the intersection of two looks which are seeking all the more a union as they know themselves to be separated by distance, opacity and the isolation of singular beings.[48]

While one would hold *projection* to be a psychological phenomenon metaphorically moulded on the physical phenomenon of the projection of shadows by a source of light, here projection becomes indeed a *physical force* but one whose source is outside vision, a long way back, and the person – the place of the shadows engendered by the source – would be only what it sees coming to the present of a surface that meets it, over there. So the fact that for there to be a *person* two sources of the look are needed, one in the background, and the other the vanishing point ahead – perhaps the same source, doubled – defines projection as the rise of sha-dows to the mirror, just as images arise in the day of the dream. Projection would thus be the physical action of anachronic temporality, which engenders a person between two looks.

> [...] through the associations that they awaken, images are doubled to infinity and complete each other, each revealing, at the heart of the visible that they hollow out and divide, an aspect unnoticed so far, so that one can wonder how vision can be distinguished from the pro-jection of imaginary figures in space [...]
>
> What absence does the image seek to fill – this absence that it des-ignates and underlines in trying to fill it –?[49]

So might not transference itself be the physical activity of the image understood in this way – generating the *person* as the optical milieu of the passage and deformation of projected shadows or again as the optical site of changes and reversals of points of view?

> The first words that Sonia pronounces in her first session, after lying down, express a quite strange sense of relief. The death of her parents in a car accident, in which she also lost her grandmother, left her alone since the age of ten, fifteen years ago, in the sole company of her now hemiplegic paternal grandfather for whom she has to care at home

from now on. In lying down here, somewhat reluctantly at first, she had the impression of the 'collapse of a wall' which for a long time had kept her 'vertiginously fixed'. It came to her mind that finding some kind of 'back' would help her 'see again'. Having lived for so long 'walled up face-to-face with her grandfather', and looking to him for what he could remember for her, her expectation has effaced her own memory and muted all words within her. Feeling herself to have 'disappeared', she doesn't know if she still has the capacity to look – she really seems to make only the same gestures she has to everyday just to 'stand upright'. She then says slowly, as if each word should at that point be carefully managed: 'It's quiet. Nothing opposite. Just a window. The light comes in just enough to not be dazzled. Don't take me as a person. I am too much one; that is why I disappeared. Here I will only be a changing, unpredictable look, a reflection of images which rise and disappear. At the shadow of my back'.

Afterwards Sonia would explain how her life with her grandfather, initially a source of delight, without her realising it became progressively an experience of oppressive waiting, waiting for an object she couldn't place – waiting for him to speak, but of what? Waiting for him to die, finally, not to be free, but so that something would happen and thus put an end to the vertiginous emptiness which she knew had filled her. As if, and it is thus that she would put it – the face to face with her grandfather had not only come to deprive her of her face and her memory, but now gave her the certainty that his presence *in front of* her made her slightest thoughts and feelings converge on him. The word *transference*, not spoken by her until later, was named thus: 'Can it happen in a life that one takes one's grandfather for an ancestor? I think this is what has happened since the death of my parents. Today I think I would rather have been put in an orphanage. It's since I've been talking here that I have begun to understand that memory stops being obsessive when it starts to be endless. Images come always changing who knows how. I am the present of an image which has already disappeared. Are these images formed in your silence? I am leaning back'.

'The Person of the Doctor'

The cure that the ill person seeks to obtain of and by themselves is considered by Freud as one of the characteristics of the 'autocratism' ('*Selbsherrlichkeit*' or '*Einmächtigkeit*') of the ego which is incapable of ceding to anyone – and thus to the 'person of the doctor' – the slightest capacity to cure their *life*, held only by them as a person. This is indicated in the 1890 text *On Psychical (or Mental) Treatment*, which considers hypnotic treatment as significant progress in relation to the archaic belief of the ego in the inefficacy or the danger of putting oneself in the hands of another and confiding in them. One could no doubt find the residues of this kind of belief in the paranoiac or in obsessional neurosis and hypochondria, a belief expressed by the increased feeling of the psychological identity of the person of the self, in the vigilance of conscious memory, and, in correlation, even in physical illness, through the negation of mortality.

In fact, the contemporary psychoanalytic clinic is certainly not unfamiliar with the expressions taken by this kind of autocratism among certain patients, even if we see the steps they take with us as an attenuated form thereof. In such cases, which appear to willingly accommodate themselves to the socialised friendliness of the analyst, it makes sense to speak of an incapacity for transference or to take the measure of the singular modalities of transference which are generally encrusted in symptoms – quite often somatic ones – which have the particularity of being both lived as a threat to life and assuring an (auto)eroticised function of self-conservation. In analytic work with cases like these what is especially striking – outside the well-known impossibility to free-associate – is the considerable effort expended to empty the person of the analyst of all presence (synonymous with contact and influence) and, through the symptomatic complaint, to try to deny them any capacity to act in a psychically beneficial way. The symptom alone appears to hold the theory and, the effects here proving the point, it is the only interlocutory – persecutory – power worthy of life's confidence. What is certain, amongst such patients, is that the *person of the analyst* is equivalent to an alterity susceptible to engender alteration and alienation while the symptom involves on the contrary the incorporation of a hostile alterity. But in reality things are not that simple. Because if there is no doubt that the symptom is an internalised hostile interlocutor, it is from it that the ego suffers and it is from the symptom that the ego retains the belief that it is the integral person capable of bringing a cure. As we learn from some treatments (generally a long time after they started), the symptom harbours a mythic character unidentifiable by consciousness, which forbids any remembrance, a character of which one knows only that it has manifested itself among other individuals of the same heritage (a paternal uncle, the brother of a grandfather) through a similar symptom. Such a genealogisation of the symptom of course invokes heredity – and eventually genetic illness – as against 'psychic treatment': it bears witness especially to the impossibility that a transference should free itself from its intrapsychic object (which in this instance is *somatic*) where the other – the analyst in person – is a stranger. And if we do admit the manifest existence of a transference (even just because the patient comes to the sessions), this can only at first and often for a long time afterward take the aspect of a negation of the person of the analyst even up to the point of identifying them as hostile. Here we could develop the hypothesis that the symptom in fact prevents a regressive access to a paternal figure of the ancestor (most of the time genealogy endows lateral figures with a similar symptom, avoiding the father), while the 'dead' father is in some sense preserved in this powerful expression of persecution or obsessive reproach. It is thus as if the immortality of the son could only be guaranteed by the autocratic activity of the symptom, reinforced by the belief of being the only one capable of curing oneself. The counterpart to this imaginary contract would be to never be in contact with the other in any form they might take and to never betray the internal persecutor by placing oneself under a foreign influence. Under such conditions the function of psychic transference is accorded to the persecutor, a function which needs to avoid the threat of the decomposition of the corpse of the self [*soi-cadavre*]. We can thus imagine that if the symptom involves the encrusted object of the transference, this object is persecutory to the extent that it demands that the ego identify with the person of the sacrificed son to whom falls the capacity to preserve life through conserving the illness from which it suffers.

In this light we can understand what Freud writes in 1890 in this text on *Psychical (or Mental) Treatment*:

> Since physicians came to realize clearly the important part played in recovery by the patient's state of mind, the idea naturally occurred to them of no longer leaving it to the patient to decide how much mental compliance he should show but of deliberately imposing a propitious state of mind by suitable methods. It is from this attempt that modern mental treatment has taken its start.[50]

'[D]eliberately imposing [*on the patient*] a propitious state of mind by suitable methods' – is precisely to produce the psychic state of 'expectation coloured by faith' (292) that is the principle of the miraculous cure – the miracle being the inversion of the action of the symptom.[51] This point of view is clarified by Georges Didi-Huberman with reference to Charcot's text *La Foi qui guérit* [*The Faith-Cure*] (1892). If *God* and *the Devil* 'have the same form' 'or rather are present as two variants of the same formal organism, the same hysterical picture', we can arrive at the recognition of the 'logical reduction' according to which 'miracle and symptom have the same effect', and this effect is nothing other than that of the symptom itself. G. Didi-Huberman continues:

> The *Faith-Cure*, where this theory has been defended, was considered as Charcot's 'philosophical testament'. A century and a half after Hume had contradictorily duplicated the evidence of miracles, without having been able to resolve the aporia from the gnoseological point of view – Charcot finally unified the field 'positively'.[52]

Hysteria is the law generative of all reunifications – hysterics being, according to Charcot, endowed with the 'maximum intellectual capacity' 'just as, in their convulsions, they can reach a maximum muscular capacity'. This law of hysteria – hysteria conceived as a law – unifies the symptomal field susceptible of producing miracles (G. Didi-Huberman). Therapeutic know-how thus consists in imitating the imitative capacity of hysteria:

> It is a question of knowing how [*savoir-faire*], of knowing how to redo [*savoir refaire*], or rather of *knowing how to reproduce the miracle*. This is a position whose coherence should be underlined: Charcot saw in hypnosis, in fact, a theoretical and 'technical' model, if one can put it that way, of the miracle of the cure. Now hypnosis is also an artefact of hysteria, a 'symptom put to work', an experimental hysteria [....] If the miracle can be understood as a hysterical symptom, deriving from suggestibility, then hypnosis, which is its experimental mastery, should allow the controlled reproduction of the miracle cures.[53]

From this point of view Freud's text *On Psychical (or Mental) Treatment*, which pre-dates Charcot's essay – goes a long way further. Freud takes care to distinguish the 'expectation coloured by faith' that one can note among patients trusting in non-medical therapists or healers (those who have 'no knowledge of the scientific basis of therapeutics'[54]) from the expectation which is directed towards the doctor. Of course we can find in the latter the same 'mental attitude' on the part of the patient, consisting in 'the faith with which he meets the immediate effect of a medical procedure' (according to the 'amount of his own desire to be cured'), but it intervenes in the case of the 'confidence that [the doctor] has taken the right steps in that direction' (a respect inspired by the art of medicine) as well as the 'the power which [the patient] attributes to his *doctor's personality* [*la personne du médecin*]' (our emphasis) and 'the purely human liking aroused in him by the doctor':

> There are some physicians who have a greater capacity than others for winning their patients' confidence; a patient will often feel better the very moment the doctor enters his room.[55]

If, then, the personality of the doctor has this thaumaturgic power 'derived directly from divine power, since in its beginnings the art of healing lay in the hands of priests'[56] it is because this *person* is a *figure of the science of occult illnesses* – of the occult and of the secret nature of illness which eludes the patient themselves, who aspires to be relieved because of their impotence to know and to cure themselves. It is also because what qualifies the power of this figure in the patient's eyes is that they abstain from any 'deliberate plan' in the manner of those who 'employ fear and fright for therapeutic ends'.[57] In this way, the *personality of the doctor* alone can produce miracles on condition that the doctor has in some way inherited the power of 'oracular dreams [while] sleeping in the temple precincts'.[58] This amounts to saying that the *personality of the doctor* does not arrogate to themselves the right to control the patient (as would be the case if the person was defined only as the representative of academic knowledge). Rather the specific psychic disposition of the *personality of the doctor* with respect to the patient makes of this *person* – the place they occupy – the *respondent* of the dream 'in the temple precincts'. Around 1910 Janet would consider a 'psychotherapy without knowledge' capable of producing a cure 'unconsciously', on condition that the one practising it knew what they were doing! The interest Freud then brings to *hypnosis* certainly resulted from his interest in hysteria, but this is already closely related to the function attributed to the *dream*, without which, one could say, one could not understand the nature of the 'harmonious' circulation of the 'magnetic fluid' – the celebrated *rapport* between the mesmeriser and the mesmerised. Inducing such a *rapport*, the personality of the doctor comes to *correspond* in some way to the dream state:

> Some of the phenomena of hypnosis (for instance, alterations in muscular activity) possess a merely scientific interest. But the most significant indication of hypnosis, and the most important one from our point of view, lies in the hypnotic subject's attitude to his hypnotist. While the subject behaves to the rest of the external world as though he were asleep, that is, as though all his senses were diverted from it, he is awake in his relation to the person who hypnotized him; he hears and sees him alone, and him he understands and answers. This phenomenon, which is described as rapport in the case of hypnosis, finds a parallel in the way in which some people sleep–for instance, a mother who is nursing her baby. It is so striking that it may well lead us to an understanding of the relation between the hypnotic subject and the hypnotist.[59]

This text is remarkable in all respects since the personality of the hypnotiser, equivalent to the *person of the dream*, is qualified by the latter – through the *words* that are spoken – as an 'influence of the mind over the body'. The *belief* of the hypnotised in the hypnotiser – which has the characteristic of the credulous belief of the dreamer in the lived images of the dream at the moment they are dreaming – is equivalent to a belief in the psychic agency of the pronouncing of certain words, leading the dream back to former perceptions and images, images that relate to that which will later be called hallucinatory, that is mnesic traces in the topical regression. The hypnotiser did not just pretend to authenticate the power of the personality of the doctor [*la personne du médecin*]:

> We then perceive that he has been seeing and hearing just as we see and hear in dreams–he has been 'hallucinating'. He was evidently so credulous in relation to the hypnotist that he was convinced that there

must be a snake to be seen when the hypnotist told him so; and this conviction had such a strong effect on his body that he really saw the snake–a thing which, incidentally, can sometimes happen even to people who have not been hypnotized.[60]

Thus: 'The words spoken by the hypnotist which have the magical results that I have described are known as a "suggestion"'.[61]

While there is no need to engage with the substance of the numerous works that have been devoted for some time and also more recently[62] to the origins of the concept of transference, it would certainly not be abusive to see expressed in this text by Freud the framework of the paradigm – that is the dream itself. This to the extent that only a small step is needed to put forward the idea that *the transference has exactly the same value, often misunderstood today, as hypnosis, on condition that the phenomenon of hypnosis is not abstracted and isolated from its intrinsic relation to the dream (rather than to sleep).* And one should not either lose sight of the fact that it is the hypnotic *value* of transference, engaged by the *person* of the 'doctor of the soul' – which in return forms the condition for listening and interpretation according to the hypnotic paradigm of the dream (Freud will say later that words should be listened to on the model of the dream). It goes without saying that if the person of the doctor is too 'real', it cannot obtain the desired effect. And we know that one of the major resistances to the psychic work of the treatment is that of the conscious 'representation-aim' of both the aimed-for cure and the presence of the doctor in person. It is also the nature of this *presence* which qualifies the status that the person comes to take on. And if hypnosis remains the paradigm for the agency of the psychic that the dream will clarify, isn't it among other things because of its power – just as with the dream – over the body, including the power of the so-called 'negative hallucination' of making such a person disappear.

> Just as a hypnotized subject can be obliged to see what is not there, so he can be forbidden to see what *is* there and is seeking to impress itself on his senses, some particular person, for instance. (This is known as a 'negative hallucination'.) The person in question then finds it impossible to attract the subject's attention by any kind of stimulation; he is treated as though he were 'thin air'.[63]

A person who is 'thin air' because they can be subtracted through *negative hallucination* thus making them *absent* from their own *presence* – one could not better describe the essence of the agency of the psychic on the part of a person who is 'thin air', or still by means of the *emptiness* of words needed for them to become magical when they are pronounced. For his part Charcot had foreseen the visuality of the hysteric and thus the correlative capacity of the therapist to act visually – thanks to their control of the coextensive visuality of the psychic – because of the phenomenon of the 'paralysis of the imagination'. But perhaps the *therapeutic person* in Charcot is still too dependent on the scenario of the show and tell of the master – it was not yet aligned with the 'temple precincts' in the sense intended by Freud. With Freud it is a question of conceiving of what will become the characteristic *neutrality* of the *person of the analyst* as engendered by the *negative hallucination* which enters into the *dream's function of internal projection.*[64]

It is in the light of this approach – which remains very happily dominated by the associationist neuropsychological definition of transference – that it makes sense to understand the 'false connection' and the 'misalliance' brought to light by the *Studies in Hysteria*. But one might say here that the 'transferences' – defined as 'new versions' and 'copies' – replacing 'a person formerly known by the person of the doctor' are indeed the 'past states' relived 'as actual relations to the person of the doctor' but also that they can be understood as such once one conceives that the 'person of the doctor' can engender the *negative hallucination* and thus become the *support* of transferences insofar as they are the hallucinatory agency of the making present of previous psychic states. If transferences can thus be 'copies' this is not, as one usually thinks, because the person of the analyst is the object of projective superimpositions but because of the negative hallucination which dismisses the representation of the person and empties it of any physical or psychical content, thus engendering absence on the basis of the particularity of their presence. This *negation* which would thus be the principle of the regressive agency of the transference – if there is indeed transference – is an operation of an animist nature applied to the person of the analyst in such a way that the latter, made of 'thin air', becomes as such the optical prism or the specular milieu of the projective engendering of a 'person previously known'. Thus, as we've described before, the *projection* involved in negative hallucination consists in the engendering of the image as a *projective surface*. And if it is the transferential image of the dream which is the projective surface, it should be added that this image is in some sense ecmnesic (and hypermnesic) of a past which is un-identifiable as such. The projection of the negative hallucination brings up within the interior (in the proper sense of *Er-innerung*) the *aspects* of the person which are thus *an-achronised*. The *aspectuality* of the person is conceivable only on condition of the negative operation brought to bear on the person of the analyst – and this is its point of departure.

It is not enough to suppose that in transference the person of the analyst becomes a 'diurnal residue' of the patient. To consider things this way would continue to credit the person with an identificatory reality. This would not fail to prompt a number of analysts to narcissistically connote and interpret such and such a figure appearing in the dream or in acting out, thus asking the patient – under the pretext of the analysis of the transference – to become aware of the resemblance of their figures with the 'image' of the analyst. It is much more interesting to pay attention to the 'faceless persons' or 'views from the back' which, in the dreams of patients, *do not 'represent' the person of the analyst* but *imagine the negation in this positive expression,* which itself is generally sensorially invested to a particularly intense degree. Such dreams can be said to be all the more important 'in' the transference insofar as they bear witness to the value accorded to *neutrality* as the *transparent surface* on which 'images' can form and be deformed. We can completely understand why, in communicating their analytic experience with borderline cases (and not with psychotics) analysts are at pains to explain the difficulty they experience in their *personal identity* and the countertransferential hatred that results as a means of re-appropriating this identity against the identity of the patient. An intersubjective conception of transference supported by the transferences of borderline patients can only lead to such a subjective derealisation of the analyst, even to something equivalent to a 'paranoisation' of identity. Harold Searles has provided numerous and personally vibrant testimonies of the confusion provoked by the patient in the analyst by means of those transferential projections that consist in speaking, in the session, as if the analyst were dismissed or directly assimilated to another figure in their life. And in view of the cases that Searles is dealing with, he certainly draws a lot from this kind of subjectivising interpretation of transference. Nevertheless, we are inclined to take a critical view when confronted by this kind of account, expressed for example in the following sequences:

> On December 11, 1965 is my first note of her perceiving a changing succession of different figures in my eyes (...) On December 15, 1965 she prepared me, in apparently conscious solicitude, but unconsciously diabolic and highly psychotic detail, for her putting into me the multitude of people, dead people as I recall, that she experienced as being within her. In the next session, two days later, I experienced a transitory sense of craziness—a sense of confusion and of estrangement from my surroundings (...)
>
> On December 24, 1965 she saw two men simultaneously in my two eyes, and when I attempted to foster her acceptance of her real identity as Joan Douglas, she bristled with startling antagonism at the name, saying, 'If I were a cat, the hairs on my back would rise.' It was evident that her aversion to her own real identity was as intense as had been her mother's aversion to her in childhood, and her own aversion to me for many years.[65]

Obviously it would not make sense to contest the clinical pertinence of Searles' interventions as he reports them. And one can hardly have reason to doubt that in such cases (with a paranoid patient) one must also be active in the direction of intersubjective realism. When, further on, the patient sees two people in the eyes of their therapist and the latter explains this perception through projection and with reference to 'the state

of intense emotional conflict', 'revealed by my eyes' (says Searles), provoked by the testing character of the sessions, what is indeed at stake is
what the *person of the analyst* can awaken in terms of the personifications
of anxiety or distress. We would say, however, that the subjective realism
of reinforced psychological identity at stake here scrambles the *value of the
person* that we have described. And this is not without provoking interventions on the part of the analyst that are too 'interpersonal', notably
soliciting a 'consciousness' in the patient of their own identity. In an inci-
dental remark, Searles notices this:

> She had started spinning a delusional fantasy, and I became alarmed
> at how much I was enjoying it, and 'conscientiously' reacted against it
> in trying to help her to become in better touch with her real, adult
> identity as Joan Douglas. This had, in retrospect quite predictably, a
> very distancing effect upon her.[66]

In fact – as we learn all the time from transferential experiences, whether
delirious or not – any intervention that aims at producing *at a conscious
level* a join between *images* and '*real*' *psychological identity* entails a 'distancing' equivalent to a psychic disappearance. What is more or less
momentarily *destroyed* is the function of *projection* inherent to *negative hallucination*; ultimately it is the latter which becomes *frozen* in the relational
aspects of an interpersonal order.

As I have already suggested, in our own practice we would distinguish
quite clearly between cases of *psychosis*, in which transference *in* delirium
(we are not speaking of delirious transference – a dubious notion) in some
sense shelters the analyst from any intervention of a personalising nature,
and *borderline* cases, closer from this point of view to neurosis, in which
the negative hallucinatory activity of transference asks of the analyst that
they contribute through a strict neutrality to the voiding of any personalised content in their own person. From this point of view the interest we
have in anorexic (often toxicomaniac) configurations is aligned with this:

> Justine had swallowed a dangerous quantity of a powerful laxative –
> leading to an urgent hospitalisation. In her first meeting (while she
> was still hospitalized) this 22-year-old young woman presented
> enveloped in a huge man's raincoat, with very short hair, crudely
> dressed in extra-large trousers with man's shoes obviously not her
> size. She would remain very silent in this first meeting and the little
> she did say would be spoken in a mannered way reminiscent of a
> little girl, not once omitting to mention what her mother thinks, so as
> to be able to say what she thinks herself, through this mirror. Before
> the treatment could begin face to face meetings proceeded for more
> than three months; it seemed at this point – and this would be con-
> firmed later – that after each session Justine would indulge in an

'effacement' of my image, an effacement that was quickly captured in bulimic episodes and the compulsion to 'make herself vomit', arising after her exit from my office.

When Justine started her analysis (extended to four times a week) she devoted each of her sessions to speaking exclusively about her obsessive alimentary rituals, the extremely detailed narrative insistence of which very quickly emerged as an act exerted on my presence – seeking to make me react either by way of an explicit personal interest or through expressions of disgust or boredom. I noted that the episodes on which she spent most time were more those set in restaurants rather than those where she was eating in secret. These restaurant episodes – generally in the company of her mother or friends – are particularly marked by the stifling proximity of 'affective bodies', leading her to eat without caring what she is swallowing and especially without any attention to what she has on her plate. Then she has the feeling of swelling up hugely, that the food is going straight to her hips and her legs, sometimes her chest. Once home she has to evacuate everything she has absorbed (which in reality is often very little it seems): 'When I eat in front of someone I forget what I'm eating. People think I make a fuss about a few grams. That's not it, it's because when I eat I don't know who I am any more'.

Some sessions are completely silent but the silence that she imposes on me on these occasions seems to me to involve an intense vigilance on her part. Subsequently she would say that she couldn't tolerate hearing my voice or hearing me moving or breathing. If the silence betrays no *manifestation* of my presence, then she can *dream*. It's not that she cannot or does not want to speak; in staying silent she has the impression that the words that come to her enable her to 'find her exact and right look'. It's a 'point of balance' which isn't gained once and for all. If she can find it then what she feels won't feel wrong. In her dealings with others it doesn't take much for her to feel deformed. The ideal, she says, would be to be sure of provoking nothing in 'the person listening to you or looking at you'. But this isn't possible because of seduction. Seduction prevents her from moving towards the other sexually, in an animal way.

Analytic practice teaches us not to underestimate the 'technical recommendations' that patients communicate to us when they talk about the mistakes made by others (parents or people close to them) about them. In Justine's case, these mistakes were always due to the same kind of behaviour: men became deliberately maternal towards believing her to be fragile and so they no longer knew how to be sexual; or she immediately sees their sexual desire for her body and immediately becomes a stranger to it; her mother fears for her health and her anxieties about not eating enough prevented her listening and speaking to her like as she would have wanted; she doesn't doubt that her father cares for her lovingly but it makes it seem like he is trying to keep her prisoner by not daring to be one way or another with her.

Her friends are willingly familiar with her but they disappear as soon as they realise that Justine doesn't like talking about herself. Every time that any of these relational avatars are mentioned the hoped for presence of the person of the analyst is also signified. She won't say anything directly about this presence. But whenever my subjective state is modified it's enough to momentarily suspend or 'inhibit' the course of Justine's thoughts.

We could find several metaphors with Justine or equally with other anorexic patients, soliciting that the neutrality of the analyst be 'pure' of any thought and language, 'transparent so that nothing is kept', 'as empty as space', etc. These metaphors, very rarely addressed to the analyst in person, are nevertheless completely determinative with respect to the transference. As for the analyst, they have no need to resort to imaginary artefacts to know that this demand for neutrality is nothing other than the need to stay on the level of the silent activity of language – precisely there where the words heard have the best chance of staying awake like dreams. It's true that under these conditions – which are never established for good and certainly not by virtue of the occupation of the 'place', which is prone to become idiotic as soon as it is identified with that of a person – we become aware of the function devolving to the dream in the 'evolution' of transference.

What is particularly striking in the psychoanalytic treatment of borderline cases – often comparable moreover to the analysis of cases of hysteria – is that a number of the patients' expressions seem to privilege the interpersonal relation with the analyst while a transferential dynamic is fully at work according to the determination of the *negative hallucination* vacating any content of the person of the analyst. Often it's as if the analyst were simultaneously solicited as a (human) person from whom proofs of personal understanding and recognition of identity are demanded *and* as a non-person therefore supposed to avoid any personalisation of their presence and on the contrary intensifying the function of *a transparent surface pure of any pre-representation*. At a certain point in the treatment Justine would express this 'expectation' that I should not in any circumstance be silent in the same way as her father, when he was present with her ('ever since I've known him my father has been psychoanalyzing me'), and moreover that I should have 'no defined form', and be ready to take on 'any form imprinted and erased by the words'. This is a remarkable expression if we compare it to the description of the *chora* (see further on) or again to this expression from a 5-year old: 'When you dream, you don't have the same face. If I tell you what I've dreamt, afterwards you won't be the same ever again'. It would be quite reductive in this case to identify the transference as a 'maternal transference' or a 'paternal transference' under the pretext of the allusion to a 'container' of the forms that are engendered through such a relation. Unless in such cases the expressions 'maternal transference' and 'paternal transference' describe the roles played by the parents as *capturing screens*, of a hypochondriacal nature, i.e. having the complementary function usually ascribed to mirror transferences (Kohut) – transference understood here in the sense of corporeal mirrors of a doubling which homothetically ensures the roles of the *phantom-bodies*. In fact in the analytic treatment of anorexics we encounter this kind of configuration, in which the body of the analyst is called on to play this kind of *mirror* function. One might be led to think however that such configurations intervene as *mirror-screens* for transferences (in relation to grasping) in some way working as obstacles to the transference. But this would perhaps come back to thinking about what becomes of the negative hallucination in these modalities of the *positivisation* of the transference – exactly as it happens in transference love.

It did not escape Freud's attention – precisely a propos of transference love – that the triggering of amorous affects taking hold of the person of the analyst and capturing them in the certainty of their electively chosen singular reality arises in the psychic process to hinder the memory of regression. In pondering the question of 'true love' (*echte Liebe*) in relation to *transference love* Freud gives scant criteria to qualify the former (doesn't all love occur via transference?), but the fact that transference love takes on a value of *resistance* clarifies in return the way in which actualisations of affect, crystallising on the person of the analyst, tend to *miraculise the symptom* and make it so that the 'real' person of the analyst is substituted for the internal persecutor. The 'Observations on Transference Love' thus lead to the confirmation that an 'ideal' transference – a sort of *echte Ubertragung* – involves the *unknown of the person* and thus the appresentation of the non-person of the person. If transference love is a kind of *freeze on the person* (in the sense of the *freeze-frame*), should we not always understand it as provoked by anxieties of death and annihilation and seeking a benign embodiment in the realisation of the person of the analyst, which it is hoped will put an end to the *hostility* of the symptom through substitution? *Transference love* could thus become the expression of the kind of transferential love that erotomania shows to us in its nosographic categorisation as a passional delirium and as paranoia. Isn't it as if the erotomaniac – or the paranoiac – makes of their very person a specular foyer for the transferential and projective intentions of others, these being hostile intentions, and threatening to the person all the more insofar as they are clothed in the expression of passional, amorous attitudes? If, for example, we hold the 'paranoiac' to be a particularly clear-sighted vestige-witness of the fundamental hostility of the human, it becomes all the more clear how Freud could have attributed to paranoia the so to speak *juridical* conditions of the *identitarian property of the person* (clearer view, consciousness, memory of inscription and recapitulation, a sense of the claims to rights of property). And is it not such a person who returns in the person of the analyst when the latter, personalising the 'relation' with the patient, moves away from the non-person of the person of transference?

The site of the stranger excludes such a relational interpretation as a matter of principle. And we know that the greatest challenge in some psychotherapies is precisely to attribute – as in the case of Zöe Gradiva – all the power of ambivalence to the words of the interpretation, which signify on the one hand the recognition of the perceptual features of the 'real' person that the patient needs in their concrete presence and, on the other hand, the indication of the figures of the non-person. In difficult analytic situations it is nevertheless not a question of relational inter-personalisation, from which there would be nothing to gain, psycho-analytically speaking.

The Totemism of Transference

The proposition that transference – as we have understood it thus far – *opens* onto an *anachronic past*, that is to a *memory of regression* in which the past cannot be deliberately thought of as the anterior horizon of con-sciousness, would perhaps justify the idea that the *interpretation of the transference* cannot be formed outside an *interpretation of dreams*. While representations of transference recurrently express cognitively genetic categories such as the 'maternal' or the 'paternal', categories which play a dynamic function of oedipal working-through in the conscious memory work of the patient, the interpretations inspired by these repre-sentations tend towards a discursive theorisation of transference, when the latter should never be deemed interpretable except as a dream inter-pretation. We should even wonder if it isn't in the *order of transference* not to be interpreted (that is, directly), since it is to the dream that the responsibility to form such an interpretation would fall. Is this then to say that the transference is interpreted by and through itself in the dream? This may be the case if we are also considering that the dream is understood here at the same time as the dream of the night, the retelling of the dream in the session, and the associations arising from this retell-ing – and as a *formative paradigm, from the analyst's attention and their interpretative speech*. If we are questioning the *discourse* of the interpreta-tion of transference – and avoiding a gross caricature of its categorial interpretations – it is because this kind of discourse legislates the repre-sentative functions of the transference and tends to reinstitute a kind of baroque legalism of the places and functions of the persons addressed as unified in the 'person of the analyst'.

Where the discourse of the interpretation of transference stumbles – the discursive strategisation of transference as a parlour game – is precisely on the need to let the transference open 'onto something other than itself'. This formula is from Jean Laplanche, whose concerns do not nevertheless depart from this conception of solipsistic disjunctions and doublings. In 'The Transcendence of Transference', taking up the case of Dora again, Laplanche seeks to 'set to work' 'three propositions':

The *first* is that in the analysis of Dora, the transference is shown to be at a second degree. What is lacking in Freud is not that he ignores the transference 'of the father' but that he misunderstands the intermediary link that we are obliged to call transferential itself, that is the transference onto Mr. K, and the transference starting from Mr. K. The transference that is shown to be strategically essential is thus defined as a *transference of the transference*. The *second point*, already noted, is that this transference onto/from Mr. K is crossed, as it were, by his relationship with his wife. Lacan's commentary on this is particularly apt: that Dora slaps Mr. K at the exact moment when Mr. K is flirting with her is expressed as follows: my wife means nothing to me. At the manifest level this can be understood in a banal sense: my wife being nothing for me (sexually speaking), the place is free for a relationship with you... and at that point Dora slaps Mr. K; Lacan interprets: if your wife is nothing for you, then *neither are you* anything for me, since you only interest me to the extent that through you I have access to Mme K. (...)

These two points echo the fact that I wanted to underline at the start and especially with my title: the transference is not closed on itself; it isn't a dual relation: transference opens onto something other than itself, as much in the chronological lineage in which we have at least three characters (Freud, Mr. K, the father) as in the actual intersubjective constellation, where it can only be understood through its referral through Mr and Mrs K.[67]

The 'third point' engages with Freud's use of the word transference (*the transferences*) notably in the analysis of the *Rat Man*, transferences which are to be dissolved one by one. Laplanche adds: 'But this is against the background of a more basic relation, which, for Freud, would hardly be of the same kind and instead would persist and perhaps not be analysed, that is, the fundamental relation to the "doctor" as father'.[68]

We might easily subscribe to this decoding of the transferential *scenario*, here in the case of Dora. Except that the 'doublings' to which the ideological representation of transference in psychoanalysis gives rise become a scenario from the moment when relations between persons are *logically* and *chronologically* privileged: in this case the transference becomes effectively a 'transference of transferences' and presupposes a *fundamental transference* – a 'transcendence of transference' – in the form of *a relation* to the *person of the doctor* identifiable as a paternal figure. In fact, as soon as transference is imagined as a dramatic action that can be transcribed 'theatrically' it becomes thinkable as an intrigue which it is easy to reduce to the kind of relationship which keeps it secret and enigmatic, thus the relation to the doctor as a father. We must acknowledge that it is this discursivity that closes transference onto itself – prevents it from 'opening onto something else' – whatever the potential multiplications of the interpretation (in the Dora case, for example, the homosexuality of the relation with the mother). But perhaps we should avoid the superseding step sought here, whereby the *person of the doctor* signifies an *accentuation of the father*? To speak of the *father of the transference* – in Freud's language – is perhaps to speak of such and such an 'image' or 'paternal figure' incarnated by the person of the doctor, but it is especially to call upon the *father* as the *mythical engendering figure* – one might say the *cause* – of the transference. And on the other hand, one could propose the idea that the *person* of the analyst is indeed the *father of the transference* or more radically, that *the transference is the memory of the father*, in the sense in which the negative hallucination is in fact concerned quite specifically with the *nature* of the *existence* of the father – and not the person themselves [*non personne d'une personne*]. To go so far as saying that transference is 'essentially paternal' would not betray our intention here if the formulation were not prone to a recategorisation, in this instance exclusive, aimed at qualifying the paternal through the elimination of the maternal. Neither can a definition of transference through the *reference to the father* be passed over as a systematic allegiance to the idea of the father as a 'symbolic function'. A formulation such as this, which is far from being accepted, poses instead the question of knowing what should be understood – from the perspective of transference – by the *symbolic* of the *imago* in the sense we have given to it here. From the perspective we are adopting here the maternal is perhaps a lot more associated in the analytic situation with the preconscious perception of the sensorial data of the presence of the person of the analyst as well as the environment of the session; it constitutes the corporeal material of this presence, and we are not unaware of the traditionally acknowledged importance of this factor in the slightest qualitative variations that the analyst induces in their relation to the patient. But here the *maternal* – and it is not certain that it can be exactly named by this word –, if it creates the (quasi-presensorial) corporeal conditions of an imaginary *exchange of the transference*, cannot be taken for the transference itself or at the very least for the movement of its *unconscious topical regression*. We have insisted enough on the fact that the analyst *in person* is sensitive to the distances and temporalities through which the expressions of the psychic life of the patient are manifested and that they tend to signify to the patient the *absence* – the non-person – of the presence they embody. Would this whole development thus come down to justifying a kind of dual partition within transference? Ultimately, would the maternal qualities belong to the frame and to presence while the father, in the negative hallucination of transference, would be the *abstract form* of *presence's lack of form*? Why not put it like that? We can of course, but if our argument works against such a partition, or rather against a transferential bivalency – whatever the 'maternal' induction inscribed in the concept of the countertransference at its origin[69] – it is because such a view remains a prisoner of the ideological imaginary of parental roles, and because it familiarises the analytic situation under the pretext of a description of the ideal qualities of the father and the mother, and thus glosses over the *phylogenetic* conceptual metaphor of the transference in the sense intended by Freud.

In this light we can see the importance of the reticence of an author like Jean Laplanche (and many along with him) to accept the function that belongs to the 'model' of phylogenesis in Freud's work. This reticence – which one can see with more clarity in Lacan – does not only express a resistance to a supposed Darwinism or biologism on Freud's part; it relates in fact, through the *problematic of language and its relation to memory* (and thus through the *status of the unconscious*), to the *question of the father* in analysis. It is as if a philosophy – and perhaps even in certain cases a Hegelian phenomenology – were underpinning the theoretical discourse here and, implicitly privileging the plane of consciousness, granting to the *symbolic function of the father* the organising power of the transference. We may see this in close proximity to the place of the sexual 'enigma' in seduction by the *Other*; its effect is to subtract from the father – from his murder and the murder of this murder, their role as the amnesiac/reminiscent memory of the transference. Because it is certainly not enough to propose that because they can't remember the states of the distant past the patient relives them in the transference and actualises them in the person of the analyst; we must also think – phylogenetically, so to speak – about the meaning of the amnesia of this reminiscent memory [*mémoire réminiscente*], both then about the murder which institutes it as well as the self-preserving value of the dead victim of this murder, maintained as such by this amnesiac memory. *It is at that very place that the father of the transference can be named* – precisely to the extent that the negative hallucination correlates with this amnesia. It is hardly possible to understand the dream and transference – and thus the role of construction in analysis – if what Freud describes as 'infant memory' isn't referred directly to the phylogenesis of the murder of the father and the avatars of his death, which factors participate in the 'glaciation' of 'psychic life'.

Perhaps the valorisation in the practice of analysis of the 'technical' (or techno-strategic) interest of the countertransference and its function as a material shield against stimuli has meant that the 'vanishing point' (P. Lacoste) of Freud's phylogenetics has been generally viewed as secondary, even outmoded, in metapsychology. We would argue that the misunderstanding by analysts of the *father of the transference* – whether in the form of their self-representation as father, a source of the ambiguity of the maternal/paternal seduction or through the operations of disjunctive doubling – is certainly not foreign to the identificatory ideology of the dead-father and his symbolic *place*. One can of course satirise, in the form of a joke, the certainty that some analysts have of being the immortal dead of their patients, and of thus being preserved from the omnipresent threat of murder! But more seriously, this comes back to what might be one of the fundamental aporias of the practice of analysis – that is *the relation of the analyst to their own death* – not in the sense of the architect Eupalinos, but in the sense explained by Marie Moscovici, to wit, the 'dismemberment' of the father. Or even according to a quasi-ontological determination of the *Versagung* of the neutral (we would say: of this renunciation), which implies on the part of the analyst in the treatment the *temporal movement of the destitution of their person through the work of language*. This movement should make manifest – on the side of the analyst – what one could call the historical (or historicising) temporality of the *trans-subjective subjectivation of death*. The *trans-subjective* dimension is to be stressed here, as long as this subjectivation through the work of language is determined by the regressive temporality of the singular transference of the patient, and insofar as it is not assimilated by the massive inertia which sometimes overcomes the analyst in the course of the treatment. And if language is indeed the site of the analytic situation, its existence means that the neutrality – the negative – of the analyst cannot be thought as a technical attitude or behaviour in the treatment unless it is affirmed as its own disavowal. The inevitable 'narcissism' of analysts is such that technique becomes laughable as soon as it secedes from language, which is to say that it solidifies outside the act of interpretation.

The advantage that the Freudian model of phylogenesis may offer in the situating of transference and the enabling of the hypothesis of the *father of the transference* certainly lies in the direction taken in the elaboration of the model by the reference to *totemism*.

From the start, it does not escape Freud that the archaic ambivalence that is constitutive of transference corresponds to that ancient state of humanity in which, under the effect of 'man's development from a primitive state to a civilised one his aggressiveness undergoes a very considerable degree of internalisation or turning inwards'.[70] Freud means that the interiorisation of hostility, which is a process of civilisation and which includes guilt in its mechanism, would be in the nature of neurosis, and also that regression – insofar as it goes back to a fixation – would constitute the neurotic specificity of transference. In the *Overview of the Transference Neuroses*, Freud returns to the distinction between the 'developmental history of the libido' – susceptible to being 'satisfied auto-erotically for quite a while' and repeating a 'much older piece of the [phylogenetic] development' – and the 'developmental history of the ego' – which 'from the beginning [is] directed at objects and thereby at reality', and represents the 'functions of self-preservation and the formations derived from them'.[71] This distinction between the two developments introduces the series which proceeds as follows: 'anxiety hysteria – conversion hysteria – obsessional neurosis – dementia praecox – paranoia – melancholia-mania'.[72] In this series the first three neuroses are referred to as *transference neuroses* due to the dynamic capacity of the libido to be displaced onto objects, as distinct from the narcissistic neuroses, since 'all three transference neuroses are directed towards the complete development of the libido'.[73] The so-called narcissistic neuroses (in the series of the three others which will be called 'psychosis'), in which the libido is withdrawn from objects toward the ego, 'return to previous phases before the finding of an object'. While the *transference neuroses* seem to exhibit a progressive mastery of thought and language (the animist hubris of understanding 'the world according to his ego'[74]), the narcissistic neuroses are characterised by such 'speech alterations and hallucinatory storms'[75] that one is justified in supposing in them a regressive tendency to heal oneself by regaining the object. According to Freud, the disposition to the later [narcissistic neuroses] 'had been acquired by a second generation, whose development introduces a new phase of human civilization'.[76] The devirilisation of the sons by the father – their castration – corresponds, in 'that primeval time', to the extinction of the libido and the arrest of individual development. It is this state which would be repeated in dementia praecox with the abandoning of any love object and evidently also of any possibility for transference onto an object – which must be reconstituted autoerotically. In melancholia-mania – the last of the narcissistic neuroses on the genealogical axis of the development of humanity – we find the essence of the totemic phenomenon at its origin:

> If one looks at the characteristic alternation of depression and elation, it is difficult not to recall the very similar succession of triumph and mourning that forms a regular component of religious festivities: mourning over the death of the god, triumphal joy over his resurrection. This religious ceremony, however, as we have surmised from the statements of ethnopsychology, only recapitulates in reverse the attitude of the members of the brother clan after they have overpowered and killed the primal father: triumph over his death, then mourning over the fact that they all still revered him as a model. So might this great event of human history, which made an end of the primal horde and replaced it with the victorious organization of brothers, provide the predisposition for the peculiar succession of moods that we acknowledge as a particular narcissistic disorder alongside the paraphrenias. The mourning about the primal father proceeds from identification with him, and such identification we have established as the prerequisite for the melancholic mechanism.[77]

Let us retain for our present purposes first of all that the essence of the phenomenon of melancholia would reside in this *identificatory passion for the dead father*, whose mourning would thereafter be impossible otherwise than in this latter form which disavows the murder – the self-conservation of the ego being assured by this 'shadow of the object upon the ego'. This turning around and withdrawal of transferential investments in the object onto the ego is indeed aligned with the concept of narcissistic neurosis, defined negatively – like the paraphrenias – as the *impossibility of transference*. And whatever forms are taken here by the effort to 'regain the object', these forms indicate not so much the absence of the capacity for transference than an inability to leave this state of transferential withdrawal – auto-erotic by nature – into the ego. It is this factor that characterises the *melancholy of the lost object* and thus of the *father kept dead by the disavowed murder*, in the transference itself. And we are aware that melancholic self-accusations arise not only from guilt, but also reproduce, in the muting of language, the murderous act as it is replayed by the ego in its identification with the dead object.[78]

But if we follow Freud's genealogical model – according to Ferenczi's 'programme' 'to bring the neurotic types of regression into harmony with the stages of human phylogeny'–, we would be tempted by another hypothesis emerging in the wake of those preceding. Would it not be appropriate to suppose that *paradoxically*, transference is a formation arising not from the 'transference neuroses' but from the 'second generation', which has to contend with the powerful image of the father, culminating in his murder, and then the unconscious memorial cult in his regard. Or should we rather suppose that it is the non-transferential neuroses – the narcissistic neuroses – which, allowing access to the dead father, are those very late instances of neurosis which conserve the topical function of regression in the transference and thus keep the memory of the traces of a lost language? It may seem just as easy – and relatively satisfying – to have the transference derive from the hysterical symptom of conversion as it would be disorienting to think that transference has a melancholic basis. And yet is on this exact point that the problem of the totemism of transference is posed. However, in staying with Freud's phylogenetic schema, nothing prevents the hypothesis that the passage from the first to the second generation – that of the sons and the neuroses – involves a conception of *transference* as a reliving or rather a remembering of the prototype of hysterical *affect*, and of its allo-erotic resource in identification with an object. This direction seems doubly underlined by Freud when he supposes the persistence of the hysterical characteristic well beyond the transference neuroses (in this case, transference would be the *prototype* of *any affective state*), and when he hints that totemic belief is itself the vestige of a vanished body that is thereafter wholly reunited – yet absent – in the name.

We are not going to repeat the whole of Freud's magisterial analysis of totemism as it is articulated in *Totem and Taboo*. This demonstration does indeed accord to the totem the function of *imagining* (rather than representing) *the dead ancestor* and expecting from the latter a filiation *not-through-blood*, ensuring the psychic protection and identity of the individual on condition that the associated taboos are not transgressed. The consanguinity of those who belong to the same kin institutes not only the interdiction of sexual congress between the *same* but also, positively, the idea of *totemic kinship* and *transferential transmission*. Initially citing Frazer – for whom the totem could be the means of identification of the individual as themselves thanks to the quite specific relation they have with the objects that surround them – and then Max Muller who thinks that the kernel of totemism lies in nomination and could result from primitive forms of writing, Freud remarks that if the origin of names may be forgotten, they nevertheless remain one of the most significant and essential attributes of the person. 'A man's name', Freud writes, 'is a principal component of his personality, perhaps even a portion of his soul'.[79] At the conclusion of *Totem and Taboo* Freud offers a striking recapitulation of the origin of totemism as reconstituted by psychoanalysis:

> One day the brothers who had been driven out came together, killed and devoured their father and so made an end of the patriarchal horde. United, they had the courage to do and succeeded in doing what would have been impossible for them individually. [...] Cannibal savages as they were, it goes without saying that they devoured their victim as well as killing him. The violent primal father had doubtless been the feared and envied model of each one of the company of brothers: and in the act of devouring him they accomplished their identification with him, and each one of them acquired a portion of his strength.[80]

The 'ambivalent father-complexes' in each of the children makes for the coexistence of powerful hatred and strong admiration. After having eliminated the father and thereby satisfied their hatred the sons discover their affection for the father in the form of their remorse: 'The dead father became stronger than the living one had been'. Freud continues:

> What had up to then been prevented by his actual existence was thenceforward prohibited by the sons themselves, in accordance with the psychological procedure so familiar to us in psycho-analyses under the name of 'deferred obedience'. They revoked their deed by forbidding the killing of the totem, the substitute for their father, and they renounced its fruits by resigning their claim to the women who had now been set free.[81]

If the totem is indeed the ancestor who figures, through its *characters*, the first graphic signs of a nomination allowing recognition of and belonging to a lineage, Freud describes it here as the *substitute for the father* – strictly speaking his effigy –, which bears witness to his murder and to its disavowal. In this case the totem – the name for the soul of the absent ancestor – will undergo an evolution, the effect of which is that the effacement of any possibility of representing the father in the totemic form first of an animal, then a God, and finally a name, will intensify both *figurability* and the power, devolved to language alone, to remember the murder and thus have language alone as interlocutor – language as the memory of the absent interlocutor. The father is nowhere to be found, even as an image. In this light we can be struck by this remark of Freud's in *Totem and Taboo*: 'the psycho-analytical interpretation of the scene coincides approximately with the allegorical, surface translation of it, which represents the god as overcoming the animal side of his own nature'.[82] In a sense the figure of the name will be its triumph over the god.

It would be tempting to conclude from this that *transference has a totemic nature* – in other words to see in transference the neurotic survival of the phenomenon of totemism and its origin in the constitution of the *religious bond*. Such a conclusion is in fact merited, based as it is on clinical considerations, and potentially developed by the reference of animal phobias to totemism (see *Little Hans*), and on the no less totemic nature of taboos with respect to the person of the analyst. Likewise – as we've seen – totemism would function in this instance as a starting point for interrogating the issue of the *psychic continuity* between one generation and another and thus for posing once more the quite fundamental question of the *genealogical nature of transference*. In fact this question is essential. It consists in considering that, in the treatment, while his memories are equivalent to a latent melancholia, the patient allows the genealogical figures of his own identifications to emerge in the dream. The more the genealogical dimension of the transference is neglected by analysts, the more they are prone to seek and interpret references to themselves. The dream is a diagnostician because it is hypochondriacal, and for this very reason it is a genealogist of the corporal insignia of the ancestors. And it is perhaps in the field of the psychoses that the genealogical dimension of transference is most telling.

To become more solid, the perspectives that arise from the totemic hypothesis merit further investigation. But we can provisionally conclude on the point we have reached. The interest of the reference to totemism is that it allows us to pursue the vanishing point of Freud's phylogenetic considerations while recognising in them their value as an account of the formation of the unconscious – between the dream and the joke – according in this instance to the person of the analyst the function not of an interlocutor but of a *name* – as much an interlocutory *mediation* as interlocutory material (to paraphrase André du Bouchet's fine title). Of course we can think of this *totemic person* as a 'substitute for the father', but we should also consider them as that aspect of the *substitute* which doesn't indicate a representative or a 'stand-in' but rather the *appearance of an image* or a *semblance*, one which belongs to the *absence of the father*, and in which this absence is the illusory focus of his presence and exists as an unimaginable emptiness.

The Enigmatic Interlocutor of Transference

If, today, analysts have come to trivialize transference and to inhibit its concept – little by little making it lose its power – is it not out of a *careless neglect of the strangeness of absence*? In other words, the disappearance of the *strangeness of transference* should be related to the forgetting of the strangeness of the absent father [*le père de l'absence*]. What our consideration of the *totem* as a form of drawing and writing [*dessin-écriture*] of the absent ancestor – an unconscious formation which can be called 'substitute for the father' – has allowed us to conceive is the *vanishing point of immemorial memory in the present*, as well as *the illusory addressee of the person* (whether designated as 'psychic' or not) of the analyst in the treatment. We might adopt J.-B. Pontalis' formulation, when he refers to this person as the 'transitory addressee',[83] while objecting that such a formulation retains the function of communication in transference and takes away the 'totemic' nature of the 'person of the doctor' such as we have proposed it, as an *effigy*, generating negative hallucination and thus – in and through the dream – leading to an intensification of the *aspects of the person themselves* in the analysis.

While Ludwig Binswanger, corresponding with Freud about certain difficult cases which necessitated analytic treatment in psychiatric institutions, was concerned to find a phenomenologico-existential basis for the phenomenon of transference in the terms of a theory of the other and their intersubjective appresentation, for his part Freud insisted on maintaining the phenomenon within the limits of a re-enacted repetition of childhood. For Freud it was not a question of relation or of interpersonal communication, since transference in fact increases – in the presence of the person of the doctor – the projections which are constitutive of the person of the ego of the dreamer themselves [*la personne propre du moi du rêveur*]. There was no need then to have recourse to a *we* (Binswanger's *Wirheit*) or an *I-you* characterised by religious spirituality. We should not expect from such a spirituality an explanation of the essence of the transferential phenomenon, and it is rather in the opposite direction we should proceed, basing ourselves on a conception of transference in continuity with psychic processes in order to account for religious affinities. At the heart of the debate with Binswanger – but also with Pfister and to a certain extent with Jung – Freud's *psychoanalytic refusal* is a radical refusal to countenance any further return, on the subject of transference, of a philosophical attitude which proposes to re-establish the claim of a theory of the other or of interpersonal communication, both of which would inevitably lead to allowing the phenomenological doctrine of consciousness an exorbitant prerogative. While it is quite legitimate – in continuity with the hypotheses of the *Sketch* to accord to the *Pcs-Cs* system the function of the sensorial organ of exchanges with others in the constitution of the *Nebenmensch* (the 'human neighbour'), it is certainly not in such a fashion that one can interpret what one calls the transference or the transferences. The fact that the word 'transference(s)' has become a concept that has been 'taken into custody', as Pontalis puts it, and that this concept has come, in the discourse of analysts, to 'misunderstand the migration which it bears with it' is not separable – as we've seen – from the phenomenological psychology currently present in the disjunctive subjective experience – itself inspired by intersubjectivity – of countertransference. With its plurality reduced, moreover, transference has been philosophically recaptured by a strategic theory of seductive counter-seduction. Aren't the appeal to mistakes about the person [*erreurs sur la personne*] or the response 'what do I represent for you?' the usual mechanisms of 'honest' rejection used by the seducer?

At its origin, it is said, the metaphorical concept of 'transference(s)' speaks of movements of transport, displacement, transfer, translation – it expresses changes of place. On this point we should indeed look for an Aristotelean Freud – the Aristotle of the *Physics*, Book IV, who sees the *physics* of place as a physics of time and language. Freud in fact conceives – with a view to a metapsychology of transference – the *meta-physics of transference*, the physic *meta* of the *psychic*, according to the psychoanalytic account of primitive animism. Transference is indeed a *process* (rather than a phenomenon) which makes for changes of place, and these are temporal movements in language. A place is the instance of a *name* – the act of naming in speech is the return, in the name, of the associative and transferential property of the physical time of *Entstellung*. Isn't speech in analysis in fact animated by transferential temporalities such that any displacement of a 'point of view' entails its transformation? And in this sense speech always carries the place along in its movement. Such a physics of the psychic may re-align with the value accorded to words by magic, making words be more like they are in Homer, *physical actions* borne by the air of the voice. It is equally on this condition that, in the act of naming specific to the words spoken, transference works through the tonal effect of resonance. In this light, transference is indeed a *field of resonances* which diffracts affect. The *meta-physics of speech of the person of the analyst* – working through an *optic*, and potentially catoptric, *physics* – thus has no other *interlocutory support* than the invisible writing of a name acting as a *site of language*. Such a *metaphysics of transference* – the prolegomenon to any metapsychology of transference – evidently excludes any semiotic philosophy of the relation between a locutor and an allocutor.

'Transference onto my person': Freud's use of this expression might well have fed the addressee's illusion which informs the crediting of their own person by analysts, in the transference. A tendentious interpretation of 'false connection' (immediately translated as an instance of mistakes about the person) has done the rest of the work on the way towards the banalisation of transference. To introduce – 'countertransferentially' – the consciousness of a false connection which is in some sense repeated is to effect a duplication such that a disavowal becomes necessary, in order to extract oneself from the error in which one is trapped ('it's not me... it's another... or "the Other"'). If the anachronicity of the past lies in *repetition*, it is all the more necessary that analysts refrain from intentionalising the 'parental images' of this past with their patients – if only through a silence which carries the *consciousness of these images* as *representations-aims* of the act of remembering. From this point of view, the self-identification of the analyst with a parental image can only engender the madness of transferential dead-ends. This is what happens with Freud and Dora as well as with the young homosexual woman.

The analyst is not the addressee of the transference. Neither are they the 'transitory addressee' because, as we've said, this would re-introduce a kind of *allocutory mediation of the person*. The word *interlocutor* might have the same drawbacks if it were taken to mean an allocutory address to another person. But the advantage of the term lies rather in the *inter* of the locutor – the latter being one, the same, but *in* two, divided. The *in two* of the interlocutor, engendered by the *situation* is, in Freud, the *zweideutig* [ambiguity] of the words of the transference through the optical effect of the other in language. If there is indeed a real person capable of being physically represented as the interlocutor of the words of images, isn't their *appearance* purely the shadow for which the word *calls* from what it is – we could say, from its nature as negative hallucination?

From Ossip Mandelstam – the author of *About an Interlocutor* – as well as Paul Celan and Du Bouchet, we know that, whatever the specific image taken by the form of the interlocutor, the *poem* is only a poem if it becomes the text *beyond* the text – the text beyond, itself unwritten, which is the interlocutor: ultimately language itself, which is non-personified, and the community of language. The word [*la parole*] is born in the interior of the written word [*la parole écrite*]: the written text is the material return or rather the *language surface* of this word. The interlocutor is this return: they are not beyond, unless this return is *beyond*. What we call the *poem* – if it has an interlocutory intention with respect to a 'real' person who inspires it – works to become the poem, in such a way that this person [*personne*] (*Jemand*) becomes no-one [*personne*] (*Niemand*): the word of the poem.

Two questions about the *Traumdeutung* are supposed to have come to Paul Celan after reading it: what or who is the interlocutor of the dream in the night of the sleeper? And who is the interlocutor of the address that the word speaks but does not intend for someone unless – under the effect of this address – they become no-one [*personne*]? In her book *In the Hand of No-one*, Martine Broda says of *Niemandsrose*: 'The question posed from the title *Niemandsrose* onwards – of whom is the poem the rose? – is among others the question of the interlocutor'.[84] Dedicated to Mandelstam, Celan's book goes beyond the indication of a distant and unknown addressee:

> Right from the start Paul Celan follows Mandelstam when the latter postulates the existence of the Interlocutor, that is the structure of address of the poem, dialogical in its essence. He follows him when the latter proposes that the Interlocutor cannot be a determinate figure. Celan's decisive or daring move is the conclusion that he draws from this point. If the poem, addressed as it is, which for Celan means directed, destined, does not for all that aim at 'a certain person', then the place of the Interlocutor is

an empty place which comes to be designated by this word: no-one [*personne*]. Because Paul Celan, with this sense of the fertility of paradox that we know him to have, goes as far as saying that the addressee of the poem is No-one [*Personne*], something that Mandelstam dare not think. But in what sense? This is what we have to understand. It is not in any case a question of the negation of the Interlocutor, since Celan's poetry as a whole is oriented toward a search for the 'Thou'.[85]

In contrast – but is it really in contrast? – to a conception of the poem as a monologue (in Novalis, for example), and also to the 'stellar' structure of language (in Rilke), the *dialogic* of the poem for Paul Celan is to be understood as the constitution of the *enigmatic Interlocutor* by means of the speech of the poem through the function of its *writing*. Since the poem is beyond its readable text and also because the reading of its writing transforms the address to *you* into the interlocution of speech, it is then the *poem* – of which the text is the support – which is the interlocutor of this speech – the speech-poem. The generation of the poem at first includes the designation of a generally feminine or feminised addressee – mother or sister – but this generation only engenders the poem through a crossing which in this sense is a *translation* or *transference* within language. This crossing through the language of barbarism – the Germanic language of Nazism – makes of the signs of the text arranged on its surface the *medium* (milieu and means) of a path towards, which is the *interlocutor*. If the interlocutor reaches impersonality it is because the poem – which universalises no-one – is the non-person of the human community of language. 'For the poem, everything and everybody is a figure of this other toward which it is heading'.[86]

About an Interlocutor (1913) inspired Paul Celan's Bremen Prize speech. The *I* turns – rises towards – a *thou* which conserves the poem of the word – the interlocutor of the regressive infinity of language, a place of withdrawal of the text and of memory to come, as a dialect of language.[87] If a poem can only arise, we might say, *out of* this to-come [*à-venir*] of the *immemorial past* which is the true figural potentiality of the interlocutor, the *transfer of the poem*, its 'transference' would thus be the coming of the interlocutor from a to-come [*à venir*] of anachronic memory in the presence of a person, in *the present of the word*. *Paradoxical temporalities*, since the *interlocutor* called forth by this transference is *embodied* [*s'incarne*] (Freud), *in the strong sense of the word*, in a person whose presence makes absence visible. Coming from the memory of time, the interlocutor is always already there, obscurely hidden, *hermetic*. They are *at the site of the epos.*

Paradoxical temporalities of the transference if one also remembers that – just as with the dream – persons are the appearances of the dead. Transference as the work of mourning then? Perhaps so, on condition that we understand this *return of the dead* in the light of the impossibility of mourning them, in search of their sepulchre in the name that names them. *To go down* and *to come back up again* are the movements which accompany the temporalities of transference. If it is difficult to think about these temporalities that belong to a time outside time, at least we know that they are, in an agrammatical manner, the places that engender the words of speech at the moment of their return.

Differently from what occurs in a text such as Du Bouchet's *Matter of the Interlocutor*, what arises in Paul Celan is a *rarefaction* of the aspiration of the poem at the point where the interlocutor must be the most exact figure of the other of language. Impasse or aporia of the poem? Still, it would not be abusive to propose that transference is thus aligned with the purity of autistic skimming – in which the *autos* has become the ascetic movement of the coincidence of the other-interlocutor in the *call of the word* alone. Thanks to painting, one might say, which in Du Bouchet is a whole language, the writing 'in the air of the immaterial interval – addressed to the support', there exists an 'outside, transient', where the support has 'power of figuration' and 'cuts into the word'. The 'air' gives *light* to figures that see. And the support is the *fragment of time* of the present.

In Paul Celan's *Conversation on the Mountain* (1959), the one to whom speech is addressed has become deaf-mute. The Jew exiled from language and condemned to wander the earth without language has no recourse to recognition aside from the *shibboleth* of the pass-word. For this Jew, there remain only simple words whose pronunciation is an appeal to an echo and already in itself the *mineral echo* returns only resonances, all the resonances. Poem of pronunciation rather than articulation. The *Conversation on the Mountain* has two Jews, 'thou' and 'me' encounter each other, and their strange dialogue, destituting language, opposes *sprechen* and *reden*.

> The babblers! They've got, even now, with their tongues bumping dumbly against their teeth and their lips going slack, something to say to each other! Alright, let them talk…
> 'A good way you've come, you've come all the way here…'
> 'So I have. I've come like you'.
> 'Don't I know it'.
> 'You know it. You know and you see: up here the earth has folded over, it's folded once and twice and three times, and opened up in the middle, and in the middle there's some water, and the water is green, and the green is white, and the white comes from up farther, comes from the glaciers, now you could say. But you shouldn't, that that's the kind of speech (*die Sprache*) that counts here, the green with the white in it, a language not for you and not for me – because I'm asking, who is it meant for then, the earth, if it's not meant for you, I'm saying, and not for me –, well then, a language with no I and no Thou, pure He, pure It, d'you see, pure they, and nothing but that'.
> 'I know, I know. Yes I've come a long way, I've come like you'.
> 'I know'.
> 'You know and still ask me: so you've come anyway, you've come here – why, and what for?'

'Why and what for... Because maybe I had to talk, to myself or to you (*Weil ich hab reden müssen vielleicht, zu mir oder zu dir*), had to talk with my mouth and my tongue and not just with my stick. Because who does it talk to, the stick? It talks to the stone, and the stone – who does *it* talk to?'

'Who should it talk to, cousin (*Geschwisterkind*)? It doesn't talk, it speaks (*Er redet nicht, er spricht*), and whoever speaks, cousin, talks to no one (*der rede zu niemand*), because no one hears him, no one and No-One (*niemand und Niemand*), and then he says, he and not his mouth and not his tongue, he and only he says: D'you hear?'[88]

The Jew, 'you know, now what he has got that really belongs to him, that's not borrowed, on loan and still owed?'[89] – the Jew is the one to whom nothing belongs, neither language nor his own *person*. He is the one who bears the person borrowed from another – from an always different and uncertain other – never given back to whomsoever. The recourse to the antisemitic interpellation 'Jud', which is the form of injury in the German language, takes in *Conversation on the Mountain* the connotative value of the barbarism of a language [*langue*] of torturers and executioners, yet nevertheless the form of a language [*langage*] – as if the latter bore the traces of a murderous violence which the poem had to cross through in order to enable the *I* to appropriate the subjective identity of a *person* in relation to a *thou*. At the start, *I* and *thou* are the incessant echoes of the 'language of no-one' in which *they* are lost. And the mountain – like Lenz's mountain – is *without place*. As Stéphane Mosès explains in his text 'When Language is Made Voice',[90] 'speech is carried alternately by different voices'. This consists of the shadows of voices syncopating a speech which has no pathway in the language of It (*Ça*). *Who I?*, as Jean-Claude Lavie might say.[91] Absence is absolute, as is the concentration camp in the last poem of *Strette*. As opposed to a site, the place of extermination has no name while also being a very real geographic place, the name of which must stay in memory, never to be effaced. But Celan's poem – nostalgically, it's true – works this coming from the most high and most radical place of language in the encounter of speech with an *I* which transforms the minerality of stone and gives *sonorous face* to the *I*. Insofar as *up there* is the summit of an ideal mountain it seems made for others and once more to expropriate the Jew from an identity in language. The *site of the mountain* is the heroic mastery of the speech of the poem – thanks to its inner dialect – at the heart of the language of barbarism. This site will not be seen and the *I* will not occupy it: it will be hidden in the poem, beyond it, in its centre which in this instance is the absence from which the *you* responds in the silence of language.

We might say that the 'reshaping' of the *I* by the movements that displace it in its speaking next to an other, an other which is neutral, whose silence demands that it confront the brutality of language, tends toward the recognition of this *I* as a locutory person. But analysis is not a philo-sophical process of appropriation. In this case the *identity* of the *I* will remain always dependent on the identifications and disidentifications of the ego. If transference does indeed reveal something essential it is that the *I* – the first-person pronoun, the concrete instance of the person speaking here and now on the couch – shows the lack of such an instance. In pro-nouncing the word *I* the analysand has already displaced and transported the place of their subjective reference to themselves, and thus modified their locutory origin. They are already no longer where they said *I*. We have accorded to the Freudian concept of *Entstellung* the responsibility of indicating how transference (*Ubertragung*) breaks away from the place or carries the place along in its movement of displacement. Now – as with the transformation of persons in the dream – this *Entstellung* is possible only due to the personal indeterminacy of the *you* that is veiled in the address of speech, a speech that is nevertheless present and yet solicits the *you* through the silence of language and the interlocutory determination of the formation of an *I*. In other words, everything happens as if the dis-placements and deformations of the *I* in the *instant* of its pronunciation had *migrated* outside a centre of articulation – this centre being signified as if in the background of all the decenterings to which this speech subjects the *I* as an instance of speech. And if the fundamental rule of association means the freedom of the *I* for delirium, is it not because this rule expressed from the *silence of the neutral* is in a sense the call of speech allowing itself to breathe upon the appearances of the *I* – to allow the latter to extricate itself from its conscious instanciation? One might of course be attracted by the Heideggerian – or rather Binswangerian – idea of a *you* which would be behind the 'language of being' and whose veiling would provoke the uncertainty of the subjectivation of the *I* while the *We* (*Wirheit*) of dialogue (*Gespräch*) is not possible. The ontological question remains open; but we would certainly not gain anything by an overhasty philosophical problematisation of transference! What appears to us to be closer to a psychoanalytical consideration of the *interlocutor of the transfer-ence* is certainly the *distance* measured by the *absence* of a *you*, of which one might say that speech awaits its manifestation as long as it exists only in the *silence* of a *language which listens*. The *act of hearing* in analysis allows the emptiness of speech [*le vide de la parole*] to form the interlocutor of the *spoken* [*le dit*] and the heard.

Transference is not a 'discursive relation to a partner' – even if the latter is 'imagined'. These words are from Benveniste, from his description of the function of *utterance* [*énonciation*] in the 'structure of dialogue'. In par-ticular, in his text 'Relationships of Person in the Verb', Benveniste writes:

> In effect, one characteristic of the persons 'I' and 'you' is their specific 'oneness': the 'I' who states, the 'you' to whom 'I' addresses himself are unique each time. But 'he' can be an infinite number of subjects – or

none. That is why Rimbaud's 'je est un autre [I is another]' represents the typical expression of what is properly mental 'alienation,' in which the 'I' is dispossessed of its constitutive identity.[92]

I thus indicates the speaker insofar as it 'refers to the act of individual discourse in which it is pronounced'.[93] Benveniste adds: 'It is in the instance of discourse in which I designates the speaker that the speaker proclaims himself as the "subject"'.[94] In analysis, we can consider that what we call transference effects this subjective *disinstanciation* of the *I*: not through alienating capture by the *it* [*il*], but due to the specific nature of the personal indeterminacy of the *you*. Insofar as it is present in the person of the analyst, we can say that the presence of this *you signifies* to the patient's *utterance* the subjective de-objectivation of the allocutory person and the re-instantiation – de-centred, so to speak – of a *you in withdrawal* at the heart of the diffractions of the *I*. As soon as the analyst in person personalises the *you* – makes themselves too personal, as it were – they massify the *me myself*, as we've seen, and they lead the *you* towards paranoia, stripping away its mobilities and temporal potentialities, in other words, its capacity for transference.

We therefore need to allow that the *you* is in this instance the non-person, the no-one [*la non-personne/personne*] of the *absent*, in the sense that Benveniste conceives of it through the example of Arabic:

> For them [the Arab grammarians], the first person is *al-mutakallimu* 'the one who speaks'; the second, *al-muhatabu,* 'the one who is addressed'; but the third is *al-ya'ibu* 'the one who is absent.' A precise notion of the relationships among persons is implied by these denominations; precise especially in that it reveals the disparity between the first and second persons and the third. Contrary to what our terminology would make us believe, they are not homogeneous.[95]

Should we describe this absent as the 'big Absent', instantiating the relation of one person to another, in such a way that the structure of dialogue only takes on an intersubjective foundation through this kind of hidden reference? This perspective would indeed merit attention in the context of a comparison of the incidences of *I* and *you* in one language with another. Arabic is certainly strongly suggestive of a function (the absent) necessary for interlocution, in such a way that the locutor and the allocutor escape from the illusion of symmetry which negates intersubjective objectivity. In other words, it is as if Arabic in fact knows that – without this reference to the *absent* – the dialogic structure of utterance of *I-you* is threatened in its 'communicative' function by the identarian instability in which the I finds itself when faced by a symmetrical other.

In a quite remarkable text by Kunifumi Suzuki – psychoanalyst and translator of some of Lacan's works into Japanese – concerning 'Cultural

Difference, Sexual Difference and Psychoanalysis', we find that the untranslatability of *I* and *you* into Japanese pronouns leads us to determine under what conditions interlocution makes foundational speech possible:

> In drawing our attention to personal pronouns Lacan makes us realize that the 'Other is the locus in which is constituted he who is speaking with him who hears'. He notes a dissymmetry between the I and the you. Lacan says of this dissymmetry: '[...] the I is never there where it appears in the form of a particular signifier. The I is always there in the name of a presence that supports the discourse as a whole, whether in direct or indirect speech. [...] It's within this enunciation that the you appears. [...] That the you is already within discourse is obvious. There has never been a you anywhere else than where one says you'. [...].[96]

Japanese etymology, for example, assigns 'the meaning "lord" to one of the second-person pronouns, *kimi*. And one of the first-person pronouns, *boku* derives from the word which means "servant" or "slave"'. However, these pronouns are used in relations of equality and even of intimacy. Kunifumi adds:

> In French the word *me* appears more as a pronoun indicating the objective and concrete aspect of the locutor. It is the same with you [*toi*]. This objective value of the pronoun is exactly how Japanese pronouns are qualified.
>
> If the Japanese pronouns *Watashi* and *kimi* are different from *I* and *you*, and closer to me and you [*toi*], the question that arises is how to take account of the dissymmetry between *I* and *you* [*je et tu*].[97]

It is as if Japanese clarifies the status of *language itself as the interlocutor*, on the basis of a *you* which may be the *you* of a speech grounding the expressive and pronunciative *I*. 'The sentence "You are my wife" is foundational, insofar as it is not simply addressed to the one who hears it, but also goes beyond the interlocutor, which is to say that it is addressed to language, from which it is suspended. This suspension means that any response from the interlocutor is never definitive (...). It is this indeterminacy that founds the subject'.[98] If Japanese reveals in some way the foundational interlocution that lies in language itself, which thus lies beyond such and such a person addressed in the uttered sentence, this has the merit of making it apparent under what conditions the symmetry of *I-you* – which is a sense that is reductive of language as interlocutor – makes of the person the paranoiac mirror of projection. In return, it is perhaps in accounting for this paranoiac projection that the time of the interlocutor in foundational speech can be understood by whoever seeks to do so.

Lacan's first two seminars on *Identification* (1961) follow the one on *Tranference*: the formula 'the subject supposed to know' has already evolved to the point where the *Other* is not conceivable as a *subject* endowed with subjectivity, somehow philosophically personalised *at the level of consciousness*. 'The Other is not a subject, it is a locus from which one strives, says Aristotle, to *transfer* the knowledge of the subject', says Lacan, in the seminar of 15th November 1961.[99] As a locus or site of language, the *Other* must be disengaged from Cartesian anthropomorphism and become the *place of meaning* for the desire of speech. With the same gesture Lacan outlines his *topology*, which we generally forget was inspired – clinically as well – in the *site of the Other* constituted by language, a proposition without which transference cannot be theorised.

'We are insufficiently amazed by the phenomenon of transference', Freud noted. In 1938, in the *Outline of Psychoanalysis*, he invites analysts not to lose sight of this sense of amazement: 'The most remarkable thing is that the patient sees in the analyst the reincarnation of a figure out of his past'.[100] It is certain that whoever is not amazed by the strangeness of transference has long forgotten or neglected the site of the stranger and certainly the virtues of the interlocutory language of transference.

Translated by Patrick ffrench and Nigel Saint

Notes

1   *Psychoanalysis and Faith: The Letters of Freud and Oskar Pfister*, ed. by Heinrich Meng and Ernst L. Freud, trans. by Eric Mosbacher (New York: Basic Books, 1963). See in particular: 'The transference is indeed a cross. The unyielding stubbornness of the illness, because of which we abandoned indirect suggestion and direct hypnotic suggestion, cannot be entirely eliminated by analysis, but can only be diminished, and its relics make their appearance in the transference. These are generally conspicuous enough, and the rules often let one down, but one must be guided by the patient's character and not entirely give up one's personal note' (p. 39). Subsequently, alluding to the curative power of love in transference, Freud adds: 'The more you let him find love the sooner you will get his complexes, but the smaller is the final success, as he gives up the fulfilments of the complexes only because he can exchange them for the results of the transference. A cure has perhaps been achieved, but the patient has not attained the necessary degree of independence and security against relapse. Now in this respect things are easier for you than for us physicians because you can sublimate the transference on to religion and ethics, which is not easy for the invalids of life' (pp. 39–40).

2   Pierre Fédida, *Crise et contre-transfert* (Paris: PUF, 1992).

3   *Crise et contre-transfert*, pp. 189–226. I have engaged with this problem mainly in two chapters of this book, 'Le Contre-transfert en question' and 'Crise et métaphore'. See also the book by Marie Moscovici, *Il est arrivé quelque chose* (Paris: Ramsay, 1988).

4   Monique Schneider, *Le Trauma et la filiation paradoxale* (Paris: Ramsay, 1988).

5   [Fédida refers to Lacan's proposition that the place of the analyst is akin to the 'dummy' hand in the game of bridge. See Jacques Lacan, *Écrits: A Selection*,

trans. by Alan Sheridan (London: Tavistock, 1977), p. 140. Footnotes in square brackets are additions by the translators.].

6   Pierre Fédida, 'L'Angoisse dans le contre-transfert ou l'inquiétante étrangeté du transfert' in *Topique* 41 (1988), pp. 49–66. [Fédida's expression 'inquiétante étrangeté', used a number of times in 'The Interlocutor', is the usual translation of *das unheimlich* into French, initially by Marie Bonaparte in 1933; since the usual translation into English of Freud's essay of 1919 is 'The Uncanny' this poses a problem for translation. We have chosen a literal option with the rendering 'unsettling strangeness' but indicated in parenthesis the allusion to Freud's essay and the conceptual cluster of 'the uncanny'.]

7   Sigmund Freud, 'Our Attitude to Death' in 'Thoughts for the Time on War and Death' in *The Standard Edition of the Complete Psychological Works of Sigmund Freud Volume XIV*, trans. by James Strachey et al (London: The Hogarth Press, 1957) [1915], pp. 289–300, p. 296.

8   Emil Staiger, *Basic Concepts of Poetics*, ed. by Marianne Burkhard and Luanne T. Frank, trans. by Janette C. Hudson and Luanne T. Frank (University Park, PA: Pennsylvania State University Press, 1991), p. 100.

9   Homer, *The Iliad*, trans. by Robert Fagles (London and New York: Penguin, 1990), Book Six [Fédida mistakenly attributes this to *The Odyssey*].

10 Staiger, *Basic Concepts*, p. 101.

11 Robert Langs (ed.), *The Therapeutic Intervention I and II* (New York: Jason Aronson, 1976).

12 Jean Laplanche, *Le Baquet: Transcendance du transfert* (Paris: PUF, 1987), p. 287.

13 Laplanche, *Le Baquet: Transcendance du transfert*, p. 287.

14 Sigmund Freud, 'The Dynamics of Transference' in *The Standard Edition of the Complete Psychological Works of Sigmund Freud Volume XII*, trans. by James Strachey et al (London: Hogarth Press, 1958) [1912], pp. 97–108, p. 108).

15 Sigmund Freud, 'Fragment of a Case of Hysteria' in *The Standard Edition of the Complete Psychological Works of Sigmund Freud Volume VII*, trans. by James Strachey et al (London: Hogarth Press, 1953) [1901], pp. 3–124, p. 116.

16 Sigmund Freud, 'Preface to the Translation of Bernheim's *Suggestion*' in *The Standard Edition of the Complete Psychological Works of Sigmund Freud Vol I*, trans. by James Strachey et al (London: Hogarth Press, 1966), [1888], pp. 73–88, p. 78.

17 Antoine Berman, *The Experience of the Foreign. Culture and Translation in Romantic Germany*, trans. by S. Heyvaert (New York: SUNY Press, 1992). See also A. Berman, 'Tradition, translation, traduction' in *Cahier du Collège international de Philosophie*, 6 (1988), pp. 21–28. [A challenge for the translator arises here due to Fédida's use of the French word 'translation' and 'traduction' in this list of terms. We have chosen to introduce the word 'traduction' which exists in English, meaning a transmission or communication, in order to avoid the repetition of *translation*.]

18 See the debate reproduced in the *Revue internationale de psychopathologie*, 7 (1992), under the title 'Freud, la langue allemande et le rapport à la *Kultur*' by Georges-Arthur Goldschmidt, Wladimir Granoff, Marie Moscovici and Patrick Lacoste.

19 [Fédida alludes to a line from Baudelaire's sonnet 'La Beauté': 'I hate the movement that displaces lines'.]

20 Berman, 'Tradition, translation, traduction', p. 33.

21 Conversation with G. Didi-Huberman (August 1993). [See Georges Didi-Huberman, 'The Molding Image: Genealogy and the Truth of Resemblance in Pliny's *Natural History*, Book 35, 1-7', in Costas Douzinas and Lynda Neads (eds.), *Law and the Image: The Authority of Art and the Aesthetics of Law* (Chicago: University of Chicago Press, 1999), pp. 71-88.]

22   Polybius, *The Histories*, trans. by Robin Waterfield (Oxford: Oxford University Press, 2010), p. 409.

23   Freud, 'Thoughts for the Time of War and Death' p. 285.

24   Sigmund Freud, 'The Unconscious' in *The Standard Edition of the Complete Psychological Works of Sigmund Freud Volume XIV*, trans. by James Strachey et al (London: The Hogarth Press, 1957) [1915], pp. 159–216, p. 169.

25   Freud, 'The Unconscious', p. 169.

26   Freud, 'The Unconscious', p. 169.

27   Freud, 'The Unconscious', p. 169.

28   Freud, 'The Unconscious', p. 171.

29   Freud, 'The Unconscious', p. 169.

30   [A translation problem arises here around Fédida's expression 'la personne propre' and associated expressions such as 'personnage', since the expression 'the own, or proper person' is unidiomatic in English, and the usual translation of 'personnage' would be 'character', losing the phonological proximity of *personne* and *personnage*. We have chosen a range of options, including 'the person themselves', and, less happily, 'personality', none of which quite capture the *making strange* effected by Fédida's commentary on the concept of the person; for this reason we have used parentheses to indicate the recurrence of the original terms in French.]

31   Freud, 'The Unconscious', p. 170.

32   Sigmund Freud, 'The Psychopathology of Everyday Life' in *The Standard Edition of the Complete Psychological Works of Sigmund Freud Volume VI*, trans. by James Strachey et al (London: The Hogarth Press, 1960) [1901], p. 255.

33   Freud, 'The Psychopathology of Everyday Life', p. 255.

34   [Fédida mobilises here the double meaning of the French word *personne*, which means both *person* and *no-one*, and draws on a similar semantic possibility in German. The duality does not exist in English, save perhaps in a diluted manner in *one* and *no-one*.]

35   Sigmund Freud, 'The Uncanny' in *The Standard Edition of the Complete Psychological Works of Sigmund Freud Volume XVII*, trans. by James Strachey et al (London: Hogarth Press, 1955) [1919], pp. 216–56, p. 234.

36   Freud, 'The Uncanny', p. 235, citing Rank.

37   Freud, 'The Uncanny', our emphasis.

38   [Wladimir Granoff and Jean-Michel Rey, *L'Occulte, l'objet de la pensée freudienne: traduction et lecture de* Psychanalyse et télépathie *de Sigmund Freud* (Paris: PUF, 1983).]

39   Pierre Fédida, 'Un organe psychique hypochondriaque – Traitement psychique autocratique' in B. Brusset and C. Couvreur, *La Névrose obsessionnelle* (monograph in the *Revue française de psychanalyse* series) (Paris: PUF, 1993), pp. 107–26.

40   Sigmund Freud, 'Jokes and their Relation to the Unconscious' in *The Standard Edition of the Complete Psychological Works of Sigmund Freud Volume VIII*, trans. by James Strachey et al (London: The Hogarth Press, 1960) [1905], p. 179.

41   Sigmund Freud, 'Metapsychological Supplement to the Theory of Dreams' in *The Standard Edition of the Complete Psychological Works of Sigmund Freud Volume XIV*, trans. by James Strachey et al (London: The Hogarth Press, 1957) [1915], pp. 217–36, p. 223. [Translation modified.]

42   Fédida, *Crise et contre-transfert*.

43   Margaret Little, *Transference Neurosis & Transference Psychosis* (New York: James Aronson Inc., 1981); H. Searles, *Countertransference and Related Subjects: Selected Papers* (New York: International Universities Press, 1979). Partially translated into French by B. Bost as *Le Contre-transfert* (Paris: Gallimard, 1981).

44 Harold Searles, 'Discussion of "The Concept of Psychoses as a Result and in the Context of the Long-Term Treatment Modalities" by Leopold Bellak' in *Countertransference and Related Subjects*, pp. 282–88, p. 286.

45 Sigmund Freud, 'Instincts and their Vicissitudes' in *The Standard Edition of the Complete Psychological Works of Sigmund Freud Volume XIV*, trans. by James Strachey et al (London: The Hogarth Press, 1957) [1915], pp. 109–40, p. 127.

46 Freud, 'Instincts and their Vicissitudes', p. 127.

47 Agnès Minazzoli, *La Première ombre: Réflexion sur le miroir et la pensée* (Paris: Éditions de Minuit, 1990), p. 137.

48 Minazzoli, *La Première ombre: Réflexion sur le miroir et la pensée*, p. 43.

49 Minazzoli, *La Première ombre: Réflexion sur le miroir et la pensée*, p. 174.

50 Sigmund Freud, 'On Psychical (or Mental) Treatment' in *The Standard Edition of the Complete Psychological Works of Sigmund Freud Volume VII*, trans. by James Strachey et al (London: The Hogarth Press, 1953) [1905], pp. 283–304, pp. 292–93.

51 Jean-Martin Charcot and Paul Richer, *Les Démoniaques dans l'art*, suivi de J.-M. Charcot, *La Foi qui guérit* (Introduction by P. Fédida and Postface by G. Didi-Huberman) (Paris: Éditions Macula, 1984).

52 Charcot and Richer, *Les Démoniaques dans l'art*, p. 155

53 Charcot and Richer, *Les Démoniaques dans l'art*, p. 155.

54 Freud, 'On Psychical (or Mental) Treatment', p. 291.

55 Freud, 'On Psychical (or Mental) Treatment', pp. 291–92.

56 Freud, 'On Psychical (or Mental) Treatment', p. 292.

57 Freud, 'On Psychical (or Mental) Treatment', p. 293.

58 Freud, 'On Psychical (or Mental) Treatment', p. 292.

59 Freud, 'On Psychical (or Mental) Treatment', p. 295.

60 Freud, 'On Psychical (or Mental) Treatment', p. 296.

61 Freud, 'On Psychical (or Mental) Treatment', p. 296.

62 George J. Makari, 'A History of Freud's First Concept of Transference' in *The International Review of Psychoanalysis* 19:4 (1992), pp. 415–32.

63 Freud, 'On Psychical (or Mental) Treatment', p. 297.

64 Freud, 'Fragment of a Case of Hysteria', p. 116.

65 Harold Searles, 'The Function of the Patient's Realistic Perceptions of the Analyst in Delusional Transference' in *Countertransference and Related Subjects: Selected Papers* (New York: International Universities Press, 1979), pp. 196–227, p. 217.

66 Searles, 'The Function of the Patient's Realistic Perceptions of the Analyst in Delusional Transference', p. 218.

67 Jean Laplanche, *Le Baquet: Transcendance du transfert*, pp. 246–47.

68 Laplanche, *Le Baquet: Transcendance du transfert*, p. 247.

69 Fédida, *Crise et contre-transfert*.

70 Sigmund Freud, 'Analysis Terminable and Interminable' in *The Standard Edition of the Complete Psychological Works of Sigmund Freud Volume XXIII*, trans. by James Strachey et al (London: The Hogarth Press, 1964) [1937], pp. 209–54, p. 244.

71 Sigmund Freud, *A Phylogenetic Fantasy: Overview of the Transference Neuroses*, ed. Ilse Brubrich-Simitis, trans. Axel Hoffer and Peter T. Hoffer (Cambridge, MA: Harvard University Press, 1987), p. 12.

72 Freud, *A Phylogenetic Fantasy: Overview of the Transference Neuroses*, p. 13.

73 Freud, *A Phylogenetic Fantasy: Overview of the Transference Neuroses*, p. 13.

74 Freud, *A Phylogenetic Fantasy: Overview of the Transference Neuroses*, p. 15.

75 Freud, *A Phylogenetic Fantasy: Overview of the Transference Neuroses*, p. 17.

76 Freud, *A Phylogenetic Fantasy: Overview of the Transference Neuroses*, p. 16.

77 Freud, *A Phylogenetic Fantasy: Overview of the Transference Neuroses*, pp. 18–19.

78   Pierre Fédida, 'Auto-érotisme et autisme. Conditions d'efficacité d'un para-
      digme en psychopathologie' in *Revue internationale de psychopathologie* 2
      (1990), pp. 395–414.
79   Sigmund Freud, 'Totem and Taboo' in *The Standard Edition of the Complete
      Psychological Works of Sigmund Freud Volume XIII*, trans. by James Strachey et al
      (London: The Hogarth Press, 1955) [1913], pp. ix–164, p. 112.
80   Freud, 'Totem and Taboo', pp. 141–42.
81   Freud, 'Totem and Taboo', p. 143.
82   Freud, 'Totem and Taboo', p. 150.
83   Jean-Bertrand Pontalis, *La Force d'attraction* (Paris: Seuil, 1990).
84   Martine Broda, *Dans la main de personne: essai sur Paul Celan* (Paris: Éditions
      du Cerf, 1986), p. 63.
85   Broda, *Dans la main de personne: essai sur Paul Celan*, p. 64.
86   Paul Celan, 'The Meridian' in *Collected Prose*, trans. Rosemary Waldrop (New
      York: Routledge, 2003), p. 49.
87   See the book by Rachel Ertel, *Dans la langue de personne. Poésie yiddish de
      l'anéantissement* (Paris: Seuil, 1993).
88   Paul Celan, *Selected Poems and Prose*, trans. by John Felstiner (New York,
      London: W.W. Norton, 2001), pp. 398–99.
89   Celan, *Selected Poems and Prose*, p. 397.
90   P. Celan, *Entretien dans la montagne*, translated into French by Stéphane Mosès
      (Paris: Chandeigne, 1990), p. 28.
91   J.-C. Lavie, *Qui je?* (Paris: Gallimard, 1989).
92   Émile Benveniste, 'Relationships of Person in the Verb' in *Problems in General
      Linguistics*, trans. by Mary Elizabeth Meek (Miami: University of Miami
      Press, 1971), p. 199.
93   Émile Benveniste, 'Subjectivity in Language' in *Problems in General Linguistics*,
      p. 226.
94   Benveniste, 'Subjectivity in Language', p. 226.
95   Benveniste, 'Subjectivity in Language', p. 197.
96   Kunifumi Suzuki, 'La Différence culturelle, la différence sexuelle et la psy-
      chanalyse' in *Revue internationale de psychopathologie*, 13 (1993), p. 30. [The
      references to Lacan are from Jacques Lacan, *The Seminar of Jacques Lacan: Book
      III: The Psychoses* 1955–56, trans. Russell Grigg (New York: Norton, 1983),
      pp. 273–75].
97   Suzuki, 'La Différence Culturelle, la différence sexuelle et la psychanalyse', p. 31.
98   Suzuki, 'La Différence Culturelle, la différence sexuelle et la psychanalyse', p. 31.
99   [See Cormac Gallagher's translation at http://www.lacaninireland.com/
      web/wp-content/uploads/2010/06/Seminar-IX-Amended-Iby-MCL-7.
      NOV_.20111.pdf. Accessed 7th May 2023. Translation modified.]
100   Sigmund Freud, 'An Outline of Psychoanalysis' in *The Standard Edition of
      the Complete Psychological Works of Sigmund Freud Volume XXIII*, trans. by
      James Strachey et al (London: The Hogarth Press, 1964) [1938], pp. 141–208,
      pp. 174–75 (translation modified).

3   Regression

'How much the phylogenetic disposition can contribute to the understanding of the neuroses cannot yet be estimated', wrote Freud in the famous 1915 manuscript, *Overview of the Transference Neuroses*, rediscovered in 1983.[1] 'Overview' – *Übersicht*: this word is very well suited to the speculative perspective of theory when it has to 'open up distant vistas' and, thanks to 'fantasy', emancipate itself from 'careful and arduous observation', which is nevertheless necessary when it comes to denominating and naming symptoms, classifying them and putting them in series. Freud continues: 'It is nevertheless legitimate to assume that the neuroses must also bear witness to the history of the mental (*animique*) development of mankind', before adding:

> Our task of understanding the neuroses would naturally be much easier if the developmental history of the ego were given to us somewhere else instead of having to proceed in the opposite direction. One thereby gets the impression that the developmental history of the libido recapitulates a much older piece of the [phylogenetic] development than that of the ego, the former perhaps recapitulates conditions of the phylum of vertebrates, whereas the latter is dependent on the history of the human race.[2]

Ferenczi, who was very tempted by the search for mutual analogies between biological and psychological facts, is very present in the notes left by Freud in this previously unpublished manuscript. We know that in 1917 they worked together on an unrealised project of Lamarckian inspiration which would have sought to illuminate the relations between psychoanalysis and the theory of evolution. Freud's reticence, doubtless not unrelated to Ferenczi's haste (since the latter was always too eager to propose as certainties what had come to him as fleeting intuitions) did not prevent him from showing his admiration for these intuitions, but Freud remained severely critical with regard to any project to extend psychoanalysis into bio-analysis, or metapsychology into metabiology. In 1924 Ferenczi published *Thalassa: A Theory of Genitality*, which consists of two

DOI: 10.4324/9781032637600-4

parts, the first devoted to the ontogenetic aspects of the genital function, while the second deals with phylogenesis. Regression is found in the right place in the development of the thesis, under the aegis of Haeckel's Law. If the analyst possesses the means to imagine, through analogy, what he hears from the patient, then it follows that an analytic session is equivalent to an ontogenetic sequence recapitulating the phylogenetic infancy of the species in the individual. What limits the use we usually make of the concept of regression is our 'psycho-morphism': it tends to deny the analyst the fantasy of forms, deformations and transformations which nevertheless suggest the teratological expressions of symptoms. Ferenczi puts this bio-analysis to practical work, in a way that does not however dismiss the extraordinary contributions of the *Three Essays on Sexuality* (quite the reverse!), and it is thanks to the analogical and metaphorical power of the analyst that the patient can draw therapeutic resources from their regression in the process of the treatment. Inversely, any conceptual mastery which lacks this kind of imagination misses the opportunity to understand the process and goes against the real restorative function of regression.

But let's go back to Freud's *Overview of the Transference Neuroses*. From a study by Ferenczi of the 'Stages in the Development of the Sense of Reality',[3] which appeared in 1913, Freud retains especially the purely speculative idea according to which the development of the original human 'took place under the influence of the geological fate of the earth, and that the exigencies of the Ice Age in particular gave it the stimulus for the development of civilization'.[4] Freud shows himself in fact tempted to 'recognize in the three dispositions to anxiety hysteria, conversion hysteria and obsessional neurosis, regressions to phases that the whole human race had to go through from the beginning to the end of the Ice Age, so that at that time all human beings were the way only some of them are today by virtue of their hereditary tendency and by means of new acquisitions'.[5] Obsessional neurosis is evidently of particular interest as a means of bearing witness to a period of development in which language and thought represent guaranteed progressions from previous states, and they mark a rebellion against regression: the passage to civilisation gives more meaning to this idea insofar as the types of neurotic regression must be put in relation to 'the stages of the genealogical history of humanity' (Ferenczi).[6] In the case of hysterical anxiety, Freud tells us, regression does not really come into the picture, because it arises very prematurely in life, and because its subsequent symptomatic forms relate back to infantile neurosis. In contrast, conversion hysteria would be 'a strong ego regression, [a] return to [a] phase without separation of Pcs. and Ucs., thus without speech and censorship' (a state of humanity particularly relevant to women in whom, due to the precarious conditions, genital life is eliminated, in spite of early impressions that are intensely stimulating).[7] As for obsessional neurosis, seen phylogenetically as especially affecting the male, it is characterised by a *regression of the libido* which 'does not serve the return [of the repressed] but rather repression' itself and 'is made possible by a strong constitutional fixation or incomplete development'.[8]

But perhaps what is most significant here is the definition of regression as a movement in time, with the aim to reach a 'fixation point':

> Behind regression are hidden the problems of fixation and disposition. Regression, one can say in general, goes all the way back to a fixation point, in either ego or libido development, and it represents the disposition (...). Fixation comes about through [a] phase of development that was too strongly pronounced or has perhaps persisted too long to pass into the next without residue.[9]

To the extent that it is difficult to be definitive about the provenance of this fixation, one can say that the later the neurosis emerges (as in the case of obsessional neurosis), the earlier and more severe is the regression.

There is every chance that this *fixation point* is situated *before language* and that in the case of obsessional neurosis (the latest of the transference neuroses in *evolutionary* terms), the violence exhibited by the symptoms of sadistic mastery hides an interiorisation of infantile anxiety, while the later acquisitions (thought and language) attempt to spare the ego from its potential annihilation in regression.

The phylogenetic success of conversion hysteria would, as Freud indicates in *Inhibitions, Symptoms and Anxiety*, be the *sedimentation of the psychic in fossil symptoms* which thus protect it from destruction. In this case, the absence of distinction between Ucs. and Pcs. as well as the prevalence accorded to the corporeal as a *memory of the fixation point* necessarily lend to regression the value of a *topical function*. Hysterical anxiety is the prototype of affect right up to the stage of its elementary physiological manifestations (the reaction of the organism to danger), and by this token it confers to hysteria the potential to be the prototype of a *memory of the psychic*, in one sense making regression possible:

> Anxiety is not newly created in repression; it is reproduced as an affective state in accordance with an already existing mnemic image. If we go further and enquire into the origin of that anxiety – and of affects in general – we shall be leaving the realm of pure psychology and entering the borderland of physiology. Affective states have become incorporated in the mind as precipitates of primaeval traumatic experiences, and when a similar situation occurs they are revived like mnemic symbols. I do not think I have been wrong in likening them to the more recent and individually acquired hysterical attack and in regarding them as its normal prototypes.[10]

The 'foreign body' of the symptom 'which was keeping up a constant succession of stimuli and reactions in the tissue in which it was embedded'[11] is equivalent to a 'piece of the internal world which is alien to it'.[12]

The metapsychological concept of regression therefore relates to two co-existent models according to whether it is referred to hysteria or to obsessional neurosis. In the case of conversion hysteria – itself referring back to the phylogenetic prototype of infantile anxiety (hysterical anxiety) –, regression truly merits the name of *regression in the topical sense*; in the case of obsessional neurosis, the model is a *dynamic* one, aiming in part at the 'defusion of instinct[s]', a 'detachment of the erotic components which, with the onset of the genital stage, had joined the destructive cathexes belonging to the sadistic phase'.[13] Here the ego imposes repression with the aim of defending itself against the claims of erotic affect – of which the fixation point nevertheless remains of a hysterical (and thus topical) kind – so as to reinforce the power of thought and language which inherit in this way a force to which they are opposed. The regressive dynamic of obsession thus leads one to accord to the obsessional symptom (of language) the vocation of the cultural production of a neo-psychic formation (a hypertrophy of consciousness), which is supposed to keep at bay an annihilation of the ego in hysterical regression at the fixation point.

If one does not lose sight of the fact that Freud's phylogenetic fantasy makes hysteria coincide with the geological destiny of the biological, one grasps more exactly the meaning given to the *psychic* by the image-metaphor of the *topos* of petrified time, in other words, the fossil. Such an image-metaphor, serving the speculative vision of the metapsychological concept, comes down to identifying the psychic with minerality.[14] As if one had in fact to risk this *vision* radicalising the opposition between the plastic manifestation (auto- and allo-) of *living forms* (symptoms) and the *construction of the psychic*, inasmuch as the psychic is the indestructible memory of a phylogenetic event (murder) having always to be pushed further back into the distant past of *humanity*. Certainly, the study of hysteria had opened the way for this stratified mineral conception of a corporeal psychism of amnesic memory. Freud's archaeological metaphor in fact serves the ends of the intuition of the minerality of the affective soul (see particularly *Delirium and Dreams in W. Jensen's Gradiva*). But the phylogenetic vanishing point determining the metapsychological fantasy underlines once more the *anachronisation of the past* and appeals this time to the *geological* as the *destiny of the psychic becoming of humanity*. Here, in contrast to Ferenczi, but also no doubt to Jung – Freud does not seek to animate the psychic through the observation of symptoms. In a sense for Freud what it is fitting to call 'psychic' is silent and inanimate; and its observation, solicited by symptoms, is regulated by the forms of language, alone capable of restoring figures, and thus the memorable. Living forms are only valuable if they determine, within language, the readability of figures. Or again: it is such a readability of figures that give forms their fortuitous *pathological* deformations. What is designated as *psychic* is thus not directly observable, as the phenomenologist might believe, focused as they are on the meaning of phenomena. That the psychic relates to a vision endowed with *readability* – exactly like a fossil – or again if one says of the psychic that it can only be inferred and that the memory that it holds can only be restoratively re-animated by the dream – this situates the diagrammatic relation of a topicality of the psychic apparatus to the (animated) hallucinatory content of the dream.

In this light we can hold the co-existence of the topical and the dynamic theories as determining for the *paradigm of regression*. As we will make explicit further on, chapter 7 of the *Interpretation of Dreams* illuminates this paradigm by means of a paradoxical fiction of an optical apparatus supposed to restore representation to the sensory image from which it derives and at the same time attribute to the psychic the 'structure' of an apparatus (schema or diagram) endowed with a direction, and thus making readable a regredience (a physical-geometric term in optics) toward an ideal point which cannot be directly seen. The phenomenon of the dream – to the extent that it takes on the 'functional' status of a symptom – acquires the value of a *memory*, through the diagrammatic schematism that it imposes. The schema (of the psychic apparatus *via* the optical apparatus) here becomes the projection of the dream into its metapsychological concept – on the condition nevertheless that such a concept is not considered in the philosophical sense but rather as a metaphysical concept, that is to say restoring the *physical* to a diagrammatic conception of the image. *Paradoxically*, it is thus the psychic apparatus – the record of a reading of a topical fossil formation – which makes possible this intelligibility; this is the 'factor of regression'.

Through an effect of logical overlap between the dream and the schema of the psychic apparatus Freud can thus conclude the section on regression in chapter 7 as follows:

> [D]reaming is on the whole an example of regression to the dreamer's earliest condition, a revival of his childhood, of the instinctual impulses which dominated it and of the methods of expression which were then available to him. Behind this childhood of the individual we are promised a picture of a phylogenetic childhood—a picture of the development of the human race, of which the individual's development is in fact an abbreviated recapitulation influenced by the chance circumstances of life.[15]

And after having cited Nietzsche ('in dreams "some primaeval relic of humanity is at work which we can now scarcely reach any longer by a direct path"'[16]), Freud continues:

> [W]e may expect that the analysis of dreams will lead us to a knowledge of man's archaic heritage, of what is psychically innate in him.

> Dreams and neuroses seem to have preserved more mental antiquities than we could have imagined possible; so that psycho-analysis may claim a high place among the sciences which are concerned with the reconstruction of the earliest and most obscure periods of the beginnings of the human species.[17]

In this text it is clear that regression – a mode of knowledge of individual childhood which has been forgotten and of which the dream places in the misrecognising present of its memory – gives access through analysis to the knowledge of the beginning of humanity and opens the way to a reconstruction of the infancy of the species. In other words, each person's dreaming animates (or animises), through regression, a petrified time which is ungraspable in our past – something that is directly readable in the content of the dream and which nevertheless comes to be read as one might read a fossil formation, here equivalent to a text which can never be materialised. And in return it is this fossil text whose writing would be readable in images, images which would make visible the living character of that which is dreamed. In 1938, Freud would still write: 'With neurotics it is as though we were in a prehistoric landscape – for instance, in the Jurassic. The great Saurians are still running about; the horsetails grow as high as palms (?)'.[18]

If regression is the dynamic of a process made possible by the construction of the *analytic situation*, we still need to fully understand that if such a dynamic were not associated with the topic of the fossil text and thus of its writing and reading, there would be merely a corporeal – psycho-pathological – regression, that our patients would allow us to note at certain moments of the cure, momentarily devoid of infantile memory. It is these moments where the frame of the treatment favours the appearance of symptoms tending to foil the retreat and the 'overhang' [*surplomb*] of the position of the analyst and in which the analytic situation is precisely dismantled. As if here one had to put forward this idea that the 'background and overhang' of the function of the *stranger* involved an anachronisation of the dynamic of the process of regression. This would come down to saying that the analytic situation as such defines regression not only as a dynamic lived by the patient but also correlatively as a topic of the memory of language to be designated by the analyst. The notion of construction in analysis derives from the latter.

The persistence of what is 'mental' (*seelish*) and that one could take as the *psychic* – in spite of the feeling it can give, in the most serious pathological forms, of having been destroyed – would not be conceivable outside this vision of a time outside time. And here again the geological is the imaginary material of this time of memory – a writing without erasure except that of the careless oblivion of human interpretation. This is a strange paradox: perishable or in any case transient life is the physiological life of vegetal and animal forms: it is from them and from their vitality that the death drive is nourished. Nothing then is closer to absolute destruction than the element in oneself which claims life. Neurosis is not ignorant of this kind of vital augmentation of the death drive, as if it sought through this augmentation the exhaustion of the disorganising forces of life. It is as if life were an addiction to death. A further aspect of this paradox is this: the vision we might accord to what is indestructible would be found in the hallucinatory dimensions of the dream and its images – the most evanescent and incorporeal elements of the body and of the living being. Dreams would come only from fossils!

> For the development of the mind (*seelische Entwicklungen*) shows a peculiarity which is present in no other developmental process (*Entwicklungsvorgang*). When a village grows into a town or a child into a man, the village and the child become lost in the town and the man. Memory alone can trace the old features in the new picture (*Nur die Erinnerung kann die Alten Züge in das neue Bild einzeichnen*); and in fact the old materials or forms have been got rid of and replaced by new ones.[19]

As fragile as it is, the memory is thus the *thought of the image* which conserves the features of a form which has disappeared and which can thus outline these features on a new form. More specifically, the ephemeral character of the things of nature has an affective relation to memory which is at once nostalgic and melancholic. One must thus suppose that memory bears witness to all the precarity of the living conscious soul; it is destined for disappearance, because it is never sure of being able to hold together what is dead. Don't some of our patients affected by grief after the loss of a loved one try desperately to cleave to an identical moulding – sometimes with several copies, out of fear of destruction due to theft or fire – of what was essential about the deceased (photographs but also casts of objects, reproduction of places, etc.)? The relic is unique, therefore it is at risk! These patients feel duped by the 'work of mourning' in which they see an attempt to make survival prevail over death. Their sensitivity to the psychic nature of memory being unable to guarantee, from one moment to the next, the persistence of the lost object, rather than the affective state in relation to this object, is so remarkable that it is accompanied by the deep naivety of the wish that the dream might re-animate the beloved dead every night. The obsessive quality of certain rituals following death has exactly this meaning: to produce a cast of time by means of gestures of thought, so that time is not the generator of destruction and is not itself destructible. For one of my patients the event of the death of the man she met and loved when we began the therapy, who was supposed to save her from too strong a transferential attachment to me, led her to encrypt materialised images of the dead man (various reflections of his everyday life) which she brought to the sessions and asked me to keep them so that they 'would not crumble into dust', and so that even if I were to die they would be preserved where the sessions took place. Having always spoken of the loved man, and at length, in each session (he was twice her age) she said that she was sure that my own conscious memory would guarantee the persistence of her memory until the end of her life, that the notebooks she kept during the treatment and as her relation to him developed would ultimately keep me from forgetting him, finally that the ideal outcome would be that she would die at the same time as me, since then her anxiety about the fear of the disappearance of the memory would stop.

In obsessional psychotic formations such as this, the analyst notes that what the patient seeks in them is an inscription of memory, an impression on consciousness of the form of psychic objects. Everything happens as if the analyst has to receive the imprint of the residues of life (*Lebensreste*), that he has the responsibility to dream in the patient's place. And the patient's ability to take account of their own dreams, immediately forgotten before then, often depends on the persistence of the repetitive details of a ritualised everyday existence.

One of the interesting features of Freud's text concerning the singular originality of psychic development is precisely to have conceived of regression as restorative of the plasticity and integrity of 'primitive mentality' (*das primitive Seelische*). We shall cite the passage in its entirety:

> It is otherwise with the development of the mind. Here one can describe the state of affairs, which has nothing to compare with it, only by saying that in this case every earlier stage of development persists alongside the later stage which has arisen from it; here succession also involves co-existence, although it is to the same materials that the whole series of transformations has applied. The earlier mental state may not have manifested itself for years, but none the less it is so far present that it may at any time again become the mode of expression of the forces in the mind, and indeed the only one, as though all later developments have been annulled or undone (*rückgängig gemacht worden wären*). This extraordinary plasticity of mental development is not unrestricted as regards direction; it may be described as a special capacity for involution (*Rückbildung*) – for regression (*Regression*) – since it may well happen that a later and higher stage of development, once abandoned, cannot be reached again. But the primitive stages can always be re-established; the primitive mind is, in the fullest meaning of the word, imperishable (*das primitive Seelische ist im vollsten Sinne unvergänglich*).[20]

'The extraordinary plasticity of mental development', i.e. of the psychic, of the soul, thus has a plasticity that living matter does not possess, however differentiated it is. *Seelische* – for which *animique* is a little obsolete, but which we hesitate to translate by 'psychic', has the merit of neither being formally delimited nor of delimiting anything. *Seelisch* avoids, one might say, the objectivation of the psychic. Such that if this 'metaphysical' word has the advantage of naming, metapsychologically in this instance, a reality which does not let itself be seen, it is precisely because its topical qualification is the true object of regression. In other words, to think the soul in terms of minerality is the only means the metapsychological imagination has to recognise the literally metaphysical reality of the soul. Under these conditions the reading of the fossil is the only knowledge possible of the memory of the soul, from the point of view of regression. The advantage of the term *Seele* and of its adjectival form *seelisch* would be to remind us that it is from these elements – sight, language, action – that what we call *animism* proceeds. So might one not say that *projection*, in the first instance the projection constituted by the dream in sleep – is inherent to regression and that, even in the dream of words, it is the only action of the memory of the soul which one can register directly? '[T]he primitive mind is, in the fullest meaning of the word, imperishable';[21] it doesn't belong to the time of remembering and in a more general sense it does not relate to the phenomenal duration of subjective states of time. In concluding this text, Freud reiterates that:

> What are called mental diseases inevitably produce an impression in the layman that intellectual and mental life has been destroyed. In reality, the destruction only applies to later acquisitions and developments. The essence of mental disease lies in a return to earlier states of affective life and of functioning.[22]

Distinguishing itself entirely from Jacksonian psychopathology, Freud's phylogeneticism sees in the most severe morbid forms 'a return to earlier states', which restore the archaic inheritance of humanity. It is the schematism of regression which is capable, in analytic treatment, of delivering a psychic qualification of this archaic inheritance in the same way as is possible with the interpretation of dreams. Freud affirms the teaching of Griesinger, according to whom listening to the dream is the technical model for the treatment of the ill. Whatever the *deformation* undergone by symptoms in mental illness, it is these *forms* of natural experimentation (the notion of *Natur-experiment* is present in the psychopathology of the early 20th-century) that bear witness to the teratological variations necessary for adaptation and self-healing (see Bleuler and his distinction between primary and secondary symptoms). Freud is barely interested in this kind of psychiatric philosophy of psychopathology. But one might nevertheless see his attachment to psychiatric nosography and its symptomatology as the sign of a faith in the idea of a natural observation of symptomal forms, inasmuch as they allow the speculative solicitation which constitutes the source and the resource of the metapsychological fantasy.[23] In contrast to Ferenczi, Freud's curiosity with regard to the symptom does not seek out analogical comparisons with elementary animal expressions. But he will nevertheless keep on looking for elementary theoretical formulations in his living imagination, just as the sexual theories of children contain the whole theory of sexuality. Under these conditions isn't each case a potential theory, capable of augmenting the theoretical capacities of metapsychology? The idea is that any symptomatic form, precisely because it is plastic and can be observed as a deformation (*Zerrbildung*), contains an enigmatic theory and is also a transferential structure that the patient is not ready to let go of, and which analysis is expected to *translate*.[24] Concerning obsessional neurosis, doesn't Freud talk of a real dialect, specific to each patient, to which, at first, analysis has no access? The translation of this dialect into language is the work of regression in the analysis, and any attempt to deal with this dialect semiologically goes against the qualification of the psychic as such, which is, in its essence, *virtual*.

In one of the first systematic elaborations of regression, in chapter 7 of the *Interpretation of Dreams*, the concept entails the co-existence of two temporal registers which in reality form a single temporality. Just as with hysterical hallucination, the dreamer believes that what s/he is living in the dream is *in the present*. The sensory images, primarily visual, which are granted to this present make the memory they contain unrecognisable to the patient or to anyone else. The incomprehensibility of the dream, as an 'asocial psychic production', is well known; it signifies that the acts of comprehension which it inevitably solicits are defeated by a kind of hermetic tautology. Now the 'putting into the present' of the unconscious wish through its disguising by the image contributes to this kind of tautology. We know that the *time of the image* has the function of making language hypnotic, in other words of making it only tell what the image has seen and describe it without being able to speak it. The *autism* of the dream image is its regressive mutism. In summary, *regression uses the present of the visual image to see a sightlessness that says nothing about what is behind it*. At most one could define the dream image as a reminiscence of having seen something, but a forgetting of whatever it was that was seen. In analysis we know that certain patients, at least at certain moments of the cure, can't 'associate' with what they have dreamed; they tell their dream or only a fragment of it and the words are paralysed by the images they relate. It is up to the analyst to produce the links in the memory of the words that have already been said. What I call *putting into language and into figures of the dream* goes through a fragmentation which is all the more feared by the patient insofar as, transferentially, it bears the threat of a psychic loss, of an annihilation of the psychic. As if any qualification of the psychic by the silence and/or the interpretation of the analyst takes on the aspect of an anxiety of disappearance. The accentuation of the visibility of images (often intensely evident in the manner of screen memories) translates, as in hallucinatory experiences, this attraction of regression.

One of our patients, 'hooking' on to certain images in her dreams, used the expression: 'the terror of tumbling back into formless white emptiness'. The same patient, by offering me her images, wanted me to dream; she said it would be 'a guarantee that the void has a bottom and words are not just holes'. There is no doubt, precisely, that the *person* of the analyst is supposed to be able to be the 'deep background', placed behind, and that this 'person' is also projectively afforded the capacity to be the *temporal background*, the *background in time*, that which can be expected of time in terms of the restitution of the forgotten dead. Or as if certain dreams equivalent to transference love wished to believe that there is nothing behind a presence of the image, that transference leads to nothing other than an affective relation and especially not to a *genealogy* of the self. Is this not, however, the strongest sense of the Latin *imago*: the image is the anteriority of the present?

For Freud, it is to the *apparatus of the soul* (*seelische Apparat*), as a *schema*, that falls the task of signifying the referral to regression. If, in metapsychological terms, the soul is unthinkable except as an apparatus whose writing is that of the (reflex and optic) schema, it is thus to such an apparatus-schema that it befalls to make readable 'when in a dream an idea is turned back into the sensory image from which it was originally derived'. 'I believe the name "regression" is of help to us in so far as it connects a fact that was already known to us with our schematic picture, in which the mental apparatus (*seelische Apparat*) was given a sense of direction'. And a little further on: 'If we regard the process of dreaming as a regression occurring in our hypothetical mental apparatus',[25] the anachronicity of time is an operation of temporal conversion which consists in winding time back towards a *virtual* site of the event that memory cannot appropriate, because what counts for it is in a sense the loss of what has taken place. Summarising what has been gained in the understanding of regression via the study of dreams, Freud writes:

> Three kinds of regression are thus to be distinguished: (a) topographical regression, in the sense of the schematic picture of the ψ-systems which we have explained above; (b) temporal regression, in so far as what is in question is a harking back to older psychical structures; and (c) formal regression, where primitive methods of expression and representation take the place of the usual ones. All these three kinds of regression are, however, one at bottom and occur together as a rule; for what is older in time is more primitive in form and in psychical topography lies nearer to the perceptual end.[26]

The *anterior site* is not a vanishing point (except when it borrows the metaphorical image of phylogenesis), and neither is it a point of view – except if one considers that the vision of the dream is blind at this point: the anterior site is a processual site insofar as it is not the object of a rediscovery but rather *time coming to an act of nomination*. It is the name given to this specific moment that *produces* the process. The fossil becomes readable.

In a very beautiful page of his recent book, *Ce que nous voyons, ce qui nous regarde* [What We See Looks At Us] Georges Didi-Huberman writes of the way Walter Benjamin understood memory, 'not as the possession of something remembered – a *having*, a collection of past things – but as an approximation, always dialectical in relation to things which happened in their *place*, that is as the very approximation of their *having taken place*'. And he adds:

> Decomposing the German word for memory *Erinnerung*, Benjamin thus dialecticises the particle *-er*, the mark of a nascent state or realisation of an aim – with the idea of *inner*, that is of the interior, the deepest inside. He draws from this (in an extremely Freudian manner, moreover) a conception of memory akin to an archaeological excavation, where the place of the objects discovered speaks to us just as much as the objects themselves, and as akin to an operation of exhumation (*ausgraben*) of something or someone long left in the earth or in the tomb (*Grab*).[27]

Didi-Huberman cites this 'thought-image' of Benjamin's:

> *Excavation and Memory*. Language has unmistakably made it plain that memory is not an instrument for exploring the past, but rather a medium. It is the medium of that which is experienced, just as the earth is the medium in which ancient cities lie buried. He who seeks to approach his own buried past must conduct himself like a man digging. Above all, he must not be afraid to return again and again to the same matter; to scatter it as one scatters earth, to turn it over as one turns over soil. For the 'matter itself' is no more than the strata which yield their long-sought secrets only to the most meticulous investigation. That is to say, they yield those images that, severed from all earlier associations, reside as treasures in the sober rooms of our later insights – like torsos in a collector's gallery. It is undoubtedly useful to plan excavations methodically. Yet no less indispensable is the cautious probing of the spade in the dark loam. And the man who merely makes an inventory of his findings, while failing to establish the exact location of where in today's ground the ancient treasures have been stored up, cheats himself of his richest prize. In this sense, for authentic memories, it is far less important that the investigator report on them than that he mark, quite precisely, the site where he gained possession of them.[28]

'Because the act of unearthing a torso', writes Didi-Huberman, 'modifies the earth itself, the sedimented ground, which is not neutral, carries within it the history of its own sedimentation, in which lie vestiges'.[29] Freudian archaeology leads to geology, the temporality of which is specific to the becoming of the soul as fossil. And if regression is memory, an archi-memory so to speak, it can only be memory on account of the *site* which determines the ground of the discovery. It does not determine it as a concept would: it installs it as a *situation* which is a knowledge of the ter-rain. While the temptation is evidently to think of the analyst as having the knowledge of this representation of the anterior site or to think of them as being the strange witness of an anachronic past, it is precisely the inevitable presence of the analyst which forms the obstacle to the anachronicity of the *seelisch*. Thus a new paradox: it is from the analysis – which takes place *à deux* – that regression receives the determinations which we have drawn out, with Freud. The analyst cannot be the repre-sentative of an anterior time even if one could imagine this to be the case through the transference. The analyst can perhaps only be the one who allows language to be the site of the anachronisation of time.[30]

We are talking about firstly a 'great memory' bringing a 'strong eye' and secondly the exact 'attention' of an infinitely curious and dependably assiduous method of observation authorising the mind to 'grasp the distant relations and bring them together', 'after having justly considered all of the probabilities and weighed the possibilities' – in other words the qualities of the *generous imagination* which makes available the discernment of details and the vision of relations, and of which whoever applies themselves to the study of living forms [*le vivant*] is the modest possessor. Living forms – in their morphological diversity and living variety – call for a language which can draw them together and articulate their imaginative logic.

It might appear rather obsolete today to recall Buffon's ideal, a kind of lesson he proposed as early as the mid-18th century. For sure, what was at stake then was the denunciation of philosophers, notably Descartes, who deliberately ignored the living in the exposition of their method. It was also a question of claiming a metaphysical pedigree for 'natural history' and of attaining in some sense the 'high point of Metaphysics, from which one can see the principles, the relations and the set of all the Sciences'. For there is a high vantage point of memory patiently acquired through description and the imaginative logic of the varied forms of life both pre-sent and past. A genealogy of the species is necessarily at work in the implicit work of *theory* and it is only a *theory of the living* if it has the power to think the processes of evolution and of development, and if allows us to see these processes in the phylogenetic production of forms of individua-tion. It is certain that as concerns theory, one can imagine that the *ideal* can easily lend itself to ideological formations! The general reception of Dar-win's *The Origin of Species*, just after 1860, looks exactly like this. The inevitable delay in the verification of its propositions and hypotheses actually afforded time for simplifying formulations to crystallise dis-advantageously around the text, accounts susceptible of producing tendentious developments. One could moreover say the same thing about Freud's texts, which, in his lifetime, were already immobilised around ideologically loaded stereotypes. In philosophy, after all, any speculative theoretical advance always runs the risk of being brutally immobilised by its ideological effects. But for Darwin this would be to neglect the exceptional moment in which his interventions took place. The moment is that of the decisive discoveries of unicellular organisms, the elementary structure of pluricellular organisms, and the physiological properties and alterations of the internal milieu of the organism: these discoveries accord to the living organism the potential to determine in some way the biological conditions of the specific constitution of its own *theorisation*.

We should not be surprised in this light that embryology played a role in identifying in advance some of Darwin's intuitions prior to being able to recognise itself in them: embryology had a mediating function between cellular theory and the theory of evolution. And, beyond embryology and cellular morphology, palaeontology also found itself drawn into a theory of the living organism in thinking the evolutive and comparative logic of forms. Temporalities and forms would thus be closely associated in the paradigm of evolution at once with respect to the history of species and to the temporalities of processes of individuation. Georges Canguilhem explains this as follows:

> The affinity between Darwin and the embryologists stemmed first of all from the fact that Darwin recognized that the embryology of his day incorporated a characteristic of the new dimension according to which he was himself attempting to understand the constitution of the world of living organisms, namely, time and history.[31]

Acknowledging, in contrast to Lamarck, the potential of duration for a serial generation of organised bodies, Darwin observed *distinct effects* whose production-time could be inferred from the *point of view of the origin*, according to the historical *perspective* of a memory of the species. Canguilhem accounts for this as follows:

> But the *Origin of Species* proposed a radically new idea, conceiving of time not as a power but as a factor whose effects could be perceived directly in distinct but complementary forms: fossils, embryos, and rudimentary organs. The fossil was petrified time; the embryo, operative time; the rudimentary organ, retarded time. Together these bits of evidence constituted the archives of biological history, in which the biologist, by reading and making comparisons, could seek to establish a beginning. In the palaeontological archive the beginning was the oldest fossil; in the embryological archive, it was the common element; in the morphological archive, it was the most rudimentary manifestation. Conceived in this way, the old comparative anatomy could be

rejuvenated. The genealogical tree was the basis of the system, not the consequence. The common ancestor replaced the archetype. Classification ceased to be a static portrait of coexisting forms and became a vast synoptic canvas woven of threads of time.[32]

In a very interesting work, *L'Arbre à remonter le temps*, Pascal Tassy discusses Lamarck's idea in *Zoological Philosophy* (1809) according to which the transformation of species over time obeys the principle of a 'general distribution of the organised beings produced by nature'. The serial representation of beings certainly involves a reference to time, but this is conceived as a function of natural order. As such, Tassy thinks, 'if the general distribution of living beings is (...) a concept analogous to that of phylogenesis', 'Lamarck does not provide a reconstruction of evolutionary lineages, nor a genealogy of the fossilised shells of the Paris basin. He does not inscribe his image of the general distribution of animals, which features in the appendix to *Zoological Philosophy*, in the dimension of time'.[33] Citing G. Laurent (*Paléontologie et évolution en France, 1800–1860*), Tassy notes that Lamarck reasons on the basis of geological facts which only provide him with a History of the Earth and a one-dimensional History of Life. Because, inversely to Lamarck, Darwinian theory implies a close articulation between 'genealogical time' and 'geological time' (see notably chapter XI of *The Origin of Species*) on 'the geological succession of organic beings'.

Darwin is a round-the-world traveller and a walker of mountainous and coastal landscapes. He looks, observes and imagines. 'It is hardly possible for me', he writes, 'to recall to the reader who is not a practical geologist, the facts leading the mind feebly to comprehend the lapse of time'.[34] 'Therefore a man should examine for himself', he adds, 'the great piles of superimposed strata, and watch the rivulets bringing down mud, and the waves wearing away the sea-cliffs, in order to comprehend something about the duration of past time, the monuments of which we see all around us'.[35] It is thus in wandering along coastlines 'formed of moderately hard rocks' that one can 'mark the process of their degradation'. In order to begin to have an idea of the 'past duration of time',[36] one must be able to imagine 'the masses of rock which have been removed over many extensive areas, and on the other hand the thickness of our sedimentary formations'.[37] The examination of volcanic islands or again the observation of faults or cracks in the surface of the land no doubt modified 'slow [ly] and effected by many starts' inform our mind of the way of how it should equip itself with respect to a past which one can only imagine changing extremely slowly over a very long duration. The information Darwin seeks in the work of geologists and the hope he places in palaeontology, which he acknowledges is impoverished in terms of its collections, catalyses a thinking of the species and its variations, or yet more precisely determines the nature of an imagination of time when what is at stake is that it is to acquire from observation an intelligence of forms and their transformations. The imperfection of geological documents certainly offers resistance to the proof of the theory of descendancy with modifications by means of natural selection. But anyone who does not allow such an imperfection should at least recognise that belief in the immutability of the species depends on the peremptory affirmation according to which geology provides no evidence of transition. Only the exact measure of the slow graduation of geological time, supported by meticulous palaeontological observation, allows one to 'understand how it is that new species come in slowly and successively; how species of different classes do not necessarily change together, or at the same rate, or in the same degree; yet in the long run that all undergo modification to some extent. The extinction of old forms is the almost inevitable consequence of the production of new forms'.[38] And a bit further on:

> We can understand how it is that all the forms of life, ancient and recent, only amount together to a few grand classes. We can understand, from the continued tendency to divergence of character, why the more ancient a form is, the more it generally differs from those now living; why ancient and extinct forms often tend to fill up gaps between existing forms, sometimes blending two groups, previously classed as distinct, into one; but more commonly bringing them only a little closer together. The more ancient a form is, the more often it stands in some degree intermediate between groups now distinct; for the more ancient a form is, the more nearly it will be related to, and consequently resemble, the common progenitor of groups, since become widely divergent.[39]
>
> Extinct and ancient animals resemble to a certain extent the embryos of the more recent animals belonging to the same classes, and this wonderful fact receives a simple explanation according to our views. The succession of the same types of structure within the same areas during the later geological periods ceases to be mysterious, and is intelligible on the principle of inheritance.[40]

We could legitimately uphold the idea that the *geological* constitutes for Darwin this *temporal vision of the continuous modification of the forms of life*, the temporality of a past reconstructed by means of the freedom afforded by *the extreme slowness of very long duration*. The forms of petrified life observed by the palaeontologist, concerning living species that have not been degraded, sketch out so to speak a schema for the imagination of current living forms, and it is then to embryology that falls the project of exemplifying the untimely in the manifestation of the living in its acts. The potentialities of the embryo allow us to imagine the development of the living being in its forms, as if in fast forward.

We know that it was Haeckel who in 1866 was responsible for identifying the embryological conditions most suitable for the reconstruction of the phylogenetic past and its 'recapitulation': if ontogenesis could thus provide the means for genealogical inference on the basis of the living forms that it puts into play it was because the living organism presents such a degree of variation that it presents time as a principle of both conservation and transformation.

One would search in vain for a theory of regression in *The Origin of Species*. If the term 'regression' seems however to bear the mark of a theory of evolution and development, associating structure and time, so to speak, it is not surprising that it is with H. Jackson that the concept of regression will take on a dynamic value as a criterion of evolutionist organisation and disorganisation with respect to the neurological normality of consciousness. In his *Croonian Lectures* (1884), Jackson says, notably, that:

> In every insanity there is morbid affection of more or less of the highest cerebral centres or, synonymously, of the highest level of evolution of the cerebral subsystem, or, again synonymously, of the anatomical substrata, or physical basis, of consciousness. [...] In every insanity more or less of the highest cerebral centres is out of function, temporarily or permanently, from some pathological process [...].[41]

For Jackson, regression indicates a subtractive pathological operation, and its 'neuro-psychological' study is only possible by dint of the evolutionist law of integrative intelligibility. There is nothing surprising in the fact that Darwinian (and post-Spencerian) theory found favour, at the turn of the 19th century, with psychologists and neurologists, notably in the context of the normative project to establish a psychology of the pathological. It cannot be taken for granted that this psychopathology (which was organodynamic *avant la lettre*) was Darwinian, but what is certain is that it was inspired in its own way by Haeckel's idea of an ontogenetic recapitulation of phylogenesis with the project of a functional description of regression, appealing to the hierarchical reference to the suppression or destruction of superior instances liberating inferior ones. Psychological perspectives of the time on the opposition of consciousness and the subconscious, will/automatism, cognition/sexuality etc. find their basis and their positive rational principles in the overall phylogenetic and ontogenetic conception of the opposition between the cortical and the sub-cortical. Whatever the case may be, what is striking above all is the reduction brought to bear by psychologists and neurologists of the influence of the temporal evolution of forms, to the benefit of a valorisation of the hierarchy of functions.

Following other quite numerous works focused on Freud's 'Darwinism', a book recently translated into French, Lucille B. Ritvo's *Darwin's Influence on Freud*, offers an honest documentation of the question. The preface by Patrick Lacoste, the volume's translator, has the distinct merit of drawing out the meaning of Freud's *transposition* of Darwin's biological theory.[42] Such a transposition definitively excludes any *psychic* 'application' on Freud's part of Darwin's hypotheses concerning death, sexuality, and descendancy. The reference made to the 'primitive horde' is immediately reinforced in its power of *fiction* to enable the phylo- and ontogenetic imagination of a *murder* – the murder of the father – organising *culture* and its neurosis. Such a 'fictionalisation' does certainly not entail abandoning biological theory for culturalism: it gathers up the imagination of a mythical event, conserves the force of the origin that it entails, but also leads Freud's work into an autonomous movement of speculation.

The epistemological challenges are not negligible, however. If it is not a question of 'influence' (this is the word used by Ritvo in the English title of her book), but rather of Darwin's *ascendancy* in relation to Freud, the antecedence of an admired ascendant, psychoanalytically speaking, involves other determinations beyond those generally admitted by the Anglo-Saxon model of influence.[43] At every stage of his work Freud does not deviate from the use of the powers of the imagination – via memory and vision – specific to the sciences of nature, to the extent that he thought that his metapsychology would one day be part of a reconsideration by biologists of the importance of the psychic and of sexuality for development.

In this light there is nothing surprising in the fact that Freud appealed to phylogenetic and ontogenetic concepts, albeit transposed, and that his spirit of observation of psychological facts was not a million miles away from the descriptive attentiveness he devoted to histology. Nevertheless the operation of transposition (*Umsetzung*) is fully present to the extent that the information drawn from biology is fictionalised by the metapsychological text. Freud's reticence with regard to Ferenczi's venture to constitute a real 'metabiology' on the basis of psychoanalysis is undeniable. Ferenczi knew this, and having hesitated to publish *Thalassa*, he then prefaced it with a sort of methodological justification.

In fact, as we have been able to see, Freudian *phylogenesis* would not deny any of Darwin and Haeckel's versions and no doubt even less so those of philologists.[44] But it is one thing to hold Darwin's theory for one of the first theories of life and living forms and another – in the light of the psychopathological clinic that remained Freud's reference point – to elaborate a metapsychological project in which death is, as we have said, the soul of the life drive and is also a murder of what we call the 'psychic'.

In certain respects the Freudian *epos* is in fact of the same order as the *epos* of great biologists like Buffon, Lamarck or Darwin. Theory is an activity of observation, of enumeration, of nomination and of storytelling. In terms of process, it could not be a theory unless it deployed the imagination of distant times and the short-term perspective necessary to the examination of the facts. *Übersicht* – the Freudian term discussed by Jean-Michel Rey – means just this: both *overview* and *blindness*, in reality two processes of a mode of seeing which has to imagine so as to see into the distance, on the one hand, and, on the other hand, a mode of seeing which leaves things out, a blundering which ceaselessly misunderstands [*de la bévue qui ne cesse de se méprendre*].[45] Observation cannot totalise anything, it can only set aside, perhaps then for the use of a vision which, for its part, can see nothing!

Translated by Patrick ffrench and Nigel Saint

Notes

1 Sigmund Freud, *A Phylogenetic Fantasy: Overview of the Transference Neuroses*, ed. by Ilse Grubrich-Simitis, trans. by Axel Hoffer and Peter D. Hoffer (Cambridge, MA: Harvard University Press, 1987), p. 10.
2 Freud, *A Phylogenetic Fantasy: Overview of the Transference Neuroses*, pp. 11–12 [translation modified].
3 Sandor Ferenczi, 'Stages in the Development of the Sense of Reality' in *First Contributions to Psych0-analysis* (Milton Park: Taylor and Francis, 2018), pp. 218–38.
4 Freud, *A Phylogenetic Fantasy: Overview of the Transference Neuroses*, p. 13.
5 Freud, *A Phylogenetic Fantasy: Overview of the Transference Neuroses*, p. 13.
6 Ferenczi, 'Stages in the Development of the Sense of Reality', p. 236 [translation modified].
7 Freud, *A Phylogenetic Fantasy: Overview of the Transference Neuroses*, p. 15.
8 Freud, *A Phylogenetic Fantasy: Overview of the Transference Neuroses*, p. 9.
9 Freud, *A Phylogenetic Fantasy: Overview of the Transference Neuroses*, p. 9.
10 Sigmund Freud, 'Inhibitions, Symptoms and Anxiety' in *The Standard Edition of the Complete Psychological Works of Sigmund Freud Volume XX*, trans. by James Strachey et al (London: The Hogarth Press, 1959) [1925], pp. 77–178, p. 93.
11 Freud, 'Inhibitions, Symptoms and Anxiety', p. 98.
12 [Freud, 'Inhibitions, Symptoms and Anxiety', p. 99. Footnotes in square brackets are additions by the translators.]
13 Freud, 'Inhibitions, Symptoms and Anxiety', p. 114.
14 See Pierre Fédida, 'L'Écho minéral' in *Musique en jeu*, 9 (Nov. 1974).
15 [Sigmund Freud, 'The Interpretation of Dreams' in *The Standard Edition of the Complete Psychological Works of Sigmund Freud Volume IV*, trans. by James Strachey et al (London: The Hogarth Press, 1953) [1900], p. 548.]
16 Freud, 'The Interpretation of Dreams', p. 548.
17 Freud, 'The Interpretation of Dreams', p. 548.
18 [Sigmund Freud, 'Findings, Ideas, Problems' in *The Standard Edition of the Complete Psychological Works of Sigmund Freud Volume XXIII*, trans. by James Strachey et al (London: The Hogarth Press, 1964), pp. 299–300, p. 299. The final question mark is in Freud's text.]
19 Sigmund Freud, 'Thoughts for the Time of War and Death' in *The Standard Edition of the Complete Psychological Works of Sigmund Freud Volume XIV* (1914–16), trans. by James Strachey et al (London: The Hogarth Press, 1957), pp. 273–302, p. 285.
20 Freud, 'Thoughts for the Time of War and Death', p. 285–86.
21 [See discussion of this expression in Chapter 5.]
22 Freud, 'Thoughts for the Time of War and Death', p. 286.
23 Pierre Fédida and Patrick Lacoste, 'Psychopathologie/métapsychologie. La fonction des points de vue' in *Revue internationale de psychopathologie* 8 (1992), pp. 589–628.
24 Pierre Fédida, *Crise et contre-transfert* (Paris: PUF, 1992).
25 Freud, 'The Interpretation of Dreams', p. 543.
26 Freud, 'The Interpretation of Dreams', p. 548.

27 Georges Didi-Huberman, *Ce que nous voyons, ce qui nous regarde* (Paris: Minuit, 1992), pp. 128–29; Catherine Perret, *Walter Benjamin sans destin* (Paris: La Différence, 1992).

28 Walter Benjamin, 'Excavation and Memory' in *Selected Writings*, volume 2; part 2 (1931–1934), ed. by Michael W. Jennings, Howard Eiland, Gary Smith, trans. by Rodney Livingstone, after a prior version by Edmund Jephcott (Cambridge, MA: Harvard University Press, 1999), p. 576.

29 [Didi-Huberman, *Ce que nous voyons, ce qui nous regarde*, p. 131.]

30 On this question of the temporality of regression, see Patrick Lacoste, 'Scène, l'autre mot' in *Nouvelle revue de psychanalyse* 44 (1991), pp. 251–66.

31 Georges Canguilhem, *Ideology and Rationality in the History of the Life Sciences*, trans by Arthur Goldhammer (Cambridge, MA: MIT Press, 1988), p. 108 [translation modified].

32 Canguilhem, *Ideology and Rationality in the History of the Life Sciences*, p. 239.

33 Pascal Tassy, *L'Arbre à remonter le temps* (Paris: C. Bourgois, 1991), p. 30.

34 Charles Darwin, *The Origin of Species by Means of Natural Selection or the Preservation of Favoured Races in the Struggle for Life* (Cambridge: Cambridge University Press, 2009), p. 266.

35 Darwin, *The Origin of Species by Means of Natural Selection or the Preservation of Favoured Races in the Struggle for Life*, p. 266.

36 Darwin, *The Origin of Species by Means of Natural Selection or the Preservation of Favoured Races in the Struggle for Life*, p. 268.

37 Darwin, *The Origin of Species by Means of Natural Selection or the Preservation of Favoured Races in the Struggle for Life*, p. 268.

38 Darwin, *The Origin of Species by Means of Natural Selection or the Preservation of Favoured Races in the Struggle for Life*, pp. 313–14.

39 Darwin, *The Origin of Species by Means of Natural Selection or the Preservation of Favoured Races in the Struggle for Life*, p. 314.

40 Darwin, *The Origin of Species by Means of Natural Selection or the Preservation of Favoured Races in the Struggle for Life*, p. 315.

41 John Hughlings Jackson, *Factors of Insanities* (London: Dent and Sons, 1894), p. 4. [Not as Fédida proposes, from the *Croonian Lectures*.]

42 Lucille B. Ritvo, *Darwin's Influence on Freud: A Tale of Two Sciences* (New Haven and London: Yale University Press, 1990). At the end of the book Ritvo provides a substantial bibliography of works concerning Freud's 'Darwinism'. French translation: *L'Ascendant de Darwin sur Freud*, trans. and prefaced by Patrick Lacoste (Paris: Gallimard, 1992). See 'Préface', pp. 25–29.

43 Harold Bloom, *The Anxiety of Influence* (New York: Oxford University Press, 1973).

44 Patrick Tort, *Evolutionnisme et linguistique*, followed by August Schleicher, *La Théorie de Darwin et la science du langage* and *De l'importance du langage pour l'histoire naturelle de l'homme* (Paris: Vrin, 1980).

45 [Perhaps an echo of the title of Jacques Lacan's 24th seminar (1976–77): 'L'insu que sait de l'une-bévue s'aille à mourre'.]

4   Where Does the Human Body Begin?

Where does the human body begin? The question is asked by Georges Bataille in his brief article 'Mouth' in the review *Documents*:

> *The mouth is the beginning or, if one prefers, the prow of animals; in the most characteristic cases, it is the most living part, in other words, the most terrifying for neighbouring animals. But man does not have a simple archi-tecture like beasts, and it is not even possible to say where he begins.*[1]

The 'bestial' *organ* of 'rending screams', and also of extreme *jouissance*: such is the human mouth. From birth, it disorients the body to the point of making itself the dark hole where everything blurs together: deep flesh and saliva, teeth, tongue. In certain respects the Deleuzian image of the blending of words and food takes full account of the impossible spiri-tuality of the organ. But for Bataille what counts above all is the disrup-tion of the individual provoked by horizontal observation.

'*On this subject it is easy to observe*', Bataille notes further, '*that the over-whelmed individual throws back his head while frenetically stretching his neck in such a way that the mouth becomes, as much as possible, an extension of the spinal column, in other words, in the position it normally occupies in the constitution of animals*'.[2]

So it's clear that civilisation, or more simply natural evolution, hasn't succeeded in making the mouth recede completely into the face! At the very least the latter has kept, in spite of sight and of expression, the vio-lence of the organ, which is nevertheless restrained and masked by the ornament of the lips. The organ of olfaction and smell has come to arrange itself in the background and to show only the axis of the face: but the mouth is a gap so opened up to the insides of the body that it seems in a sense devoted to regression. And here the word 'regression' itself should be taken to designate the flesh – an organ of flesh for immediate plea-sure – tumescent and detumescent. We could say that dreams may be formed in the mouth, from which they might borrow internal forms and deformations, as well as drives: *organ pleasure* or perhaps a pleasure that makes use of a kind of autonomy of the organ. This liminary designation

DOI: 10.4324/9781032637600-5

of autoeroticism, in its phantasmatic disengagement from alimentary self-conservation, serves precisely to make the human mouth the focal point of the *primitive* and so of the animal analogy in regression. What we would call 'regression' here would be the infinite vanishing point where the human body begins.

At the *origin* of psychoanalysis, the dream of 'Irma's injection' – the dream of dreams, and as such the dream of the organ of dreams – imagines regression on *the side* of the analyst. In his dream, Freud sees the patient with her mouth open (which Lacan notes she cannot do in reality), and what he sees he sees deep inside: the nasal cortices covered with a whitish-grey membrane. The vision to which the dream gives rise is thus a vision of the flesh of the organ – female genital mouth-organ. The wise ordinances of Fliess no longer hold: the dream *of* psychoanalysis thus produces the organ in its materiality or in its horrible state as sick meat. This *vision of the back of the throat*, moreover, can mix the organ of the mouth with the horrible image of the female genital organ.

'There's a horrendous discovery here', writes Lacan, 'that of the flesh one never sees, the foundation of things, the other side of the head, of the face, the secretory glands par excellence, the flesh from which everything exudes, at the very heart of the mystery, the flesh in as much as it is suffering, is formless, in as much as its form in itself is something which provokes anxiety'. And Lacan adds immediately: 'Spectre of anxiety, identification of anxiety, the final revelation of "you are this" – You are this, which is so far from you, this which is the ultimate formlessness'.[3]

It is upon this that the mouth opens deep inside: the formlessness [*informe*] (a Bataillean word) of the flesh is a form that engenders anxiety. Better still, anxiety seeks out this form of the formless of the organ in flesh. The regression in the dream of the analyst takes thus the image of such a sight, of which the *Lösung* (solution) is found in the formula of Trimethylamine which relates to the sexuality of (sexual) substances. The *Lösung* would be the solution as a word issued from the flesh –psychoanalysis itself, one could say. And Irma's suffering expressed in front of her therapists who hear nothing of her screams comes from the depths of her throat; it is suffering made flesh. The organ is that too. Compare with another mouth, that of Célina straining towards her scream – which makes the visibility of the image 'float'. Medical observation offers us a *sonorous body* (*corps sonore*) (screams, vociferations, cracks...).[4] In his presentation of the possessed (*les démoniaques*) in art, Didi-Huberman writes on this point that 'The paradox can be grasped through the essential aspect presented by the clinical case: it is a sonorous, invocatory aspect, which is terrifically mobile. Célina's body is a charivari, a shouting body; her bones crack, her teeth grind; it is often endowed with an intense and chaotic motricity. (...) Secondarily, Célina's cries, her vociferations, her constant refusals and her violence (she "makes piercing cries", writes Bourneville) rise up, fall down, writhe about, dispute; all of this, strictly speaking, *resembles nothing*'.[5]

But let us return to Irma's throat. Lacan makes the association between the sight of Irma's throat and the terrifying appearance of the head of Medusa. What is unnameable and thus terrifyingly anxiety-provoking is *'the back of this throat, the complex, unlocatable form, which also makes it into the primitive object par excellence, the abyss of the feminine organ from which all life emerges, this gulf of the mouth, in which everything is swallowed up, and no less the image of* death *in which everything comes to its end'.*[6]

This is to say that regression grants to the sight in the dream a status such that, *seen from there*, it has no distinct form and by the same token cannot be named. Regression is a 'spectral decomposition of the function of the ego' (Lacan).[7] There is no person there, or rather *no person (who) can say 'I'*. The 'egos' of doctors or therapists are grotesque in their wish to assure themselves of identity faced with this medusa-mouth which is indeed, and originally in this instance, *the organ in psychoanalysis*. Or at least, the mouth *open to anxiety* can only be known by the analyst through their own dream, plunged so to speak into their own impotence when it comes to curing a sick organ.

Behind the prone patient, the opening of the mouth for speech is an opening onto the origin of the body, of which it will no longer be possible to say where it begins. A drawing of a young child could make of this opening the door of a house, a mouth whose tongue may well also become a serpent penis as well as a path looked over by windows, which are eyes. The drawing of the door is imperfect and the child knows this when he says that at night he wants to be sure that his mouth will stay closed like his eyes. But lips are not eyelids and for going to sleep the thumb closes nothing, quite the reverse!

Human architecture is certainly simpler than the composition of animals, but its complexity arises in our representation from the fact that we want it to be the projection onto our internal and external body of the supposed complexity of our brains. And a definition via anatomical description *ab capite ad calcem* belongs to the modern ideal of *vertically* ordered perspective, the anatomy of which would be a melancholic consciousness. It is not solely a question of the hierarchy of parts of the body and of the carefully distributed and arranged organs; it is the *axis* of the body assured as a function of symmetry, which solicits verticality as the assurance of spiritual humanity. The corpse, a horizontal body delivered to the decomposing intelligence of death – perhaps allows for a spatial image of the differentiated organs as well as of the beginning and end of the human body. But as Freud underlines, mental thought has need of the decomposition of the corpse to neutralise hatred and, correlatively, to make possible the narcissism of mourning, which in some way saves the pure verticality of the body of the human among its fellows. Popular belief, so influential in what we call 'psychotherapy', may secure the representation of the organs and cast them in wax ex-votos as if, in this way, such and such a part of the suffering body or such and such an organ could be withdrawn from anxiety, suffering and the threat of decomposition. Perhaps our dreams are literally made of similar ex-votos figuring organs in search of their image. Let us note that a theoretical schematism of the concept of regression leads us to a spatial hierarchisation of a temporality of the upright body from head to toe. The hierarchy of the organs and their functions is that of the erection and progression of the human supposed thus to have extracted itself from the animal realm of contact with the ground dominated by olfaction.

The thoroughly Nietzschean operation carried out by Bataille *on the basis of* the 'mouth' has the value of a method. It is the regressive method of the formless [*informe*].[8]

The animal figurehead of the mouth engages a beginning of the body because the mouth is an *organon* – in itself an organ of prehension and predation as well as of butchering and ingestion. To the extent that it is this violence of the mouth as beginning of the body which makes us imagine, in the strong sense, the anxiety-provoking threat represented by the animal. If the animal *has* this beginning, then it is the beginning of fear. Animal phobias speak volumes about the beginning and its effects. The termination of the body by the anus is no less violent, moreover; it belongs so to speak to this imaginary way in which the body began. The organs which lie between the mouth and the anus are reserved for the hypochondrias of the digestive tract and the reassurance that they bring will not succeed in domesticating the mouth-anus from the physical violence of love![9]

Indeed Freud's vision of the face here does not leave it at peace in its own look: the sight of the face throws the face back and draws the whole body into a vertiginous rotation. This kind of vision does not only submit verticality to a violence that destabilises it through the intervention of the horizontal field, it gives back to vision the scopic angle of the dream and the materiality of flesh. Would it thus be the mouth that is the materiality of the organ made concrete by the organic matter of the piece of liver hanging there? This is *to see flesh*, as we saw with Lacan, when the form of the organ is formless: but the anxiety is not only what is produced by seeing to the back of the throat, it is an anxiety of and in the eyes which constitutes the materiality of vision.[10] If the mouth can open onto the abyss of anxiety dispossessing the human body of any beginning, it is because it is incapable of defining a space and because it turns this vision into the materiality of a space nowhere to be found. Beyond the uncanny (*l'inquiétante étrangeté*), is the face not decomposed by its own disappearance in the mirror?

The explanation of this movement of materialist visuality implicating the animal emergence of the formless has been very clearly set out by Rosalind Krauss:

> [T]he camera looking steeply up at the recumbent form to catch, or to fabricate (or is it to imagine?), the nude body revealed as beast [...]. Bataille

contrasts the mouth/eye axis of the human face with the mouth/anus axis of the four-legged animal. The former, linked to man's verticality, and his possession of speech, defines the mouth in terms of man's expressive powers. The latter, a function of the animal's horizontality, understands the mouth as the leading element of the system of catching, killing, and ingesting prey, for which the anus is the terminal point.[11]

If the term 'sublimation' can find its full meaning here, one must in fact take account of the civilisation of the face in which verticality structures a transcendence of the human and in which 'interpersonal' communication imposes the face-to-face encounter. But the work of such sublimation, making possible the community of equals, entails the avoidance – forgetting or repression – of the mouth and the lips whose anxiety-inducing force of uncontrolled aspiration and cannibalistic amorous devouring brings us back to the hallucinatory materiality of speech. Doesn't Melanie Klein say much the same thing of the observation of infants, that they incite us to see the noise of words as phantasms inasmuch as they are *still in the mouth*.[12] Maybe the psychoanalytic situation and the prone position that it imposes – outside the face – make use of horizontality as a form of visual listening to the indistinct materiality of the organ. Or rather, this situation opens onto the anxious excess of aggressivity and destruction, in doing violence to the anthropological dimension of vertical mastery which belongs to the temporality of the project in the act of enunciation and communication.[13]

Roland Barthes justly notes that Freudian discourse recapitulates a bipolarity of the two *terms* 'mouth' and 'anus'.[14] It is a question of a semanticisation of the meanings which grant two openings to the human body and support libidinal genesis by means of the conception of stages. So in this account Freud would have opened up the human body through a decentring of the organs and then through an indefinite displacement of the sexual function, no longer exclusively the province of the genital organs alone. In other words, Freud thoroughly *disoriented* the human body but also gave back to it a beginning and an end through the inscription of the organs in an onto-phylogenetic history whose decryption escapes systematic symbolic interpretation according to the representation of masculine/feminine. Through just such a symbolic interpretation Stekel misunderstands the imaginary imbrication of the organs and the erogenous force of displacements and transformations. Although characterised by a forceful clinical and metapsychological fantasy, Ferenczi's imagination of the organ is perhaps not immune from the criticism of too strong an inclination to make the medical representation of the organ coincide with its uncertain definition in psychoanalysis. Because if – just like in rudimentary animals – the penis can be imagined as the prolongation of the intestines or again if the infantile sexual theory of the form or shape and positioning of the organs gives imaginative force to the symptom, it makes sense not to lose sight of the starting point of the observation of anatomical difference which remains the phantasmatic resource of interpretation. Groddeck did not shy away, for his part, from amplifying the allusions to equivalence, as if the organ of which the sick person was complaining justified the adjustment of the symptomatic and the therapeutic. Freud took care not to move in the direction of such a schematic approach and he certainly never refrained from reminding doctors that they would gain nothing, in analysis, from the appeal to the knowledge of the organs they had acquired. It is language and its usage which gives form to the organs of which the sick person is complaining. It is the word spoken in the opening of the mouth which invents the organ, just as in the image of the dream. It is about *listening with the dream*, so Freud suggests with the *Witz*. The sexual organ does not have to be represented there in an image: it differentiates a masculine and a feminine that can't be validated by symbolist allusions. It is also infantile sexuality which incites modifications of all sorts. Lacan reminds us of this with Melanie Klein: it is listening to dreams which implies regression in and of words.

Nevertheless, the wholly intellectual position explained by Roland Barthes is of interest because it reintroduces a vectorisation – a meaning (*un sens*) – of the body via the implicit reference to the Freudian primacy of the genital organ and the male libido. Thus the lack of definition and the indistinction of the limits of the human body originally brought to light by the mouth are blurred. It is as if the genital organ – particularly the erect male genital organ – in taking on the value of a prototype for all the organs, reinstates the representational ideology of the oriented human body. Moreover, even in the conception of female sexuality this erect male genital organ would model and modulate the exemplary form of the body, first masculine and then feminine, insofar as the latter is supposed to be the mirror of the former. *This organ would thus be perfect!*

But the indeterminacy of the organ persists in Freud's thought, even within the formulation of the prototype. Of course it is no longer a question, in the essay on narcissism, of a bisexuality of the organ according to Fliess' idea. And even if the reading of this text gives us the intuition of the male organ, this is not said explicitly. What counts above all in the designation of this organ is its capacity to be *modified*:

> *Now the familiar prototype of an organ that is painfully tender, that is in some way changed and that is yet not diseased in the ordinary sense, is the genital organ in its states of excitation. In that condition it becomes congested with blood, swollen and humected, and is the seat of a multiplicity of sensations.*[15]

Beyond the earlier discovery that the erogenous zones can replace the genital organs and are analogous to them in their function, the idea must be put forward that '[f]or every such change in the erotogenicity of the organs there might then be a parallel change of libidinal cathexis in the ego'.[16]

I have developed elsewhere some considerations, regarding hypochondria, on the impact of the organ on the psychic and on language, to the point that in schizophrenia words become the organs themselves.[17] The metapsychological reversal towards which Freud proceeds in his contribution on narcissism tends in fact to privilege the model of the genital organ in a state of excitation and to profit from this state so as to recognise in it the happy imperfection of being capable of modification under the effect of the libido. This amounts to saying that the genital organ is less the evolutionary paradigm of the corporeal axis (might the penis be a vesitigal bone?) than that *form* subject to deformation familiar to the dream, even in its diagnostic capacity to amplify alterations which have not yet been felt in the states of the body. It is this 'magnification', Freud says, which is 'hypochondriachal in character'.[18]

The *Three Essays on Sexuality* had already recognised 'the use of the mouth as a sexual organ'.[19] Such a use 'is regarded as a perversion if the lips (or tongue) of one person are brought into contact with the genitals of another, but not if the mucous membranes of the lips of both of them come together'.[20]

The claim of the buccal and anal mucous membranes is to be treated as genital parts. The rapprochement here of the buccal and anal with the genital organ makes perversion into a method for the understanding of the imbrication of the zones and organs with each other, with the genital organ as the apparent point of reference, while also exploiting the *genitality*, so to speak, particularly of the buccal membranes. We might be tempted to think that if the mouth is the organ in which are formed the dream and the autoerotic phantasm (with its intense physical hallucinatory activity), then the genital organ is in some way prefigured there and recognises the role of the mouth. On the subject of thumb-sucking, Freud underlines the detachment from any alimentary aim:

> *A portion of the lip itself, the tongue, or any other part of the skin within reach – even the big toe – may be taken as the object upon which this sucking is carried out.*[21]

The rhythmic economy or thumb-sucking is of course based on the model of sucking at the breast, but what matters above all is the libidinal genesis of the autoerotic phantasm – of sexuality – in the secondary instance of detachment from auto-conservation.[22] This is to say that the organ is indeed the site of sexual imperfection in search of auto-generated satisfaction. The skin is 'more convenient' than any other part of the body and assures independence from the external world.[23] The erotogeneity of this 'second region', which is 'of an inferior kind', doesn't for all that diminish its continuity with the mouth, and moreover establishes for the latter a protective surface for the organ.[24] The child teaches us in this way how sexuality is formed through the lack of an external object.

> *The inferiority of this second region is among the reasons why at a later date he seeks the corresponding part – the lips of another person. ('It's a pity I can't kiss myself', he seems to be saying).*[25]

In its autoerotic origins sexuality would thus be marked by the imperfection of the organ and by its inadequation to the intended aim. It is a strange particularity of the human not to begin anywhere and because of this to make use of all parts of the body, all of the organs and the entire body, as equivalents for the genital organ, while each of these organs appears to be sexually conceived as standing in for an organ which is absent. Of course the big toe or a piece of skin apparently signify another absence – that of the other –, but one should not rush to think that sexuality is oriented toward an *other* when analysis tells us that neurotic symptoms tend individually, and each in their own way, to establish an other in the form of an organ of auto-satisfaction. Is it the fetishist's privilege to construct an organ that would perfectly unite the organ and the other in a shoe or a female undergarment?

So Freud imagined making the child say 'It's a pity I can't kiss myself'. Any nostalgia for sexual completion is thus left mouth wide open on a word which never ends but which especially does not proceed from any beginning of the body. The mouth would thus be the real *nowhere space* of the dream and of the imperfect organ of sexual sight. Genetic embryologists know today that the differentiation of the organs of the body represented in the genome co-exist virtually, and that their specification – their form and position – results from durations of genetic expression. Would an organ thus be the materialisation of duration? If the same developmental genes are expressed as much in the form of the penis as in that of the fingers of the hand, one should expect that the mouth, lips and tongue respond to a temporality which does not afford them any anteriority or originality, as a beginning, due to their position in the head.[26]

Unless we trust in this remark from Marcel Proust's *The Guermantes Way*:

> *Man, a creature clearly less rudimentary than the sea-urchin or even the whale, nevertheless lacks a certain number of essential organs, and notably possesses none that will serve for kissing. For this absent organ he substitutes his lips, and thus perhaps manages to achieve a more satisfactory result than if he were reduced to caressing the beloved with a horny tusk.*[27]

Translated by Patrick ffrench and Nigel Saint

Notes

1 Georges Bataille, 'Mouth' in *Visions of Excess*, ed. and trans. by Allan Stoekl with Carl R. Lovitt and Donald M. Leslie, Jr (Minneapolis: University of Minnesota Press, 1985), p. 59.

2 Bataille, 'Mouth', p. 59.

3 Jacques Lacan, *The Seminar of Jacques Lacan Book II: The Ego in Freud's Theory and in the Technique of Psychoanalysis 1954–1955*, trans. by Sylvana Tomaselli (New York and London: Norton, 1991), pp. 154–55.

4 See Georges Didi-Huberman, 'Image, organe, temps' in *Le Fait de l'analyse* 5 (September 1998), pp. 245-60.

5 Georges Didi-Huberman, 'L'Observation de Célina (1876–1880): esthétique et expérimentation chez Charcot' in *Revue française de psychopathologie* 4 (1991), p. 271.

6 Lacan, *The Seminar Book II*, p. 164.

7 Lacan, *The Seminar Book II*, p. 165.

8 See Georges Didi-Huberman's book on Bataille, *La Ressemblance informe ou le gai savoir visuel selon Bataille* (Paris: Macula, 1995).

9 Colette Rigaud, doctoral thesis on animal phobias, Université Paris VII – Denis Diderot, 1997, 'L'Animal dans l'imaginaire infantile'. [See Colette Rigaud, *L'Animal d'angoisse: Aux origines de la phobie* (Toulouse: Érès, 1998).]

10 See Pierre Fédida, 'Anxiety in the Eyes' in *Psychoanalysis and History*, 25:1 (2023), pp. 83–94.

11 Rosalind Krauss, 'Corpus delicti' in *October* 33 (Summer 1985), pp. 31–72, p. 34, pp. 41–43.

12 [In English in the original. Footnotes in square brackets are additions by the translator.].

13 Erwin Straus, *Upright Posture*, collected papers. [See Erwin Straus, 'Born to see, bound to behold: reflections on the function of upright posture in the esthetic attitude' in *Tijdschrift voor Filosofie* 27:4 (December 1965), trans. by Erling Eng, pp. 659–88.]

14 Roland Barthes, 'The Outcomes of the Text' in *The Rustle of Language*, trans. by Richard Howard (Berkeley and Los Angeles: University of California Press, 1989), pp. 238–49, p. 241.

15 Sigmund Freud, 'On Narcissism: An Introduction' in *The Standard Edition of the Complete Psychological Works of Sigmund Freud Volume XIV*, trans. by James Strachey et al (London: The Hogarth Press, 1957) [1914], pp. 67–104, p. 84.

16 Freud, 'On Narcissism: An Introduction', p. 84.

17 Pierre Fédida, 'L'Hypochondriaque médecin' in Marilia Aisenstein, Alain Fine and Georges Pragier, *L'Hypochondrie* (Paris: PUF, 1995); a volume in the *Revue française de psychanalyse* series.

18 [Sigmund Freud, 'A Metapsychological Supplement to the Theory of Dreams' in *The Standard Edition of the Complete Psychological Works of Sigmund Freud Volume XIV*, trans. by James Strachey et al (London: The Hogarth Press, 1957) [1915], pp. 217–36, p. 223.]

19 Sigmund Freud, 'Three Essays on Sexuality' in *The Standard Edition of the Complete Psychological Works of Sigmund Freud Volume VII*, trans. by James Strachey et al (London: The Hogarth Press, 1953) [1905], pp. 125–243, p. 151.

20 Freud, 'Three Essays on Sexuality', p. 151.

21 Freud, 'Three Essays on Sexuality', p. 180.

22 Jean Laplanche, *Life and Death in Psychoanalysis*, trans. by Jeffrey Mehlman (Baltimore: Johns Hopkins University Press, 1985).

23 Freud, 'Three Essays on Sexuality', p. 182.

24 Freud, 'Three Essays on Sexuality', p. 182.

25 Freud, 'Three Essays on Sexuality', p. 182.

26 Alain Prochiantz, *L'Anatomie de la pensée* (Paris: Odile Jacob, 1997).

27 [Marcel Proust, *The Guermantes Way*, trans. by Mark Treharne (London: Penguin, 2003), p. 362.]

5 On the Primitive

When Émile Benveniste writes about Freud's error, is it not that Freud sought to '[transpose] what seemed to him to be "primitive" in man' into a temporal representation?[1] And in that way, to have started the illusion of a domain lying beneath the surface of history and civilisation, and inaccessible to them?

The idea of an 'original primitiveness' certainly does support the illusion of a state that can only be called archaic, removed from the work of civilisation, thus attributing an irreducible naturalness to psychic life. As Benveniste writes: 'for it was indeed into the history of this world that he [Freud] projected what we could call a chronology of the human psyche'.[2]

Benveniste's assessment is not an exact translation of what Freud intended in appealing to a notion of the primitive. Benveniste's starting point is an *intellectual* critique of a use, attributed to Freud, of the opposition between myth and history, which in fact is of very little interest to Freud the psychoanalyst. But even accepting that to imagine an original primitiveness is an 'error', as Benveniste suggests, suddenly we are faced with the fertile character of that notion. For it increases the imaginary tension in the word 'primitive', a word inspired and amplified by Goethe's conception of origin. The primitive is *not of this time*, and for that reason cannot be historicised. But on the other hand, this *not of this time* allows the presence of the psyche in each and every event to become distinctly and intensely evident. The eddy of thought which, according to Walter Benjamin, takes historians out of their discursive representation of things, aspires to a vision of origin – *of the primitive in the vision itself of origin*: it discourages commentary and narrative, always far too concerned with unfolding of things in time; and could even lead to a reassessment of the rather confused idea we have of process.[3] Let us say, in short, *that to think the primitive requires an unmediated contact with the materiality of the thing; and to achieve that, it needs to refrain from any recourse to the idea of process.* For surely thinking, of itself, as though out of deference to subjectivity, tends towards respecting the time of process. And so thinking is slowed down, and in taking too much time, the acuity of its vision is dulled. Whereas the imposition of an idea of the primitive generates a sort

DOI: 10.4324/9781032637600-6

of sacred anguish, which is the sacred anguish of silence. Sometimes it is reached in a single word, through the vision of an interpretation. So to have the 'primitive' slide into 'original primitiveness' sharpens and reinforces *the psychic in itself*, in the light of everything in the psychic that could not be more physical. We should be reminded once more, as Freud wrote in 1924, to listen to the psychic materiality of every utterance in the same way that dream is listened to; all the while knowing that to do so is essential for the analyst to become analyst with their patient.[4]

It is certainly true, following Benveniste further, that Freud's task was not to ask of the language of history [*langage*] what he was able consistently to find in myth and poetry.

All the more so since, 'as it happens in "primitive" societies, far from language reproducing the appearance of a dream, it is the dream which is brought into the categories of language [*langue*], in that the dream is interpreted in connection with actual situations'.[5] Which comes down to maintaining, not inaptly, that language [*langue*], in the words of Ludwig Binswanger, dreams well before we ourselves begin to dream.[6] Dreams are not formed, perhaps, from diurnal residues, but from *diurnal residues of language* [*langue*]. It would then seem that dream fashions its images from the generosity of metaphor to be found in the things of language [*langue*], in the sense that Ponge understands it.[7] And so the primitive emerges as images that themselves allow external reality to emerge in its fullness.

The influence of Carl Abel's book *The Antithetical Meaning of Primal Words* (1884) on Freud is well known – I could go further and say that Freud thought it an entire mine of resources for developing a theory of dream and interpretation. A *singular* origin of language is certainly the issue. Yet Freud is neither a Herder nor a Schelling. For him the question of origin only matters in the context of opposing meanings, an ambiguity – literally: *Zweideutigkeit*, a *double entendre*, a dual understanding – by which opposing ideas coexist in language [*langue*], and in the words that are uttered [*parole*]. The idea of words functioning as utensils for human communication is part and parcel of assuring human mastery over the things of nature, and of the progress aimed for by civilisation. It then becomes possible to conceive of objects, in their object-ness as well as their objectivity. But manifestations remain of what is materially primitive in both the thing and the psyche. And even though language [*langue*], in its various expressions, bears witness to civilisation, it cannot eclipse the phonic-gestural primitiveness of words. In seeking - *in the very moment of psychoanalytic listening to utterances* [*parole*] – the phonic gestures of meaning which are a kind of primary, if not fundamental language [*langue*] of the unconscious, Freud carefully investigates these units of the primitive, and their capacity to guarantee non-destructibility: as opposed to the perfection of the civilised state, which is a sign only of its own fragility. For the primitive is unalterable, a consequence perhaps of the extraordinary material plasticity of its forms. Whereas the 'civilised' – bearer of the multi-faceted training in compromises that produces it – is ruled by a powerful human destructiveness, which alone should dissuade anyone from preaching the humanism of civilisation.

'"The primitive Egyptian", Abel believes, communicates by calling upon 'images, known as determining images, that lie behind letter-signs which specify the meaning of those images, without themselves being intended for utterance'.[8] Here Freud calls on a notion of the *unutterable in exchange*, as performed by dreams recounted in the analytic situation: psycho-analytic listening is rendered far more receptive to this unutterable than through verbal representation, always intended for communication and signification. And surely the analyst senses the domains of regression in a *hallucinatory* way, so to speak; and in an equally *hallucinatory* way, forms their interpretation from within their own regression. The role of the hal-lucinatory in interpretation has been insufficiently understood, along with the phantasmatic (or the oneiric) elements that interpretation presses for in the psychic apparatus.

It is therefore clear that the civilisation of a language, in allowing its popular oral idioms to survive, its tales, legends, and poetic magic, oppo-ses all the more strongly the destructive forces of inter-subjective, con-scious communication. Thus the notion of an 'originary primitiveness', *Urpflanz*, or *Urmensch*, moves towards that of an *image-of-before*, *Vorbild*, which might be even be called transcendental, or a 'prototype' of a form not encountered in the external world, and whose production would effectively mutate over time. But the *a-temporality*, the *Zeitlos* of the unconscious, is not simply a type of immutability, but more *the regressive condition of psychoanalytic listening*, a condition that provides access to the primitiveness of living forms. We should then be able to name living forms just as they appear in language [*langage*], without even having to describe them. Or if not, then write them without describing them. The written or drawn traces of the living form belong to the *petrified time* of the fossil. Fossils detain life preserved in inanimate form. In an earlier work on regression (in *Le Site de l'étranger*, 1995[9]), I have already proposed thinking of the dream as the *animate* psyche of the primitive, which is both alive and *inanimate*; and that the *psychic apparatus* in Chapter 7 of *The Interpretation of Dreams*, where regression is conceptualised topologically, can also be thought of diagrammatically as a fossil. I would like to add to this that fossils, which preserve the living in an inanimate state, contain the immutability of the primitive in a state of flux. For while the fossil is a petrification of time, deprived of mutation, it nonetheless retains a *stylistics of form*, which is essential to theorising regression in the analytic situation. (I'm thinking of the anthropological, History of Art context, in which Aby Warburg envisioned form in movement.) Negative hallucination, which is a property of dream, consists in *rendering a present person absent*. We might then speculate that the stylistics of form is the trace-writing of the primi-tive in movement. In which case why not go still further, and following

Freud's commentary on *Gradiva*, say that *the primitive emerges as the pure phenomenon of the person in their presence, or survival made manifest.*

The more ephemeral, the more transient, the more appearance shows its indestructibility. Freud's formulation is quite exemplary in this regard: 'das *primitive Seelische ist im vollsten Sinne unvergänglich'* – 'the primitive psyche, in the fullest sense, cannot pass'.[10] The ephemeral, that which passes, can assume the appearance of any natural form; whereas the type of being made up of the acquisitions typical of the civilised state is the one internally most threatened with destruction. But such destruction leaves the primitiveness of the soul untouched. Without that *vision*, the survival of the 'psychic', of the 'soulful' [*animique*], leaving aside the feeling right across pathology of it having been destroyed, is inconceivable. Geology very much provides the material for an imaginary conception of time outside the time of memory: it is the bearer of a writing with no efface-ment, or if not that, then only the effacement that is the negligent or fear-ful obliviousness of mankind.

In his text 'Thoughts for the Time on War and Death', Freud is eager to highlight what is particular in psychic [*animique*] development. He writes that 'the development of the mind shows a peculiarity which is present in no other developmental process. When a village grows into a town or a child into a man, the village and the child become lost in the town and the man. Memory alone can trace the old features in the new picture; and in fact the old materials or forms have been got rid of and replaced by new ones'.[11] However fragile in conscious memory and its expressions, *memory of the feelings of memory* – reminiscence of regression – is *thought-in-image*: it preserves the living features of form in movement.

> The earlier mental state may not have manifested itself for years, but none the less it is so far present that it may at any time again become the mode of expression of the forces in the mind, and indeed the only one, as though all later developments had been annulled or undone (*rückgängig gemacht worden wären*). This extraordinary plasticity of mental developments is not unrestricted as regards direction; it may be described as a special capacity for involution (*Rückbildung*) – for regres-sion (*Regression*) – since it may well happen that a later and higher stage of development, once abandoned, cannot be reached again.[12]

The primitive psychic [*l'animique primitive*] – that which 'in the fullest sense, cannot pass' – is outside the scope of the past as it appears in memory, for it is not determined by the phenomenological duration of subjective states in time: regression restores the memory feelings of a living form, a form that might have been thought destroyed. Freud goes on: 'What are called mental diseases inevitably produce an impression in the layman that intellectual and mental life have been destroyed. In rea-lity, the destruction only applies to later acquisitions and developments'.[13]

But while regression attests to the plasticity of psychic [*animique*] development and shows what the human conditions are for their complete restitution, regression in such an understanding, i.e. topological, can only take place in a situation so arranged as to allow its recognition. If that arrangement is in the least veiled or falsified, the meaning of regression can be reversed, and the body is put to the service of sending the soul to sleep. In the same way as he wrote about 'Some Points of Agreement between the Mental Lives of Savages and Neurotics' in 1912,[14] Freud appeals to what is *primitive (primitiv)* so as to denominate, re-name and name the disturbing strangeness of the human. This same disturbing strangeness is involuntarily sought after in the analytic situation. It brings us up close to the sacredness of the non-human, its presence. The primitive, as I said a moment ago, is contrary to process. In the anxiety of a divided self – the division or split without which there can be no analytic listening – the primitive is anticipatory, like a full-frontal obscurity sucking up any capacity to see. The human and its excess, writes Freud, produces 'an intellectual uncertainty', a doubt that arises from the phenomenon of no longer knowing 'whether something is animate or inanimate'.[15] What can also happen is that 'the inanimate extends too far its resemblance to the living'.[16] For surely, *regression in the transference* sometimes has the anxiety-inducing intensity of a manifestation of present formlessness? And surely here we have the first point of contact with interpretation?

In his review of G.H. Luquet's *L'art primitif*, Georges Bataille seeks a relation between 'crude and deforming art' and 'representations of the human form'.[17] 'Only through an abuse of the term', Bataille writes, we call 'primitive' an art which is really a practice of impairment [*altération*][18]: impairment, that is, and even the destruction, of its medium and its material; but also impairment in the sense of allowing one form to pass into another. The form resulting from this impairment, though unknown to the formless, proceeds from the violent action of formlessness itself and the impulse that drives it. In so-called 'primitive' re-creations of animal forms, the most remarkable detail is rigorously observed, making the animal in question perfectly recognisable. But Bataille adds that 'the drawings and sculptures that represent the Aurignacians are nearly all formless and much less human than those that represent animals'.[19] Primitive formlessness in representations of the human figure is therefore on a different level from the practices that enter into human culture. And here we see that in one sense, the art of impairment is an art that restores the strangeness of the human, in its passage through death.

This art of impairment, as we should call it, is not only a matter of technique, or changes of state brought about by technique: one might call it corpse art, in that a corpse can putrefy, but also produces phenomena of psychic survival [*phenomènes animiques de survivance*]. Bataille specifies, in a footnote: 'The term "impairment" expresses both a partial decomposition analogous to that of corpses and the passage to a perfectly heterogeneous state corresponding to what the Protestant professor Rudolf Otto calls the "wholly other", which is to say the sacred, realized, for example, in a ghost'.[20] This association is called to mind by quasi-totemic thoughts on the progressive encroachment of animal forms. As soon as they are captured in representation, the decomposition and putrefaction of cadavers present to the mind something that is absolutely horrible. Under threat from a *mortal melancholia* beyond any hope of mourning, humans choose a totemic denial, by which the form of the animal head is a mask that the human face, for its own salvation, pays as a due to horror. What is called a primitive mask expresses human feelings through its animal appearance. (I am thinking here of West African animal masks, from Burkina Faso, for example.[21]) Impairment reveals the face; and ultimately, the mask restores strangeness to the human face – everything that is fundamentally terrifying, so to speak, about the relation to the other.

'The term *primitive*', notes Lévi-Strauss in *Structural Anthropology*, 'now seems to be safe from the confusion inherent in its etymological meaning and reinforced by an obsolete evolutionism'.[22] The consequent stability of the term is then an expression of what cannot pass – in the sense that Picasso once declared that 'there's no passing beyond primitive sculpture'.

At the end of his book titled *Negerplastik*, Carl Einstein proposes that 'the mask has meaning only when it is inhuman, impersonal, which is to say a construction purified of the lived experience of the individual'.[23] Theatre has provided a way for Europeans to share some of the African practice of the mask. All the excesses of subjective psychology often characteristic of European theatre go against the 'construction' imagined by Einstein, and which beckons a *contact with the divine*. 'I would like to call the mask fixed ecstasy', Einstein adds.[24] And later on: '[W]e should also comment on the peculiarly rigid expression that has been formed on the faces of these masks. This rigidity is nothing but intensity of expression, freed from every psychological origin; above all it makes possible a lucid formal structure'.[25] Thus with the mask and through the mask, the face displays a primitiveness that consists of a *fixed immobility*, and that conveys presence at its highest level of intensity – a presence like that of an ancestor or a god. At this point the mask is seen to capture, possess and reveal everything in the face that is at once transient, and the most living, the most fragile. In a mask, the choice between human and animal never applies – *it is the mask between human and animal*. The mask holds what Carl Einstein calls '*the power of auto-metamorphosis*'. It is clear that animal masks have the specific quality of saving the human face from destruction. Furthermore, the act of killing an animal is related, with equal clarity, to the pursuit of salvation dependent upon on a payment in return, 'the tribute to the slaughtered animal, through which to come closer to the god'.[26] Horror involves the cadaveric decomposition of a human face – which is the absolute void, and equivalent to the elimination of the primitive. I wrote in 'The Site of the Stranger' that when there is no face opposite, the mask of ancestors is restored to the face through the memory of regression in the transference.[27] But now it seems that the mask in its essence presents as nothing other than sketches and drafts of faces, that disappear in their very approach. Thus transference entails a totemisation of the animal which conveys the imago of the ancestor: nothing is ever explicitly recognisable, and by means of reminiscences, resemblance itself, and only that, will have the power to convey further resemblances. The avoidance of the melancholy that might arise from transferential regression depends precisely on this: the recall that saves the face from the void. For surely dehumanisation, in the day-to-day life of people, always begins with the disappearance of faces?

Let me return to Einstein's text and pay closer attention to it. Having reminded readers of all the different errors resulting from the evolutionist prejudice against the primitive, presumed to be inferior, he then goes on to highlight the highly relevant opposition of 'European' systems of representation (and the discourse upon which they are organised), and the primitive modality of the sacred found in African sculpture. For our purposes what this reading draws attention to more specifically is the primitive/civilised opposition which appears at the same time, and in the same cultural moment, in the work of Sigmund Freud. In Freud, the opposition is not properly speaking dialectical: as we have seen, it turns on the destructibility of the work of civilisation, and the indestructibility of primitive forms. Insofar as it preserves these forms (in dream, delirium, symptom), the *paradigm of neurosis* is, in effect, a model of understanding neurosis in terms of the workings of civilisation, and that understands neurosis as keeping alive within civilisation, under certain conditions, the means humans use to prevent destruction. By design, as well as by its method and its processes, surely psychoanalysis responds to the hope of seeing the work of human civilisation fulfilled at the individual level, by means of a return through regression to what is primitive in each one of us. But nothing is acquired once and for all, and the works of human beings, regardless of how modest they are, are quick to fall into chaos once more. From which results the lack of confidence in the institutions achieved by civilised beings: fiasco is at the heart of any project that fails to recognise the fragility of all acquisition. And from 1918–1920 onwards, Freud is sure to warn psychoanalysts against the temptation of 'psycho-synthesis' and especially of seeking psychotherapeutic results using medical-type or philosophical-type methods. Freud is referring to any approach aimed at reducing the time of psychoanalysis, and at adopting modes of representing the psyche that fail to grasp the unconscious. And so in the psychoanalytic cure, the only belief left to the analyst is animism!

Doubtless Carl Einstein does not have the same approach, but his analyses at this level intersect with those of Freud.

To say that Giacometti, Picasso and Brancusi helped discover a certain primitiveness in the sculpture of African art, is the same as saying that the tectonic power of all sculpture is revealed in the space of Cubism. Carl Einstein analyses the modalities of a particular repression of the primitive, which is the primacy accorded in painting to covering over, to the detriment of the *plastic* and therefore the *living*. Repression proceeds like *per via di porre* in painting. This is also a consolidation in conscious thought of the three-dimensional illusion, concentrated in the frontal representation of the face, and the appearance which that gives of simple foregrounding. This illusion is related to rhetoric in discursive thought, and it eliminates the frontality of the dream. The representation of space *in perspective* supports and amplifies the internal/external opposition and vindicates the exteriority of the object. In its grammatical-philosophical conception, time itself is represented spatially, i.e. in perspective: the present/past opposition does not only relate to the memory of recall, it also legitimises an idea of depth anchored in interiority, thus devaluing the *surfaces of appearance*. In that light, what the European mind seeks to achieve is a formal coherence just like that of the object, and congruent to the objectivity of thought. Thus presence no longer effects *appearance*; and in objectifying themselves, the temporalities of an art work become external to the living forms of creation.

What in this context might be called cognitivism in representation, is in effect physicalism in approaching the objects of thought. One of the consequences is a conversational dimension in the function of spectatorship, right into the heart of *theory*. '[The] spectator', writes Carl Einstein, 'was woven into the sculpture; he became an inseparable functional component of it (e.g., perspectival sculpture) [...] The sculpture was the subject of a conversation between two persons'.[28] It is therefore one and the same to conceive of the object as the 'spectacle' of its representation, on that basis to produce a theory of thought, and finally to cast the object in the discursive features of intersubjective communication. Trying to produce an effect on someone who is no longer there to see – a *spectator in conversation* – transforms sculptures into 'paraphrases of the effects they produce'.[29] As a result, a 'civilised' European creative sculpts as someone who is already a spectator. In theoretical terms, the discursiveness of the spectator produces the sculpture. The disappearance of the primitive – its major repression, and subsequent forgetting – passes for civilising progress at the point where the ingenuity of the mind, in producing this object-sculpture, is regarded in theoretical terms as promoting community in the conversations of looking. 'The construction of space', Einstein adds, 'was sacrificed to a secondary, indeed to an alien means, namely that of material movement; cubic space, that precondition of all sculpture, was forgotten'.[30] Imprisoned in a representation of form governed by spectatorship, plasticity now only stifles the materiality of the mass itself. When space is externalised time can no longer be seen. 'The work of art must provide the entire spatial equation'; it should 'totally absorb cubic space'.[31] To which one could add that *a-temporality* – which increases the sculptural qualities of space – is co-extensive with primitiveness, and in effect excludes the discursiveness of the spectator's position. The increasing force of spectatorship demands the concentration of the time-dimensions into mass, now at the forefront. Yet this is not to say that the work of art is deprived of its own generative powers, or its living materiality. A-temporality demands only that nothing should induce the discursive effects of the perspectival representation of objects to be re-established. Thus what should properly be called regression in motion involves a process of unravelling discursivity.

What Carl Einstein calls 'pure plastic vision' has nothing to do with any sort of aesthetics of beauty (which he radically challenges), but rather with a quality of perception that might be called 'endopsychic'. The purity of plastic vision is not determined by sighting the sculpture from the outside, but by the action in space produced by the sculpture, and overwhelming (i.e. setting inner forms in motion) anyone who welcomes it, anyone who embraces anxiety. Carl Einstein's analyses explore the religious strength of this eminently corporeal vision of the soul *by* the soul and *in the presence* of sculpture.

> [Black African art] is above all determined by religion. [...] The maker creates his work as the deity or its guardian, i.e., from the beginning he maintains a distance from the work, which either is or contains the god. The sculptor's labour is a form of remote adoration [...] [African sculpture] signifies nothing, it does not symbolize; it is the god, who preserves his hermetic mythic reality into which he draws the worshiper, transforming him, too, into a mythic being and dissolving his human existence. Formal and religious unities correspond to one another; so, too, do formal and religious realism.[32]

The development of form, to the point 'where it is entirely contained within itself', makes a god into a mythical, secretly closed reality. The formal power of 'compact mass', complete in the same way, sees the exclusion of signification as well as symbolism. The materiality of form appearing frontally, in its mass – such is presence personified.

In *Black Sculpture*, Carl Einstein guards against the risk of the term 'primitivism' slipping not only into evolutionist prejudice, but also towards a Romantic exoticism, which would destroy its capacity to describe the equally physical and psychic nature of vision.

Georges Didi-Huberman's current research on Carl Einstein, as well as on Aby Warburg, should help us extend still further the field of psychoanalytic thought on regression. His recent work on 'The Surviving Image: Aby Warburg and Tylorian Anthropology' addresses exactly this *Nachleben*, somewhere between symptom and spectre, where an anachronic past is brought to the light in present reminiscence.[33] A focus on the notion of regression, as against a simplistic evolutionism, without question involves a better, and more appropriate evaluation in psychoanalysis of the function of dream, as much in silence as in interpretation.

Translated by Timothy Mathews

Notes

1 Émile Benveniste, 'Remarks on the Function of Language in Freudian Theory' in *Problems in General Linguistics*, trans. by Mary Elizabeth Meek (Miami: University of Miami Press, 1971), pp. 65–75, p. 72.

2 Benveniste, 'Remarks on the Function of Language in Freudian Theory', p. 72 [translation modified; footnotes in square brackets are additions by the editors].

3 [Fédida may allude to the proposition, in *The Origin of German Tragic Drama*, that: 'Origin is an eddy [*tourbillon*] in the stream of becoming, and in its current it swallows the material involved in the process of genesis'. Walter Benjamin, *The Origin of German Tragic Drama*, trans. by John Osborne (London: Verso Books, 1998), p. 45.]

4 [Fédida may allude to Sigmund Freud, 'A Short Account of Psychoanalysis' in *The Standard Edition of the Complete Psychological Works of Sigmund Freud Vol XIX*, trans. by James Strachey et al (London: The Hogarth Press, 1961), pp. 191–209, p. 199.]

5 Benveniste, 'Remarks on the Function of Language', p. 72.

6 [Fédida may allude to Ludwig Binswanger, 'Dream and Existence', in which Binswanger proposed that: 'Language is that which, for all of us, "dreams and thinks" well before the individual themselves comes to dream and think' (translation modified). In Michel Foucault and Ludwig Binswanger. *Dream and Existence*, trans. by Jacob Needleman (New Jersey: Humanities Press International, 1993), p. 81.]

7 [Ostensibly an allusion to Francis Ponge, *Le Parti pris des choses* [1942].]

8 Sigmund Freud, 'The Antithetical Meaning of Primal Words' in *The Standard Edition of the Complete Psychological Works of Sigmund Freud Vol XI*, trans. by Alan Tyson (London: The Hogarth Press, 1957), pp. 155–61, p. 158 [translation modified].

9 [See Chapter 3.]

10 [Fédida cites from the original German of Freud's *Zeitgemäßes über Krieg und Tod*, translated as 'Thoughts for the Time on War and Death' in *The Standard Edition of the Complete Psychological Works of Sigmund Freud Volume XIV* (London: The Hogarth Press, 1957) [1915], pp. 289–300. However the French translation he cites here – 'L'animique primitif, au sens plein, est incapable de passer' – differs from Strachey et al's version ('the primitive mind is, in the fullest meaning of the word, imperishable', (p. 286) and from a French translation by Jankélevitch (revised by Freud himself) – 'ce qu'il y a de primitif dans notre vie psychique est, au sens littéral du mot, impérissable' (*Considérations actuelles sur la guerre et la mort* (Paris: Payot, 1920), p. 15). Fédida appears to cite from Vol. 13 of the translation of Freud's complete works published by PUF – 'L'animique primitif, au sens plein, est incapable de passer' ('Actuelles sur la guerre et la mort', *Œuvres complètes de Freud*, vol. 13 (Paris: PUF, 1988), pp. 127–55, p. 139).]

11 [Freud, 'Thoughts for the Time on War and Death', p. 285.]

12 [Freud, 'Thoughts for the Time on War and Death', pp. 285–86.]

13 [Freud, 'Thoughts for the Time on War and Death', p. 286.]
14 [This is the subtitle of 'Totem and Taboo' in *The Standard Edition of the Complete Psychological Works of Sigmund Freud Volume XIII*, trans. by James Strachey et al (London: The Hogarth Press, 1955) [1912–13], pp. ix–164.]
15 [Sigmund Freud, 'The Uncanny' in *The Standard Edition of the Complete Psychological Works of Sigmund Freud Volume XVII*, trans. by James Strachey et al (London: The Hogarth Press, 1955) [1919], pp. 217–52, p. 230.]
16 [Freud, 'The Uncanny', p. 233.]
17 Georges Bataille, 'Primitive Art' in *The Cradle of Humanity: Prehistoric Art and Culture*, trans. by Michelle Kendall and Stuart Kendall (New York: Zone Books, 2002), pp. 35–44, p. 40 [translation modified.]
18 [Bataille, 'Primitive Art', pp. 39–40.]
19 Bataille, 'Primitive Art', pp. 39–40.
20 [Bataille, 'Primitive Art', p. 193. Bataille's reference is to Rudolf Otto, *The Idea of the Holy*, trans. John W. Harvey (Oxford: Oxford University Press, 1923) [1917], pp. 25ff.]
21 Gabriel Massa, *Masques d'animaux d'Afrique de l'Ouest* (Saint-Maur-des-Fossés: Éditions Sépia, 1995).
22 [Claude Lévi-Strauss, 'The Concept of Archaism in Anthropology' in *Structural Anthropology*, trans. by Claire Jacobson and Brooke Grundfest Schoepf (New York: Basic Books, 1963), pp. 101–19, p. 102.]
23 Carl Einstein, 'Negro Sculpture', trans. by Charles W. Haxthausen and Sebastian Zeidler in *October* 107 (Winter 2004), pp. 122–38, p. 137 [translation modified].
24 [Einstein, 'Negro Sculpture', p. 137.]
25 Einstein, 'Negro Sculpture', p. 138.
26 [Einstein, 'Negro Sculpture', p. 138 (translation modified).]
27 [See Chapter 1.]
28 [Einstein, 'Negro Sculpture', p. 128 (translation modified).]
29 [Einstein, 'Negro Sculpture', p. 128 (translation modified).]
30 [Einstein, 'Negro Sculpture', p. 128.]
31 [Einstein, 'Negro Sculpture', p. 131.]
32 [Einstein, 'Negro Sculpture', pp. 129–31.]
33 [Georges Didi-Huberman, 'The Surviving Image: Aby Warburg and Tylorian Anthropology' in *Oxford Art Journal* 25: 1 (2002), pp. 59–69. Originally published in French in the same issue of the journal *L'Inactuel* (no. 3, 1999) in which the present essay by Fédida was published, under the title 'L'Horreur du primitif'.]

6   The Dream's Hypochondria

> The 'diagnostic' capacity of dreams – a phenomenon which is generally acknowledged, but regarded as puzzling, becomes equally comprehensible, too. In dreams, incipient physical disease is often detected earlier and more clearly than in waking life, and all the current bodily sensations assume gigantic proportions. This magnification is hypochondriachal in character; it is conditional upon the withdrawal of all psychical cathexes from the external world back on to the ego, and it makes possible the early recognition of bodily changes which in waking life would still for a time have remained unobserved.
>
> Freud, 'A Metapsychological Supplement to the Theory of Dreams'[1]

Glasses, hairpieces, false teeth…. Such are the accessories, among others, which human beings sometimes use 'as [supplements] to their bodily organs (so far as they have succeeded in making good those organs' deficiencies by substitutes)'.[2]

The substitutive value of these accessories underlines not only a deficiency of the organs but confirms, so to speak, their physical and rational functionality or even their practical 'use value'. Anatomical knowledge defines the condition of physiological functionality according to rational positivity.

> Every night human beings lay aside the wrappings in which they have enveloped their skin […] when they go to sleep they carry out an entirely analogue undressing of their minds and lay aside most of their psychical acquisitions. Thus on both counts they approach remarkably close to the situation in which they began life.[3]

This is what Freud says at the beginning of his 'Metapsychological Supplement to the Theory of Dreams'. On entering sleep, man casts off the envelopes and devices which waking life imposes upon him in order to produce, defend himself and adapt to his surroundings; he abandons them to the strange darkness of a space – which Brauner has described as 'the gloaming' [entre chien et loup] – a bric-a-brac of allegorical accessories momentarily emptied of their function and ready, as if surrealised, to enter

DOI: 10.4324/9781032637600-7

into the space of dream. Magritte says this in his paintings: a dress made of skin is a nude. In another instance, abandoned to the passing of time, in the dream, Dali's watch goes soft. The *Strange Case of Mr. K* by Victor Brauner – a tale told backwards so that the dream can find its place – tells us in its own way of the instrumental modifications and animal, vegetal and even mineral metamorphoses of a pot-bellied man akin to Ubu who, in the course of adorning himself with decorations, machine-guns, geographical maps, prostitutes, masses and monuments allows the glimpse of a strange form of nudity, grasped by humour.[4] *The dream resembles the joke: it resembles the body seen as a joke.* The nudity of a sleeping man relates to the infamous denuding (*mise à nu*) which Bataille told us was a putting to death (*mise à mort*). If it weren't for the dream keeping the sleeper asleep, they might encounter their own corpse. So dreaming is perhaps a means of preventing sleep from just being death. But the dream is also the only clothing woven from our own body – the infantile body of fantasy – which allows the truth of nakedness to be discovered. The accessories which human beings take off to sleep are thus pledges left to the real as relics of the familiar. Described by Freud as the 'instigating agents' of the dream, the day's residues lend the dreamer, so to speak, the loose change of the scenario; the anodyne detail of familiar objects is what the dreamer discovers where they least expected to find it, once these objects finally gain a mode of reality which is intensified (a mode of sur-reality), once they have been de-functionalised.[5]

Psychical acquisitions are the montages of things we have learnt, our thoughts and conscious acts, in a word, everything that constitutes the psychological object of our productive and defensive behaviour. These acquisitions relate to a function analogous to that which we accord to clothes and accessories of all kinds intended to complete our corporeal organs, to 'make good their deficiencies' or compensate for their lack. This analogy, reproduced in various forms in Freud's work,[6] concerns the functional system of our objects inasmuch as they figure the role given by knowledge to our organs – corporeal and psychological – and it allows us to finally situate psychology as a truly functional anatomy, which informs and is represented by a mechanistic physiology. Consciousness, which forms the 'surface' of the psychic apparatus, is nothing other, in its systematic and functional determination, than an 'organ of the higher senses'. Placed in contact with the exterior world, this organ corresponds to a prosthetic function assuring the 'organism' a differential protection against external excitations (cf. the image of the 'living vesicle'[7]). If the psychological equipment of human beings is the projection of their anatomic-functional organisation, should we not allow that the regime of the conscious *production* of human beings in the waking state and the *work* implied by this production (conscious thoughts, actions, etc), obey the criteria of a mechanistic projection of a model acquired through scientific knowledge of the body? Organs are *organa*, that is, for Aristotle, parts of war machines, and we all know, without all this falling into a naive anthro-pomorphism, the economic, social and political meanings that underlie the mechanistic idea of an animated anatomy.[8] In other words, and it is Freud who invites us to discover this – would it be possible to understand any-thing about sexuality if, bracketing the unconscious, we saw in this mechanistic vision the sole functional privilege of what are conventionally called the genital organs? Conversely, we have to ask: what does the genital organ figure if it is taken as the model for any of the corporeal organs? More pointedly, of what order is the anatomical transgression that makes psychoanalysis possible?

It is not our purpose here to re-evaluate the meanings that have been attached to the organs in psychoanalysis.[9] In recognising that human beings are *anatomically equipped* with corporeal and psychological organs which render them capable of defining themselves within a system of conservation, production and exchange – averaging out as the ability to recognise themselves corporeally in their *property*[10] – we see them as all the more admirable inasmuch as they adorn themselves (Freud writes 'they dress themselves') with 'all of their auxiliary organs', making them-selves into veritable prosthetic gods.[11] And human beings are indeed such 'prosthetic gods' with respect to the sovereignty of scientific and technical knowledge of their organs. Surrealism, contemporary with a hyper-func-tionalism of objects which it also denounced, called precisely on dreams to re-establish a reality of the everyday, and just as much with things as with words. As a compromise formation, the dream deals with something like a transgression of the functional law of the object: it welcomes the object back as all the more true insofar as it has been distorted. Paradoxically, it is the defunctionalisation of the object which authorises the latter to take on the significations of the body as a whole. Under these conditions it is not surprising that Freud affords any representation the power to connote, in the dream, a part of the body or the body in its totality[12]: the images produced in the dream recover for the sleeping human this reality of the object – a lighter, a knife, a book, hat or lamp – which, beyond its figura-tion, resides in a play on words of the everyday, in that very place where the dream finds its first inscription. Speaking of Magritte's shoe-foot or again of his woman in a dress of skin hanging in the wardrobe, Bau-drillard writes precisely that: 'everywhere surrealism plays upon the dis-tance instituted by the functionalist calculus between the object and itself, or between man and his own body [...] Fusion of the skin and breasts and the folds of a dress, of toes and the leather of a shoe: surrealist imagery plays with this split by denying it, but on the basis of separate terms legible in the *collage* or *superimpression*'.[13] The procedure of *collage* – Max Ernst has given us particularly remarkable examples – is perhaps one of the most effective means to engender a spatiality of the *screen* on which effects of *condensation* and of *displacement* are produced together. What comes to reality in and through the 'hallucinatory satisfaction of desire' finds its projection screen at the level of the body itself [*au ras du corps*] – *in that place where the somatic can recover all of its meaning as a site, without a surface, of desire or of primary erotogeneity.*

In that case, is not a metapsychology of dreams above all the only possible means to understand the somatic? This is to say that the only possible understanding of the somatic is the *metapsychology of sleep* which renders any possible psychology of dreams non-existent. The dream is perhaps not only the guardian of sleep: it is paradoxically the guarantor of a reality which, as an originary reality, cannot be revealed except through desire and as *inscribed* in the very body of fantasy. The dream is at the same time the *myth* of the body itself and the only place possible –analytically – for its interpretation. We should not be surprised that the somatic, disencumbered of its accessories, should finally find its meaning there, in the dream.

***

Before reminding us that 'the psychical state of a sleeping person is characterised by an almost total withdrawal from the surrounding world and by a cessation of all interest in it', Freud notes that 'Somatically, sleep is a reactivation of intra-uterine existence...'.[14]

These two remarks, as banal as they seem, establish a two-pronged question: is entering sleep not in a way a simulation of mourning, and dream a resolution of this mourning as far as sleep is concerned? As if in accepting to sleep – thus abandoning oneself to the somatic, human beings were to entertain, every night, the *illusion* of loss, finding in dreams the satisfaction of their lack and the proof of their own immortality. The simulation of one's own death in sleep and the power accorded to dreams to stage it represent for interpretation a sort of humoristic response (full of wit) on the part of a melancholic person busy shuffling things around and shamelessly digging around in themselves in search of their own corpse.

The work of mourning is so to speak the condition demanded by the *reality* of a *no longer* such that is no longer threatened by the 'evil spirits' which Freud says arose first from corpses.[15] Mourning does not only accomplish a work of liberation in relation to the lost object; the 'narcissistic gain' of remaining alive only takes on meaning if one admits in parallel the *necessary* limits of the *representation of our own death*. The specificity of this representation is to be blind if not deaf to any auto-scopy of oneself-as-corpse, which would provoke in anyone an intolerable horror whose only equivalent is the thought of castration. The representation of our own death has something 'impenetrable' about it, and Freud locates this characteristic among those which concern the unconscious wish for the death of the stranger and in ambivalence with respect to the loved one.[16] To welcome death into our representation is to be able to make of it an object of inclination – a kind of tenderness toward oneself – it is to guarantee in any case a thought with an object and constitute it as a definitive modality of the only figuration of the self possible with respect to an Other whose primitive desire we signify in the narcissism of the loved one. Moreover, does it not enter into the strange power of madness to remind us, as Artaud put it, that the only possible suicide signifies, on the contrary, a death 'without inclination', and therefore an impossible representation of death which makes it, in psychosis, a violent auto-scopy, a kind of radical resolution of the desire to know in an excess of inter-pretation?[17] This would be a punctual actualisation of the untimely unconscious: this death which finds in itself the freedom to 'fall down like a lopped tree' (Artaud) defies spectacular imagination, as well as reasoned language, which we habitually use to guarantee, even in the face of death, the unconscious belief in our own immortality?[18] This belief makes of the soul the imaginary act of our narcissistic sovereignty and the stakes of the ownership and integrity of our bodies. It was always such: the image of the body is the specular effect of a 'jubilant assumption'.[19]

In this sense also the work of mourning resembles somewhat what one might call the *work of infantile amnesia*. The elaboration by the infant of the death of the other is, throughout the period of latency, the putting into effect of the means that will permit them to acquire a capacity to *believe* independently of the existence of *knowledge*. The corpse can thus enter into knowledge on condition that it is abstracted from the lived experience of the infant which underlies their amnesia. If the corpse is the prototype of the encyclopaedia of the body constituted by anatomy, it also figures the fetishist or superstitious index of a knowledge of death which confirms in return the unconscious belief in immortality. The adult human is as amnesiac in relation to their own death as they are of the archaic body of their terror and their distress. The contemporary ideology of the body rests on a conservationist plastification of the image of oneself: the nudity of the sleeping humans is decidedly the only such nakedness to find its truth in the humour of our death.

In other words, we should acknowledge that it is not straightforward to conceive of the *mourning of oneself*. More precisely, melancholy might tell us that there is something of this order at play in it: the 'extraordinary diminution in his self-regard', 'an impoverishment of the ego on a grand scale' participate for the melancholic in this *work* of the disinterment of past faults, indignities and awkwardness with which it knows itself to be dressed.[20] The constant repetition of the melancholy complaint is offered in fact as the actualisation of a *totalitarian knowledge* of oneself, the alleged expression of a *lucidity* of consciousness or even the resolution of a radical knowledge of oneself. The melancholic lacks prudishness or shame; in denuding themselves, they seek to be seen according to the *truth* of what they are. '[...] it may be, so far as we know, that he has come pretty near to understanding himself; we only wonder why a man has to be ill before he can be accessible to a truth of this kind', says Freud.[21] The *transparency* of the ego to consciousness is perhaps the worst of the resistances of the unconscious. The melancholic mobilises so much energy in searching in themselves for what is bad that one is led to ask if the faults that they attribute to themselves don't relate in fact to 'someone else, someone who the patient loved or has loved or should love'.[22] The work of mourning in melancholy passes through the '*identification* of the ego with the abandoned object' and through *regression* to primary (or originary) narcissism.[23] The regression of the libido into the ego is, one could say, specific to the work of mourning in melancholy and takes account of the form taken by primitive narcissism in the experience of all-powerful mania.

To stick to the clinical description of the melancholic state, one might justly propose that the ill person only looks inside themselves to discover a corpse – in the sense of a cruel nakedness – on condition that the corpse had been substituted, or, more exactly, that their complaint was *moral* to the extent that it was an alibi for a complaint addressed to the lost object (cf. *Ihre Klagen sind Anklagen*).[24] The ambivalence attached to primitive narcissistic identification, as Abraham points out, is such that devouring is the archaic form of the cannibalistic assimilation of the elected object. The melancholic creates the allegory of their own *psychic* (or moral) *corpse* to hide what they devour: an *exquisite corpse*. Organic inferiorities, corporeal deficiencies, ugliness, we know, rarely feature in melancholic complaints: the moral corpse can thus be all the more exhibited insofar as it functions as the nudity from which the melancholic protects themselves so as not to threaten their own integrity and thus to preserve the immortality of their own body.[25] The consumption linked to melancholic work thus allows self-knowledge [*connaissance de soi*], the knowledge [*savoir*] of oneself in truth, to have the acuity and penetrating intensity that one would associate with an insomniac consciousness and its reclusive lucidity; one might add that evil spirits latch on especially to a lost sense of humour. For there to be humour, the skin of the moral corpse must not be given as nudity: the psychological or moral denuding is melancholic.

From one point of view we could say that the hypochondriac bears a certain clinical likeness to the melancholic[26]: we find the same lack of interest in the exterior world, the loss of the capacity to love, an exclusive investment of the libido in the painful organ, the figure for the bad object in the body. The re-distribution of the organic complaint – posing the question of the relation between corporeal and psychic pain – in the perpetual search for a medical witness (a search whose function seems linked to the ongoing sense of frustration) and the lack of satisfaction linked to the denial the relevance of health, these factors would allow one to characterise hypochondria as both a *melancholy of the organ*, as an effect through pain of the *transparency of the body to consciousness*, or again as the depression of a *body which has become an evil spirit*, in the insomnia of consciousness. The hypochondriac, however, has this particularity of living their self-consciousness not as the constitutive condition of a knowledge of their psychological or moral truth but as the discovery of a bad body – a body injured through modification, threatened with modification. In a sense the hypochondriac is indeed haunted by their own corpse, insofar as the latter comes to reveal not so much death as the pain associated with the modification of the organ. If it were necessary to pursue here the question corresponding to the work of mourning one would be led to ask how, for the hypochondriac, the regressive process of ego libido leads the ill person to the primitive narcissism of identification with the bad object. The hypochondriac's identification with the diseased organ, the 'stasis of the libido' indicated by the latter, turns the hypochondriac into the mother of their own pain, in their relation to themselves. We can say then that the hypochondriac's mourning resembles a kind of work of pregnancy in which on a somatic level the subject would be the one who carries in themselves the separated penis whose suffering is such as to let itself be taken as that of a certain castration. The identification of the somatic with the material involves a kind of inversion of the myth of a return to the paradise of the mother's body and intra-uterine existence: the traumatism of birth illustrates, in hypochondria, a function of the dead child (a penis-relic of the castrated father) conserved as an organ in the maternal body, therefore in the somatic itself. The equivalence between child, faeces and penis plays out here in the sense of a kind of pregnancy-constipation: the somatic complaint of the hypochondriac and the lived experience of suffering that it connotes are not only to be heard as a demand to 'take care of me', but also as a recurrent fascination with the organ in speech. This kind of *verbal hallucination of the organ in speech* seems specific to the hypochondriac's position and characterises precisely the meaning of the word for the organ (it is thus comparable from this point of view with hysteria). Or again: this hallucination of the organ in the word makes of the latter the only possible site – perhaps one could say the only *screen* – for a ritual mourning of the dead child (repetition of the castration of the father in a castration of the self), such that there is at the same time mourning but also hallucinatory satisfaction and thus conservation of the organ. The hypochondriac suffers – and enjoys – precisely from not being able to evacuate the diseased organ since, if it were thus, they would be threatened by a death due to the lack (lapsus) of having suffered. The insomnia of the hypochondriac is the guardian of the organ and of their suffering: to keep watch over the organ is as much to keep watch over the child as over death. The somatic is nothing other than this analytic word that makes itself heard alone in *word-representations*.

***

Melancholy, hypochondria and the dream appear, according to the metapsychological project, to define respectively a series of complementary positions differentiated by the structural and dynamic modalities of the work of mourning.

If sleep and dreams appear to 'simulate' a melancholic process and a mode of hypochondriachal investment as if to 'prevent' us from becoming melancholic and hypochondriachal it is because they define each of these states in relation to the other in an essential complementarity. This therefore means that one can't constitute a psychology of dreams without having embarked upon a metapsychology of sleep, as I've said: such a metapsychology has the twin specificity of providing us with a truth of the somatic and of only recognising it as such on condition of understanding the dream as its specific interpretation.

Thinking that the entry into sleep has something to do with a *mourning of the self*, it immediately becomes possible to say that this *self* can only be identified with the *object of primary narcissism* – an object whose particularity is to guarantee against any destruction of the self. Such that the mourning of the self is like the necessary return to the lethal state of a potential death and its hallucinatory resolution. The primitive object is only conserved on condition of being 'accepted' as lost by sleep. This situation exactly evokes *acute hallucinatory psychosis*, Meynert's *amentia*, which Freud calls 'hallucinatory wishful psychosis', and which is 'the reaction to a loss which reality affirms, but which the ego has to deny, since it finds it insupportable'; reality being set aside, wishful fantasies *maintain, in a hallucinatory* mode, a 'better reality' or an element of reality which can be conserved as essentially good against all the rest.[27] As concerns the dream, we could say that the surreality of the objects which compose it is not at all a deformed reality but a primary reality such as exists in representations of the object outside any functionality and such as can be restored through hallucination in a kind of primary truth of libidinal investment. 'It seems justifiable to assume', writes Freud, 'that belief in reality is bound up with perception through the senses. When once a thought has followed the path to regression as far back as to the unconscious memory-traces of objects and thence to perception, we accept the perception of it as real. So hallucination brings belief in reality with it'.[28] If sleep is thus the acceptance of a mourning of the self along with what it entails in terms of a suspension of interest in the exterior world, retreat from reality and so on, the dream is the corresponding condition of sleep which allows the sleeper restitutive access to what reality has retained as essentially good.

At this point in our research we can thus summarise what links and differentiates dream and hypochondria: hypochondria's regression to a primitive narcissism fits well with the sense of a mourning of the self in a form avoided by melancholy – thus this auto-scopy (auto-gnosis) of the bad self, radicalised in the painful figure of the functional organ. With the hypochondriac the self needs to take on the expression of the bad organ so that the complaint can be good and so that it can figure a compassionate maternal super-ego. The 'reactivation of intra-uterine existence' is the paradisiacal myth of the good object of primitive narcissism; it excludes any trauma.[29] In hypochondria, if the organ takes the place of the painful child-penis, the traumatic event (separation, castration) engages a process of internal projection which is itself based on an identification by the self with the dead child as castrated penis, with respect to an ego itself identified, in its complaint, with the desire of the mother. In a way then we can speak, in the case of hypochondria, of an *anatomical melancholy* if we recall that in melancholy, precisely, there occurs an 'identification of the ego with the abandoned object'.[30]

The transparency of the body to consciousness, the illusory reassurances that the ill person gives themselves through the anatomical representation of their organs and their functions,[31] the power of the organs to be hallucinated in the words of a reiterated complaint: all of these aspects confirm the impression that the hypochondriac lives a true insomnia of their body and has as if lost the capacity to dream and thus to find in thing-representations the wishful hallucinatory satisfaction which the somatic can attain only through sleep. We are certainly hypochondriacs in our dreams. But should it be said at the same time that we cannot be when our body is symbolically figured there thanks to this travesty which gives to the body of desire the only possible appearance: that of familiar objects?

> The image of a cat expresses a state of angry ill-temper, and the image of a smooth and lightly-coloured loaf of bread stands for physical nudity. [...] The human body as a whole is pictured by the dream-imagination as a house and the separate organs of the body by portions of a house. In dreams with a dental stimulus, an entrance-hall with a high, vaulted roof corresponds to the oral cavity and a staircase to the descent from the throat to the oesophagus. In a dream caused by a headache, the head may be represented by the ceiling of a room covered with disgusting, toad-like spiders [...] The dream features numerous symbols for the same organ: thus the breathing lung will be symbolically represented by a blazing furnace, with flames roaring with a sound like the passage of air; the heart will be represented by hollow boxes or baskets; the bladder by round, bag-shaped objects or more generally by hollow ones. It is of special importance that at the end of a dream the organ concerned or its function is often openly revealed, and as a rule in relation to the dreamer's own body. Thus a dream with a dental stimulus usually ends by the dreamer picturing himself pulling a tooth out of his mouth.[32]

These explanations by Scherner (cited by Freud in *The Interpretation of Dreams*) can be compared to the electromechanical descriptions the model of which was proposed by Baglivi in his *Practice of Physick* (1704 [1696]).[33] While accepting the thesis of a symbolisation of the somatic state in dreams, Freud confessed himself 'shocked' by such explanations because 'once again the mind is saddled with the dream-work as a useless and aimless function'.[34] We must also add that to assign to any somatic excitation a specific symbolic representation leads at most to a reintroduction of the principle of a univocal correspondence between the functionality of the organ and the functionality of the represented object. Paradoxically, *the work of the dream ceases being 'a useless occupation' once it has thrown doubt on the functionality of the organ as well as that of the object.* If 'every successful dream is the accomplishment of a wish' to remain asleep, the dream-work defines real *somatic work* which represents something like the necessary transgression of the functionality of the organ. This is why the symbolics of dreams which Freud unveils in the *Interpretation of Dreams* excludes the systematism of someone like Scherner: it can only be based on a theory of the unconscious which alone is capable of accounting for a *metapsychology of the somatic.*

If we can allow with Freud that any dream image relates to a symbolic meaning of a sexual nature, such a proposition is only of value if it is understood not as an interpretative postulation but as the *law of the unconscious elaboration of the somatic.* In other words, it would make sense to account for the potential of the genital organ to constitute the *interpretative model* of any representation of objects, in such a way that its presence in the register of sexuality would in the dream be connoted by the single law of a denial applied to the functionality of the object. 'It is highly probable', writes Freud, 'that all complicated machinery and apparatus occurring in dreams stand for the genitals (and as a rule male ones); in describing which dream symbolism is as indefatigable as the "joke-work"'.[35]

To speak here of the *model of the genital organ* under the rubric of a real functional transgression cannot but remind us of the meaning recognised by Freud of the 'familiar prototype of an organ that is painfully tender, that is in some way changed and that is not yet diseased in the ordinary sense, [...] the genital organ in its states of excitation'.[36] The erotogenic zones – considering that any part of the body can be an erotogenic zone and that 'the body as a whole is erotogenic' – are conceived on the model of the genital organ ('they may act as substitutes for the genitals and behave analogously to them'[37]) which ceases by the same logic to possess the privilege of sexual activity (in the sense that a physiology could speak of sexuality as a *function*). The erotogeneity of any of the organs ensures for the somatic the power to be understood according to a law of unconscious trans-functionality; it is thus under the same condition that excitations of a somatic order are never enough to account for such and such a symbolic representation by means of the play of a functional correspondence with such and such an organ. In which case the somatic is understood in the full meaning of erotogeneity of which only the unconscious of mnesic traces can assure the meaning given to desire. Since it goes without saying that the dream fulfils the function of hallucinatory satisfaction on the condition that the somatic be in some way, and at the same time a 'magic writing block',[38] re-inventing the fiction of the psychical apparatus and the screen, without surface nor depth, of the defensive mechanism of *projection*. The notion of the *dream-screen* brought out by B.D. Lewin[39] is the somatic itself interpreted as the maternal breast hallucinated at the moment of falling asleep; it is thus the silence of the analyst in the cure, and, in this way, it relates to the acoustic space in which the visual images of the dream take form.

Theories of the anatomical and functional symbolism of the dream do not only misunderstand the nature of the dream-work but allow a kind of naïve belief in the visibility of images. It's true that the notion of the screen supports, in psychoanalysis, that of a visual projection of representation while risking leaving as given the defensive and conservative meaning nevertheless present in the object of hallucinatory psychosis. That the dream-work should be in some way present and denied in the hallucinatory object gives to the latter the power to be a screen in the triple sense of being that which provokes and reveals, allows to be figured, and finally protects. The visibility of the oneiric image responds to the same functions: it is the illusion necessary so that desire can be *figured*, travestied and at the same time defended in its own recognition. If the dream is a *projection* – 'the externalisation of an internal process'[40] – the visual character of representations is necessary for consciousness so that interpretation takes the form of a misrecognition and so that nothing can thus be understood about unconscious desire. About the dream-work, Freud tells us, 'It is very noteworthy how little the dream-work keeps to the word-presentations, it is always ready to exchange one word for another until it finds the expression which is most handy for plastic representation'.[41] The transposition of thought into visual images is thus the result of a work consisting in drawing back word-representations to *thing-representations* 'as if in general the process were dominated by considerations of representability'.[42] We know that Freud gives a *topographical* value to the difference between word-representations and thing-representations: the thing-representation 'consists in the cathexis, if not of the direct memory-images of the things, at least of remoter memory-traces derived from these'.[43] Thing-representations belong to the Unconscious; this must be understood according to a conception of *regression* which makes of representation itself the result of a re-investment of mnesic traces or thus of this specific modality of the inscription of the event.[44] The hallucination of the dream is precisely the *actualisation* (the satisfaction) of a primitive perception (which is so to speak inactual) of the object by the effect of its absence. If the dream therefore undergoes a topographical regression – differently from in schizophrenia – it is because connections remain possible between cathexes of words and cathexes of things. The words which weave a network of an attentiveness in thought (Pcs) are, in schizophrenia (the work of elaboration of the primary process), the restitutive acts of the lost object. In the dream, the potential play of cathexes of words and things alike give to the visual figuration of images the property of participating at the same time in sonorous material and a visual conversion into form.

These remarks can lead to greater precision about how hypochondria differs from the dream. In hypochondria, we proposed, the organ is hallucinated in the word. We should understand by this that 'the predominance of what has to do with words over what has to do with things' affords the organ a representation in thought on the basis of an analogy (or an identity) in verbal expression.[45] The functionality linked to the model of the genital organ and to sexual activity (generally linked to masturbation) is indicated by the play of verbal identities (what 'spurts out' in the squeezing of a blackhead and '"a hole is a hole" is true verbally'[46]): *words are thus* – to the extent that they are primitively cathected – *the site of the modification of the organs.* In return, the organ is reconfigured in the body by means of an *internal projection,* the organ thus re-endowed functions as an auto-scopic allegory of the word. It is clinically observable that the hypochondriac 'refuses' to understand what is expressed in words while at the same time keeping the painful feeling of not being understood in their evocation of the diseased organ. What results is a situation in which the organs can only relate to the words actualised in the complaint and thus that speech is the only projective surface available for the somatic.[47] What is thus lacking in the hypochondriac is to not be able to cathect thing-representations, as if these alone – on the model of the dream – were able to restore the true meaning of the somatic. Hypochondria makes a kind of hypothesis of a denial of infantile amnesia: the body of the hypochondriac makes of the painful organ the only vestige of childhood under the image of the dead child.

The somatic is the space of a text. The text which associations reveal in analytic work is precisely the only possible space of dream. This text woven in the event restores the infantile body: the dream, says Freud, 'might be described as *a substitute for an infantile scene modified by being transferred into a recent experience'.*[48]

In assimilating the work of the organic symptom into the dream-work, Groddeck[49] recognises the existence of a *somatic work* thanks to which symptoms can be read and interpreted in terms of the principle of condensation and displacement. However he reinstitutes a thickness to organicity which obscures, in a way, the sense of the somatic as a *screen.* The dream is precisely that which affords the body the necessary projection, as a myth, of what is going on there. But, emerging out of a psychologism of the dream, we can see that it is valuable only as a text and that this text is that of the *body-event.* If – as is the case with hysteria and in a different way with organic illness – the somatic is the site of a dramatic actualisation (illness, the pain), it designates with respect to the dream the space and screen of an *instigating* scenario of its hallucinatory representations.

If it were necessary to find someone that best understood how one could render such representations, one might think of Eisenstein. Speaking of 'a type of "post-painting" passing into a distinctive type of "pre-music"',[50] Eisenstein designates a quality of the image whose surface on the screen is in some way engendered by the acoustic nature of sounds and whose dramatic content is as if produced by the musical material (pathic function), which carries the *event* within itself. The visual figuration thus takes on the power to reveal something like a meaning – that which is present through its absence in primitive reality.

Translated by Patrick ffrench and Nigel Saint

Notes

1 [Sigmund Freud, 'A Metapsychological Supplement to the Theory of Dreams' in *The Standard Edition of the Complete Psychological Works of Sigmund Freud Volume XIV*, trans. by James Strachey et al (London: The Hogarth Press, 1957) [1915], pp. 217–36, p. 223. Notes in square brackets are added by translators.]

2 [Freud, 'A Metapsychological Supplement to the Theory of Dreams', p. 222.]

3 [Freud, 'A Metapsychological Supplement to the Theory of Dreams', p. 222.]

4 [Fédida refers to a 1933 painting by the Romanian-French Surrealist artist Victor Brauner depicting a portly individual in various states across 40 vignettes.]

5 [Sigmund Freud, 'The Interpretation of Dreams' in *The Standard Edition of the Complete Psychological Works of Sigmund Freud Volume IV*, trans. by James Strachey et al (London: The Hogarth Press, 1953) [1900], p. 169.]

6 See *An Outline of Psychoanalysis, The Interpretation of Dreams* and other texts in which Freud describes the psychical apparatus. See also Ludwig Binswanger, 'Freud's Conception of Man in the Light of Anthropology' in *Being-in-the-World*, trans. by J. Needleman (New York and Evanston: Harper and Row, 1968), pp. 149–81.

7 [Sigmund Freud, 'Beyond the Pleasure Principle' in *The Standard Edition of the Complete Psychological Works of Sigmund Freud Volume XVIII*, trans. by James Strachey et al (London: The Hogarth Press, 1955) [1920], pp. 3–66, p. 27.]

8 See Georges Canguilhem, *Knowledge of Life*, trans. by Paola Marrati and Todd Meyers (New York: Fordham University Press, 2008), pp. 61–64; Jean Starobinski, *L'Idée d'organisme* (Paris: Centre de documentation universitaire, 1956).

9 I have proposed an initial approach to this problem in my contribution to the issue of the *Nouvelle revue de psychanalyse* (3, 1971) on 'Sites of the Body' [*Lieux du corps*], entitled 'Anatomy in Psychoanalysis' (pp. 109–26).

10 See Pierre Klossowski, *Living Currency*, trans. by Vernon Cisney, Nicolae Morar and Daniel W. Smith (London: Bloomsbury, 2017).

11 Sigmund Freud, 'Civilisation and its Discontents' in *The Standard Edition of the Complete Psychological Works of Sigmund Freud Volume XXI*, trans. by James Strachey et al (London: The Hogarth Press, 1961) [1929], pp. 59–148, p. 92. [NB. The original text of Fédida's essay has 'dieu prophétique'.]

12 Sigmund Freud, 'The Interpretation of Dreams' (Second Part) in *The Standard Edition of the Complete Psychological Works of Sigmund Freud Volume V*, trans. by James Strachey et al (London: The Hogarth Press, 1955), p. 356.

13 Jean Baudrillard, *For a Critique of the Political Economy of the Sign*, trans. by Charles Levin (St. Louis, MO: Telos Press, 1981), p. 193. In the same passage, Baudrillard writes: 'In surrealism the symbolic relation no longer appears

except as the phantasm of subject-object adequation. The surrealist metaphor defines itself as a compromise formation, as a short circuit between the two orders of functionality (here transgressed and made ridiculous) and the symbolic (distorted and made into a phantasm). [...] To the rational calculus which "liberates" the object in its function is opposed surrealism which liberates the object from its function, returning it to the free associations from which will re-emerge not the symbolic, in which the respective crystallisation of subject and object does not take place, but subjectivity itself, "liberated" in the phantasm' (p. 193, p. 194).

14 Freud, 'A Metapsychological Supplement to the Theory of Dreams', p. 222.

15 Sigmund Freud, 'Totem and Taboo' in *The Standard Edition of the Complete Psychological Works of Sigmund Freud Volume XIII*, trans. by James Strachey et al (London: The Hogarth Press, 1955) [1913], pp. ix–162, p. 59.

16 Sigmund Freud, 'Our Attitude towards Death' in 'Thoughts for the Times on War and Death' in *The Standard Edition of the Complete Psychological Works of Sigmund Freud Volume XIV*, trans. by James Strachey et al, (London: The Hogarth Press, 1957), p. 289, p. 247.

17 Friedrich Hölderlin, 'Remarks on Oedipus' in *Essays and Letters on Theory*, trans. by Thomas Pfau (New York: SUNY Press, 1988), pp. 101–108, as well as the fine preface by Beaufret [See *Remarques sur Œdipe. Remarques sur Antigone* (Paris: UGE, 1965)]. See also André Green, *Un œil en trop* (Paris: Minuit 1970). Finally, my article 'L'Inceste et le meurtre dans la généalogie' in *Szondiana VIII: Contribution à l'analyse du destin* (Louvain and Paris: Neuwelaerts, 1971).

18 [The reference to Artaud is to 'Sur le suicide' (*Le Disque vert*, 3:1 (1925)), trans. by David Rattray as 'On Suicide' in *Artaud Anthology* (San Francisco: City Lights, 1965), pp. 56–58 (translation modified).]

19 [Fédida refers here to Jacques Lacan, 'The Mirror Stage as Formative of the Function of the I as revealed in psychoanalytic experience' in *Écrits: A Selection*, trans. by Alan Sheridan (London: Routledge, 1989), p. 2.]

20 [Sigmund Freud, 'Mourning and Melancholia' in *The Standard Edition of the Complete Psychological Works of Sigmund Freud Volume XIV*, trans. by James Strachey et al (London: The Hogarth Press, 1957) [1915], pp. 237–58, p. 246.]

21 Freud, 'Mourning and Melancholia', p. 246. See also: 'Feelings of shame in front of other people, which would more than anything characterize this latter condition, are lacking in the melancholic, or at least they are not prominent in him. One might emphasize the presence in him of an almost opposite trait of insistent communicativeness which finds satisfaction in self-exposure', p. 247.

22 Freud, 'Mourning and Melancholia', p. 248.

23 [Freud, 'Mourning and Melancholia', p. 249.]

24 [Freud, 'Mourning and Melancholia', p. 249: 'their complaints are really "plaints", in the old sense of the word'.]

25 In my seminar this year [1971–72] on depression and melancholy at Saint-Antoine University, I have engaged with the problem of melancholic suicide. [See for example 'La grande énigme du deuil', *L'Absence* (Paris: Gallimard, 1978).]

26 See on this point the descriptions provided by Esquirol, Greisinger, etc.

27 [Freud, 'Metapsychological Supplement to the Theory of Dreams', pp. 230–33.]

28 Freud, 'Metapsychological Supplement to the Theory of Dreams', p. 230. It would also be useful to refer to Freud's commentary on Jensen's *Gradiva*.

29 [Freud, 'Metapsychological Supplement to the Theory of Dreams', p. 222.]

30 [Freud, 'Mourning and Melancholia', p. 249.]

31 See Louis Wolfson, *Le Schizo et les langues* (Paris: Gallimard, 1970).

32 [See Freud, 'The Interpretation of Dreams', p. 225, p. 320. Freud cites Karl Abraham Scherner, *Das Leben des Traums* (Berlin: Heinrich Schindler, 1861).]

33 'Examine with some attention the physical economy of man: What do you find? The jaws armed with teeth: Are they anything but pliers? The stomach is but a

retort; the veins, the arteries, the entire system of blood vessels are hydraulic tubes; the heart is a spring; the viscera are but filters, screens; the lungs are but bellows. And what are the muscles, if not cords? What is the ocular angle, if it is not a pulley? And so on', Giorgio Baglivi, *The Practice of Physick (De praxi medica)* (London: Midwinter, 1723). Fédida cites from Georges Canguilhem, 'Machine and Organism' in *Knowledge of Life*, trans. by Paola Marrati and Todd Meyers (Fordham: Fordham University Press, 2008), pp. 75–97, p. 78.]

34 [Freud, *The Interpretation of Dreams*, p. 226.]

35 Freud, 'The Interpretation of Dreams' (Second Part), p. 356. The essay by Tausk 'On the Origin of the "Influencing Machine" in Schizophrenia' [*Journal of Psychotherapy Practice and Research* 1:2 (Spring 1992), pp. 184–206], the French translation of which appeared in *La Psychanalyse* 4 (1958), merits wider attention and comment. In terms of the interests of the present article, I would draw attention to the notion of *somatic paranoia*. If the *apparatus* represents the genital organs, it does not represent them alone but 'obviously' writes Tausk of his patient, 'her whole person. It represents the projection of the patient's body on to the outer world. At least, the following results are unquestionably obtained from the patient's report: the apparatus is distinguished above all by its human form, easily recognized despite many non-human characteristics. In form it resembles the patient herself, and she senses all manipulations performed on the apparatus in the corresponding part of her own body and in the same manner. All effects and changes undergone by the apparatus take place simultaneously in the patient's body, and vice versa. Thus, the apparatus loses its genitalia following the patient's loss of her genital sensations; it had possessed genitalia for as long a period as her genital sensations had lasted'. [Tausk, 'Influencing Machines', p. 192.]

36 Sigmund Freud, 'On Narcissism: an Introduction' in *The Standard Edition of the Complete Psychological Works of Sigmund Freud Volume XIV*, trans. by James Strachey et al (London: The Hogarth Press, 1957) [1914], pp. 67–104, p. 84.

37 Freud, 'On Narcissism: an Introduction', p. 84.

38 Sigmund Freud, 'A Note upon the Mystic Writing-Pad' in *The Standard Edition of the Psychological Works of Sigmund Freud Volume XIX*, trans. by James Strachey et al (London: The Hogarth Press, 1961), pp. 227–32.

39 B.D. Lewin, 'Sleep, the Mouth and the Dream-Screen' in *The Psycho-Analytic Quarterly* 15 (1946), pp. 419–34. Translated into French in *Nouvelle revue de psychanalyse* 5 (1972), pp. 211–23.

40 Freud, 'A Metapsychological Supplement to the Theory of Dreams', p. 223.

41 Freud, 'A Metapsychological Supplement to the Theory of Dreams', p. 228.

42 Freud, 'A Metapsychological Supplement to the Theory of Dreams', p. 228.

43 Sigmund Freud, 'The Unconscious', in *The Standard Edition of the Complete Psychological Works of Sigmund Freud Volume XIV*, trans. by James Strachey et al (London: The Hogarth Press, 1957) [1915], pp. 159–216, p. 201.

44 Freud, *The Interpretation of Dreams*. See the very important chapter devoted to *Regression*.

45 Freud, 'The Unconscious', p. 200.

46 [Freud, 'The Unconscious', p. 200.]

47 Freud, 'The Unconscious', p. 200.

48 [Freud, 'The Interpretation of Dreams' (second part'), p. 546.]

49 Georg Groddeck, *La Maladie, l'art et le symbole* (Paris: Gallimard, 1969). See in particular the text on 'The Dream-work and the Work of the Organic Symptom'.

50 [Fédida cites from Barthélemy Amengual, *Que viva Eisenstein* (Paris: L'Age d'homme, 1990), p. 92. For the English translation see Sergei Eisenstein, *Non-indifferent Nature*, trans. Herbert Marshall (Cambridge: Cambridge University Press, 1987), pp. 202–21.]

7   Day's Residues, Life's Residues

In his 1896 essay *The Names of Gods* ('An Essay toward a Science of Religious Conception'), [Hermann] Usener, cited by [Ernst] Cassirer, distinguishes between 'momentary deities' and 'special deities'. Momentary deities belong to a distant period of mythical thinking and are named in common language when a representation issuing from a psychical event appears and disappears instantaneously, whilst in these very conditions maintaining potential significance for the person surprised by this happening in their life. These *gods of the moment* take shape in language as a vital individually-experienced concrete event, but – like the words used to name them – they acquire an objectivity and stability which entrust them with a quality of universal jurisdiction beyond the event, whereby their memory is not effaced.

Commenting on Usener's essay, Cassirer says:

> The same function which the image of the god performs, the same tendency to permanent existence may be ascribed to the uttered sounds of language. The word, like a god or a daemon, confronts man not as a creation of his own, but as something existent and significant in its own right, as an objective reality. As soon as the spark has jumped across, as soon as the tension and emotion of the moment has found its discharge in the word or the mythical image, a sort of turning point has occurred in human mentality: the inner excitement which was a mere subjective state has vanished and has been resolved into the objective form of myth or of speech. And now an ever-progressive objectification can begin.[1]

The reciprocal structuring of myth and language is fostered by the progressive transformation of passivity into activity: the establishment of everyday tasks has the function of constituting the mythico-linguistic identity of the cultural community and it is then – as we see in Ancient Rome, for example – that momentary deities are personified as gods of activity (gods of the home and of the threshold, of the forest, the pastures, of sowing, the harvest, growth, flowering and bearing fruit...). The world

DOI: 10.4324/9781032637600-8

acquires exterior objectivity more easily insofar as *action* emerges from sensory experience and is differentiated in a system of representation which governs the temporality of events *discursively*.

Yet let us not leave the deities of the moment so hastily. It is Greek poetry (and what survives of it in the Classical period) which inspires Usener with the idea of the religious quality of any psychical event worthy of surprising each particular individual in their own existence:

> By reason of this vivacity and responsiveness of their religious senti-ment, any idea or object which commands, for the moment, their undivided interest, may be exalted to divine status: Reason and Understanding, Wealth, Chance, Climax, Wine, Feasting, or the body of the Beloved. Whatever comes to us suddenly like a sending from heaven, whatever rejoices or grieves or oppresses us, seems to the religious consciousness like a divine being. As far back as we can trace the Greeks, they subsume such experiences under the generic term of δαίμον [*daemon*].[2]

Now according to etymology δαίμον comes from δαίο, which means to share, to divide and in the linguistic and mythical tradition has the sin-gular operative function of hiding and showing at one and the same time, of bearing the imprint of the ambiguous and making of this a quality of speech which gives voice to an event by naming it. The *daemon* arises – by surprise – in speech which relates the event as if to prevent it from being caught there *intentionally*. It is the figure of a passive-active *interplay* in whose power each modality may be reversed into the other.[3]

As we can see, what is interesting about the position which Cassirer takes and elaborates from Usener is that it places us – perhaps fictionally – at the constitutive moment of the metaphorical capacity of a language, the origin at which symbols are formed, or furthermore at the internal threshold of transformation between images and words, between the mythical and the linguistic. Not that one should hasten to distribute myth, symbol and metaphor along the same axis, at the expense of losing the complex intelligence which maintains their diachronic separation at dis-tinct levels of effectuation. Yet to have them coincide at the place and event of momentary gods inevitably means keeping in mind and not only at a minor level that this is one of the major challenges of psychoanalysis, and that in thinking about their reciprocal complication one might just touch on the significance of the remainder as an event occurring on the scene of fantasy or of the dream.[4] This then allows us to avoid losing sight of the fact that language is the only shared community between the ana-lyst and the analysand.

At the end of his book on *Language and Myth* – in which he demon-strates the close correlation between myth and language in shaping the construction of thought – Cassirer seeks to uncover *in regress* 'the ways of myth and language ..., to regress back to the point from which those two divergent lines emanate'.[5] From this point it is the function of the *meta-phorical* to decide on questions of both identity and difference between the 'mythical world' and the 'linguistic world'. Simplifying to the extreme the debates between linguists, specialists of myth and philosophers, we might say that metaphor can be considered either as the mnemic remainder of myth, the memory of which language has the capacity to preserve, or that the mythical material inherent in languages – provided we hear them speak – might be composed out of their essentially metaphorical, primitive quality. That metaphor should correspond to a sort of internal spiritual dilation of language – no longer simply serving the purpose of translating or expressing needs, but in the act of nomination that of ensuring their *corporeal transference*, the very event of their meaning, only serves to recall the evidence according to which metaphor and transference mean exactly the same thing. Both involve transport and exchange and it is speech in the presence of another which has the role of using all the resources of language to ensure the transformation of the body's state of need into the event of desire. The equivalence between metaphor and transference in Cassirer's thinking undoubtedly involves that same dimension discovered by Freud as early as *Studies on Hysteria* and even in his thinking on hypnosis; but his emphasis on the movement of *signification* as occurring with the advent of metaphor – as the moment at which naming and saying liberate language from being arrested in mythico-magical images, restoring the 'concrete actualisation' of 'pure feeling' and of the plenitude of sensation – in no way excludes the other as the advent of metaphor.[6] The reciprocal support of language and myth founds the conditions for symbol formation in culture. In some ways the symbol arises at the end of a process of mental activity, concentration and heightening of 'simple sensory experience'; it concludes the interpretive work in which language and myth are in close correlation and makes this work available – through a process of renewed interpretation – to whoever will take the trouble to garner it at the source of its auto-creative potential. Directly formulated, such an interpretation would only uncover an outline of thematised lexical signification; in other words, it would produce a dictionary of symbols. Yet interpretation is speech resonating in answer to speech and as such it is speech's debt to meaning, the heightening of what it is by what it has one hear/understand.[7] According to its anthropological definition, metaphor is language's giving birth to the presence of the other, the significance of each life event for memory that of a shared existence whose horizon is language. Once again quoting Usener, Cassirer reveals that same intuition:

> It is not by any volition that the name of a thing is determined. People do not invent some arbitrary sound-complex in order to introduce it as the sign of a certain object, as one might do with a token. The

spiritual excitement caused by some object which presents itself in the outer world furnishes both the occasion and the means of its denomination. Sense impressions are what the self receives from its encounter with the not-self and the liveliest of these naturally strive for vocal expression; they are the bases of the separate appellations which the speaking populace attempts.[8]

Cassirer continues, 'Now this genesis corresponds precisely, feature for feature, with that of the 'momentary gods'.[9]

As Strachey's *Standard Edition* of Freud's work attests, successive editions of *The Interpretation of Dreams* (between 1901 and 1914) gave Freud the opportunity for considerable complementary editing and updating, principally focused on *symbolism* in dreams (the addition of a supplementary section). There is nothing particularly astonishing about that if we recall that during this period Freud was in open discussion not only with Jung, but with Stekel, Abraham, Reik and Rank and that the point in question will be the source of continued debate between psychoanalysts well beyond this period. It is not our intention to re-establish the tenets of an extensive controversy, the interest of which has not escaped our attention.[10] What matters is rather that dimension of the Freudian wager which determines which part of the doctrine cannot be renounced – without which the dream can no longer uphold its function as a paradigm in the face of theory. The dream itself and the evident untimeliness of the transference in the present constitute the memory of *archaïsche Erbschaft* (archaic heritage). Yet insofar as the dream/transference is a memory (*Traumgedächtnis*) of infancy which defies childhood memory, it is so on an individual (ontogenetic) level, corresponding as such to an individual's singular experience of life events. These are events of perception, the importance of which recedes from consciousness and makes them meaningful for that memory which is the antimony of consciousness.[11] Insofar as dream is the principle and function of the intelligibility of memory of infancy, it constitutes the meaning of life events – but on the condition that these be heard through the dream, beyond the temporal reach of consciousness, outside the knowledge the subject has of their life. The value here accorded to dream does not lie in making of it an individual archetypal (ontogenetic) synthesis of (phylogenetic) universal mythical formations, but of recording it, in its quality of nocturnal accident, as that asocial psychical (necessarily egotistical) product whose value is commensurate with the unexpected quality it brings to thought, to remembering and to speaking before another who can *hear* it. The dream thinks, remembers and speaks transferentially. Unlocked by associative speech emerging from the hallucinatory sensoriality of its visual images (manifest content), the dream awakens the powerful hidden resources of a common language. These resources are named through the mythical dimension of language itself insofar as speech carries the dream; as Laurence Kahn has observed, it constitutes the endo-psychical.[12] We think then that for Freud – beyond mythical images and their configuration – the mythical tradition ensures the silent, veiled condition – hidden even to speech itself – of the trans-ferential metaphor signifying the event. It is this understanding of myth which makes language 'daemonic', restoring its ambiguity. Without that element of ambiguity nothing can be heard. Nothing can be heard because that would only leave a *solus ipse* and each individual would be abstracted from what they have in common with others. Belief in the dream as a solipsism, is it not upheld by *symbol interpretation* which short circuits common language, addressing itself rather to directly reading the images of manifest content and translating them into *symbols*? Freud says that symbols are at once silences (symptoms) interrupting the associative chain and cultural residues serving the purpose of resistance.[13] No *psychoanalytic interpretation* would be possible without the latent thoughts uncovered in the train of associations and would have no resonance for the patient if it did not engage with the metaphorical ambiguity of dream in the common language. In this sense interpretation is an isomorphic paradigm of the dream even as we consider that it is formed out of the dream's forgetting, with the precise purpose that it does not become hermeneutic. This is the condition according to which analytic interpretation remains individual (from someone to each one), whilst being formulated in the common lan-guage, out of its extensive metaphorical resources. When it becomes cate-goric and synthesises (through *symbolism*), analytic interpretation is a *contradictio in adjecto* especially if it emerges from a knowledge of myth and collective symbolism (the analyst would then become a *Traumdeuter* – an interpreter of dreams), even if that knowledge happened to be con-stituted by psychoanalysis itself.

The coherence of the Freudian doctrine on dream at the basis of psy-choanalytic theory is axiomatic in the sense that one could not hope to change a term or a proposition without having to change that axiomatic quality. Freud's discovery of a general theory is not issued from some kind of dogmatisation of the *Traumlehre* (theory of dreams), but rather this latter is elaborated as foundational for the site of the psychoanalyst on a clinical and technical level and of the meaning and the reach of meaning thus uncovered by the act of listening.[14] In its time Jacques Lacan's exceptional 'Rome Lecture' served to recall this.[15]

Indeed, the effects of modern psycho-sociology on psychoanalytic thinking have led to the events of a life related during the clinical encounter being conceived in line with the principles and the linear determination of temporal causality. As such, the account of the experi-ence of an event (a break-up, loss, illness, an accident) seems destined to be believed in its lived reality, understood in terms of the emotional upset produced, in the hope that a final explanation might prevent it being repeated. In this vein Freud first developed his theory of the trauma of seduction as a real event, whereby the etiological meaning of the patient's words led him to trace their symptoms back to passively experienced events of a sexual nature occurring in the early years of their childhood.[16] Freud's abandonment of Charcot's clinical thinking prevents him from relinquishing the theory (as did Breuer), but rather leads him to the discovery that the patient's account should be heard *as it is told* – in the full force of its phantasmatic conviction – and in *a state of speech in which the event of psychical trauma takes place*. The account is dramatised with the intent of influencing the thinking of the one who listens, securing their belief in the historical reality of the traumatic event and thereby posing the hysterical challenge of rendering the addressee powerless, unable to change the past unless it be 'redeemed' by a gift of love. The 'reality' of the past event is thus summoned to give credit to words spoken, which means that as their addressee the other can but *imagine* the content of the event. And the hysteric of course knows that one can only represent the content of someone's life to oneself through the imagination, and does not the hysteric's art consist in remaining forever immortal after leaving their addressee historically compromised? With the discovery of the auto-erotic function of fantasy, of screen-memory and of the persistence of infantile sexuality in the act of speech, the moment Freud designated as a veritable reversal of *for* and *against* involves the discovery of theory as the capacity to listen to speech – through the paradigm of the dream – and to hear the transferences it carries.

But let us take time to pause and reflect on this reversal of perspective, first asking ourselves if this is the right way to name a revolution which has all the appearances of a return to tradition; and if, in the wake of Freud's discovery we can even talk figuratively about perspective? For perspective is a spatial fiction produced by an objectifying conception of time; the central question here is the impossibility of putting things into perspective when faced with the a-temporality of the unconscious. Then if we uphold the view that psychoanalysis recalls the clinical tradition and medical practice of the Greeks, it is precisely in terms of that philosophical questioning in the Hippocratic corpus which sees the event as the act of a patient speaking and remembering before a doctor listening. This is the literal meaning of *anamnesis*, remembering as going back. 'It is then for each patient simply a question of remembering – while listening to the doctor – what it is that happened. If one fails to make oneself understood by laymen and does not induce this state of mind in one's listeners one will fail to reach the truth'.[17] The event is that which occurs between the patient and the doctor as long as the latter's listening has the insistence of a question for speech which does not know what it has to say. If clinical attention focuses intentionally on the scenic content of the recounted event, it denies these words their transferential potential (tantamount to the forgotten dream), thereby creating or reinforcing the hallucinatory pregnancy of the image. With that intentional attention, by dint of abstraction, psychical isolation, and the annihilation of the implied temporalities of speech, the event is rendered psychotic. The anamnesis of Hippocratic practice founds those conditions whereby the dissymmetrical positions of patient and doctor are regulated according to their distance one from the other and to the temporality of memory and forgetting, not according to the order of knowledge. 'What it is that happened to them' the patient does not know and the doctor has no knowledge of this. Unlike during a maieutic process, anamnesis has at its basis a form of remembering which concerns the opening up of words in speech. Psychoanalytic attention depends on the capacity of that speech to accord itself memory. In this sense the event is *a cluster of temporalities* which the Greeks bring together in the concept of the *aorist*. The event's exceptional quality emerges from the obscure depths of forgetting and its unpredictable becoming is a result of the immutability conferred on it by amnesia.[18] 'The Greeks understood personal life as a suspended totality, known only at its end, when it is found to have been and – whether a happy or unhappy life – only found *because it has been*'.[19] In the absence of perspective on a life and its events what we are given to know is nothing – *the life's residues in the day's present*. Yet are we led to know them only through a nocturnal disguise which has them appear as what they are not? In the psychoanalytic cure the associativity of speech is not simply present in order to undo images and fragment the dream; it demands of the analyst that s/he hear through the memory of infancy (the dream) and that while *constructing* the event that memory renounce the genetic temporalities of explanation.[20] Named in a past present, the event attains historical truth without having ever been known as remembered. Its historicity could not be that of a past time – of childhood, for example – and if we say that it puts the past transferentially in the present (*präsentisch*), it is because that past has never ceased to be present, and in a sense has never ceased to not yet happen. Freud's notion of trauma and Winnicott's notion of catastrophe both point in different ways to that manifest presence of the event in the residues of life, which for the dream are the day's residues. We are tempted to say that removing any causal quality from the event as having really taken place in the memory narrative recounting it constitutes the event as a historical truth, sealed in the intense present of sensory dream images and formed out of the day's residues which belong to *the latency of thought*. Known as *pre-conscious*, that thought is, in a sense, the activity of metaphor. And when, deserted by metaphor and rendering impossible the presence of the day's residues for dreaming or remembering the dream, the body sleeps in its waking state, this might be called depression. Is depression the albeit provisional destruction of the day's residues – of life's residues?

Analysts have trouble adhering to the idea that the dream is *Wunscherfüllung* – a wish fulfillment. Supposing that there exist dreams of confession, of mourning, reflection, relief, of hope, etc., they find it somewhat difficult to renounce the emotional connotations of the day's events, henceforth thought of as the day's residues directly transposable into dream.

According to Freud, the repetition of the 'pre-psychoanalytic error' is evident in the work of all those who, claiming to practise psychoanalysis, continue to interpret dreams by naming the affects associated with the preconscious thoughts of the previous day, knowledge of which they have obtained through the patient's free associations. This mistake comes down to according a causal function to life events experienced during the day – and thus in the same way as indigestion or any other somatic impression – to giving these the *explanatory quality* of the dream itself. This misapprehends precisely what had to be abandoned in order for psychoanalysis to be discovered: the etiological theory of the traumatic event. As we have suggested, the very abandonment of that theory signified the foregrounding of *infantile* sexuality as it inhabits the hallucinatory activity of fantasy in (transferential) speech and thus the temporal dis-intentionalising of the past event in its causal capacity. To allow a dream interpretation which concentrates on an affect attached to the previous day's lived events to subsist is in effect tantamount to making a 'pre-psychoanalytical error', a technical contradiction, the consequences of which have repercussions on the psychoanalytical status of theory. And as Freud repeats after Griesinger in his work on the *Witz*, it is the role of the dream to be that presence thanks to which the patient's symptom might be heard. The reference to the dream paradigm in psychoanalysis makes of the act of listening an act of language from which the words of interpretation emerge and that because to hear is to accord speech to the unpronounceable dimension of the infantile in the masked evidence of its manifestation in the present. Unconscious desire brings the infantile into the present while masking it. In these conditions so called 'free-floating' attention (*gleichschwebende Aufmerksamkeit*), derived from Freud's analysis of his own dreams, is precisely that associative attention (the correlative to *free association*) which espouses the anachronic time of the infantile as long as this latter is manifest (*präsentich*) and cannot be constituted as an event in the past. If the infantile event is targeted through a wish to understand the present in terms of the past, instead of being reconstructed, attention is re-intentionalised in favour of causality. We might then grasp that these representative categories of time no longer have any place in psychoanalysis.

The advantage of the notion of the *day's residues* is clearly that of thinking through the previous day in terms of the dream-work and the associations solicited by that incomprehensible nocturnal event, the dream. The event is *ultimately* that which the subject does not apprehend, that which remains unnoticed. The event is a residue of the day – and of life – that the dream's own interpretation may well make into sensory images, before spoken interpretation releases it from conscious wish-fulfilment. As a remainder, the event of the day is thus restored to its essential ambiguity, revealed precisely through the dream, by being put into words. Any wish to give the day's event a single meaning corresponds to a compliant resistance formation, with the apparent function of making the analyst's attention waver and rendering their interpretation suggestive and tendentious. The phenomenon of trauma is related to this. It is either due to a dramatisation of the event, as exposed in the narrative recounted to the analyst, or the result of a collusion between the analyst's intentional attention and the event as pre-constituted in the speech of the transference addressed to the latter. In which case the notion of dramatic event is tantamount to a protective shield-formation with the peculiarity of distancing attention from the dream to the profit of the affective charge of the day's events as lived experience and of forcing interpretation to be *responsible* for this. If interpretation engages with the day's events in this way, it is soon experienced by the patient as a direct expression of the analyst's desire and of their suggestive influence. The paranoid inversion of interpretation is one example of intentional attention to events in the patient's life and thus of that function that only the dream can accord to these in accordance with the day's residues. Furthermore, in certain difficult cases it is significant that the patient seems to seek out the sway of this attention (in an attempt to inhibit the analyst's capacity to think freely) and to succeed thereby in annulling the value of their own dreams and fantasies. The forgetting of the dream, whether by the patient or the analyst, has the correlative of reinforcing the value attributed to (often truly dramatic) events recounted from life, and captivating the analyst's attention. *Analysis in the present* – as we have named it elsewhere – consists precisely in the negation of the paradigm of the dream as referring to the a-temporality of infancy and thereby of the day's residues as such.[21] One never forgets with impunity the function of 'dreaming', the place of dream memory and the account of the dream in psychoanalytic treatment. If by any chance that happens, one soon notices that speech loses its metaphorical quality and is alienated in the expectation of exclusive comprehension from its addressee. We have called this the threat of language destruction.[22] Maybe even this threat of language destruction is related to the analyst renouncing that state between sleep and wakefulness which constitutes his/her attention to words spoken [*la parole*].

The negation of the dream and of the day's residues has the simultaneous result of the analyst's losing sight of their true *place*. Nothing can distinguish the analyst from the hypnotiser, only that s/he is unaware of intending to be one! Whereas *to be* an analyst – or to become one in relation to a certain situation regarding speech and silence – is to be able to constantly evaluate the function of the day's residue that one occupies as analyst in all the patient's forms of psychical protection.[23] Without this the transference and analytic interpretation are no doubt almost inconceivable. Let us not forget that the transference is primarily defined according to the day's residues and that its primordial significance as event draws its meaning from the intelligibility of dream.[24] This reminder serves to uncover the analyst's ego formations in the event that, failing to consider him/herself as a day's residue, s/he colludes with the patient's resistance to the extent of no longer seeing it. It is not a minor function of the dream in analysis to guarantee the operativity of the analyst's place in discerning the patient's resistance. The analyst's qualifying their own persona before the patient and for the patient inevitably brings in its wake a reactional conception of the countertransference in symbolic terms – the paternal or maternal imago – or in terms of emotional attitude (the notion of the experience of the countertransference). Technically speaking, this concept of counter-transference introduces the actuality of the event into the treatment and, favouring subjectivisation in a familiar mode, amounts in fact to another way of denying the day's residues as such.[25] The seduction scenario is left unanalysed until – wanting to be distinguished from the hypnotist – the analyst takes on the responsibility of their role. From this perspective, the whole problem of a metapsychology of psychological functioning comes to the fore. It is of no minor importance to recall that Ferenczi was the first to allude to this, that his own perspicacious judgement of psycho-analytic treatment led him to conceive of a moral psychology of the ana-lyst's consciousness (for example, the sincerity with which the analyst must be able to communicate their mistakes to the patient).[26] But that is the question concerning the difference and also the disagreement between Freud and Ferenczi – under what conditions can the theory of the dream be changed? And can that theory still be called psychoanalytic? And can we call a practice which is founded on the notion of the day's residues analytical without drawing it out of the theory of the dream?

Let us now quote the passage of 1913 from 'An Evidential Dream' in which Freud returns to the function of the day's residues:

> The so-called 'day's residues' can act as sleep disturbers and dream constructors; they are thought-processes cathected affectively from the day of the dream and which have resisted the general lowering of energy through sleep. These day's residues are uncovered by tracing back the manifest dream to the latent dream-thoughts; they constitute portions of the latter and are thus among the activities of waking life – whether conscious or unconscious – which have been able to persist into the period of sleep. In accordance with the multiplicity of thought-processes in the conscious and preconscious, these day's residues have the most numerous and varied meanings: they may be wishes or fears that have not been disposed of, or intentions, reflections, warnings, attempts at adaptation to current tasks, and so on. To this extent the classification of dreams that is under consideration seems to be justified by the content which is uncovered by interpretation. These day's residues, however, are not the dream itself: they lack the main essential of a dream. Of themselves they are not able to construct a dream.[27]

We now know that repressed childhood desire is the only factor in the formation of the dream, which accords itself modes of figurability issued from the day's residues thanks to the apparent insignificance of what appears to be negligible. In this sense, cannot the tonalities of affect associated with the day's residues be understood as infantile desire itself and thereby form the content of the analyst's interpretation? 'It is this unconscious wish that gives the dream-work its peculiar character as an unconscious revision of preconscious material'.[28] Whatever the dream's manifest content as regards the affects of preconscious thinking, *it remains* the accomplishment of repressed childhood desire. Which means that latent thoughts cannot be attributed to the dream per se. It is evidently not fortuitous that some residues are more invested in than others, but to some extent one might assume that in certain conditions every infinitesimal detail of waking life be recuperated and named associatively as a day's residue.

It is certainly not easy to know or to characterise the conditions according to which a barely noticed 'detail' of waking life may be thought of as a *day's residue*. The criteria of apparent insignificance is certainly not sufficient in justifying how this fragment of waking life is engaged, nor in explaining the release in censorship which allows the dream to make use of this apparently negligible material. Ferenczi's response might be considered in the light of the critique Freud made of those who – tempted to resort to the day's residues to give meaning to the dream – fail to recognise the presence of infantile phenomena in the dream-work, thereby cancelling the difference between the dream and latent dream thoughts. In a sense, the question as to whether a dream can be provoked by *suggestion* and whether the analyst in person has the power to influence the patient into the night hours here returns to the debate. That infantile desire at work in the dream is not influenceable is an unavoidable point of doctrine which Freud explained at length. But the position adopted by Ferenczi – in contradistinction to that of Freud – leads to a re-evaluation of what might be called the waking state and even more precisely *the daytime event of treatment* in its quality as a *life event*.

In conceiving of trauma as veritable 'psychical commotion' (*Erschütter- eung* in the sense that this word contains the idea of debris, *Schutt*), and thus as 'inhibiting every kind of mental activity and thereby provoking a state of complete passivity devoid of any resistance, the inhibition of perception and (with it) of thinking, [...], the complete defenselessness of the ego', Ferenczi has in mind the idea that the waking state corresponds to a veritable state of shock.[29] Occurring intermittently, conscious thinking is not so far removed from an activity involving suffering, and it would be preferable to assume that the waking state is generally characterised by defensive attitudes reinforcing the self's 'massification'.[30] The traumata endured by psychical life in a micro-cumulative way have an anaesthetic function through the partial disconnection of perception and motricity (passivity of many impressions in the course of waking life). Furthermore, the origin of trauma does not have its source in memory, and it is only by dint of certain lived experiences (of which the cause escapes us) that a necessity to repeat the trauma comes into play, so that it may find an outlet at the level of motricity. Then the dream occurring as a crisis amidst the paralysis of the night's sleep reestablishes the conditions for a highly sensory image perception of traumatic impressions of psychical life. Despite the dream having visual image content at its disposal, we must concede that these images are really paradoxical condensations of movement, and their intensity is equivalent to a veritable hallucinatory mode of motor discharge. According to Ferenczi, the traumatological function of the dream consists in the return of unresolved traumatic impressions seeking resolution. If the dream thus has a therapeutic function, it is because it takes on those impressions through an active metabolisation of their quality of excitement. The idea that trauma is at once a form of intrusion through an increase of internal excitement and a form of anaesthesia in the face of the awakening of psychical life is the idea implicit in the conception of the hypnotic phenomenon at the foundation of the experience of terror.[31] In these conditions the dream is indeed an activity of *psychical awakening amidst the sleep of the night*, whereas the very definition of the waking state includes a strong prevalence of hypnotic numbness which prevents what we call factors of consciousness and acts of memory having any credibility in the resolution of trauma.[32] In other words, says Ferenczi: 'the repetition tendency of the trauma is greater in sleep than in waking life; as a consequence in deep sleep it is more likely that profoundly hidden, very urgent sensory impressions will return which in the first instance caused deep unconsciousness and thus remained permanently unsolved'.[33] And a little further on he adds: 'The therapeutic aim of dream interpretation is the establishment of direct access to sense impressions'.[34]

It thus becomes apparent that Ferenczi adopts a technical perspective, which, whilst recognising a debt to the *Traumdeutung*, still leads him to join the ranks of those adept in interpreting dream through the day's residues. In so doing he introduces a small revolution into psychoanalytic thinking which does not send it back to a 'pre-psychoanalytic' era. It is through the dream that the day's residue is what it is and by attaching this to a micro-cumulative repetition formation Ferenczi meta-psychologises the day's residue in line with the theoretical paradigm of the dream, whilst in terms of technique ensuring it a referential value in the understanding of counter-transference. Thus on the basis of the analyst's recognition of aporias and difficulties occurring during the treatment there ensue original technical modifications relating principally to their perception of the traumatic impact (in line with the day's residue) of their role as analyst (the notion of sincerity in the analyst's recognition of their mistakes). The analyst's affects regarding the patient, and modifications in their attention and variations in subjective attitudes hardly perceptible to the analyst him/herself have a considerable impact on events in the psychic life of the patient. So, in what conditions can the analyst's intra-subjective perception – made manifest by ruptures in the patient's psychical process – take the form of an *experience* capable of making the traumatic event intelligible to one and the other? The answer would quite simply be that the condition is that the event be recognised as a *residue* of life and that it be brought to encounter language. It is worth noting that without going that far, Ferenczi clearly inflects his reference to Freudian dream theory in terms of the relation of dream to the development of trauma neurosis (see *Beyond the Pleasure Principle*).

In a certain way the *day's residue* has a singular quality of eventfulness [*événementialité*] which can only be understood in relation to what can be thought of as process. Thus, according to Ferenczi, the constant threat to analytic interpretation posed by symbolic interpretation is avoided:[35]

> In Freud's *Interpretation of Dreams* the wish-fulfilling transformation of the disturbing unpleasurable residues of the day is represented as the sole function of the dream. The importance of these day's and life's residues is elucidated with almost unsurpassable accuracy and clarity; I think, however, that the recurrence of the day's residues in itself is one of the functions of the dream. While following up the connections, it strikes us more and more that the so-called day's (and as we may add, life's) residues are indeed repetition symptoms of traumata. As is known, the repetition tendency fulfils in itself a useful function in the traumatic neuroses; it endeavours to bring about a better (and if possible a final) solution than was possible at the time of the original shock. This tendency is to be assumed even where no solution results, i.e. where the repetition does not lead to a better result than in the original trauma.[36]

Thought of as an endeavour to bring 'a new, more favourable and possibly lasting mastery of the trauma',[37] the dream is the nightmare *par excellence*, the nightmare which is less the 'bad dream' than it is the dream in which painful images have a quality of *insistence* at the moment of awakening and in this way demand to be related to the day's impressions concealing the symptom whereby the trauma is repeated. And as we know, the infiltration of forgotten dreams into the impressions of the previous day often refers back to that insistence of the dream which at night takes on the dramatic appearance of nightmare.

Ferenczi continues: 'Day's and life's residues are accordingly mental impressions, liable to be repeated, undischarged and unmastered; they are unconscious and perhaps have never been conscious; these impressions push forward more easily in the state of sleep and dreaming than in a waking state, and make use of the wish-fulfilling faculty of the dream'.[38] The deeper the sleep the more the impressions linked to trauma repetition are likely to appear – and this because of the anaesthetic function exerted by the traumatic event. Unlike Freud, who links trauma to an event haunting memory (at once incapable of grasping it and being released from it) and which is perhaps the motor of this remembrance in the treatment, Ferenczi defines the traumatic as an irrevocable experience of trance, which creates a silent blank, a break in speech associations.[39] We ourselves would say that the traumatic is that which makes manifest a psychical place for the destruction of language in the body (a state of being struck dumb, or hypnotised). Without the dream nothing would be metaphorisable any longer and the *essential nightmare* would be precisely a state of terror in a waking state without representation, a state of terror in which, no longer having any internal echo, words would be condemned to the status of residues of sensibility being repeated in a complaint which itself fails to become melancholic. Our clinical intuition of that state emerges from certain cases of serious depression: the patient lives constantly in the lucidity of an artificial light which is none other than the Sartrean *No Exit*. This lucidity means that the patient expresses absolute despair, without a single word being capable of naming impressions of the outside world. Things no longer provide words with sensory nourishment and so words no longer have any metaphorical capacity. This is what we mean by a destruction of language. As is here suggested, it is remarkable that such patients *cling* to the analyst in person (their voice, face, eyes, etc.) as if the dream of the night might emerge from this alone, and from this dream, language as a *resource*. Yet despair is well named precisely if it includes the failure of dream and if the person of the analyst becomes the exclusive addressee of an arid complaint [*plainte sèche*]. What has often caught our attention as regards this type of depression is that the violent cry to be heard in repeated speech renders impossible *the constitution of the day's residue* as an imprint of life possessing language. Now we must put forward the hypothesis that dream uses the day's residues and that its role is to confide them to speech which remembers its images as long as the day's impressions are pre-metaphorised in their pre-conscious state. This would amount to saying that the sensory images of the dream's manifest content are formed from the however infinitesimal linguistic implications of any perception. In such cases of depression as mentioned, we have the impression that the absence of dream does not signify the absence of dream memory, but the existence of a state of sleep in which dream can no longer take place. If we were to reserve the term *nightmare* for a waking state in which language is destroyed by unnameable terror, this would involve pointing to an extreme limit of the human, deprived of the melancholy of which the night's dream is made, so that humans may mourn the dead within their touch. In the words of Heraclitus to touch the dead is the expression of the waking thought of the dream; Freud remains Heraclitean in his insistence that the dream is our only knowledge of the event of infancy, since it is its memory. It is through the mythical (and metaphorical) potentiality of common language that analyst and patient have access to the knowledge of that event. The melancholic psychosis of dream, which is the unwitting nocturnal experience of each of us, signifies that mourning which preserves us from death while sleeping.[40]

There is a way of thinking through the event using a theory of narrative speech. In a sense speech forms seduction theory in its relation to hysteria. The event is recounted in such a way that the addressee remembers it while attributing to it a determining quality of historical causality. Whether the event is an accident, an illness, the loss of a loved one, a break-up or any other experience of violence, the event as such seems to emerge out of a narrative addressed to an absentee. This absentee is transferentially imagined as possibly being the analyst, who is expected to understand what has happened. The experience of conducting psychoanalytic treatment provides abundant illustration of the meaning here attributed to a 'real' event. Insofar as the analyst might reinforce the imaginary role of her or his own comprehensive presence, s/he in return receives in the analytic session events from the life of the patient, who seems to have experienced them as *already* related to the analyst at the very time they were being experienced. Evaluating the risk of a transferential production of the event is not a minor technical difficulty in certain treatments. In other words, what is at stake here is an event which the hysteric relates as having 'really' happened; the causal implication of this event makes the addressee a witness, and thereby responsible for it! From a technical point of view Ferenczi anticipated the condition underlying the production of the event, whereby the analyst is responsible for any event occurring in the patient's life insofar as s/he makes mistakes and doesn't recognise them. This comes down to thinking about the analyst's influence, about its source in their personal narcissism and their misrecognition of it. The analyst, for example, only needs to fall under the power of a dramatic event related by the patient for the representation of the event in the analyst's mind to have him/her speak and assume the power of their reassuring presence, without realising that the event itself is being attributed to that very presence. The apparent addressee of the narrative of the event, the analyst, is in fact its author – in exact accordance with the patient's desire to implicate them. In fact, all of the implicative aspects of analytic technique present in an exemplary way the illustration of seduction theory, here understood as a theory of the production of the event. As Deleuze has us observe, in extending an intuition belonging to Stoicism: 'The event is not that which happens (by accident), it is in what happens the pure expressed which beckons to and awaits us'.[41] We notice that in the best of cases psychopathology is the pupil of a school in the Stoic tradition, for which, as long as human experience has not accorded temporality to what happens in a possible narrative, the event does not exist.

The Freudian discovery of fantasy and of dream is involved in a process of mutation here. The fact that the event is that of the day's residues as restored by the dream and known by the dream's latent thoughts in no way detracts from the critical function habitually attributed to them. That critical function is quite simply not directly accessible and is literally incomprehensible. In Leibnizian terms (terms not indifferent to Freudian thinking) if we say that the day's residues belong to the infinitesimal realm of small perceptions it must also be said that the dream composes these in their entirety. On the condition that this entirety should become the conceptual basis of memory and not that of perception.

Dream memory has no memories [*souvenirs*] to speak of. It has only images which the dreamer believes to be in the present of their dream. The day's residues are the stuff dreams are made of. Let us say then that the day's remainder is that life event which speech uncovers while speaking – for as long as common language has access to its metaphorical resonance.

Translated by Anne-Marie Smith-Di Biasio

Notes

1 Hermann Usener, *Göttemamen.Versuch einer Ichre von der religiösen Begriffsbildung* (Bonn, 1896), frequently quoted by Ernst Cassirer in *Language and Myth*, trans. by Suzanne K. Langer (New York: Dover Publications Inc., 1946), p. 36.
2 Quoted by Cassirer, *Language and Myth*, p. 18.
3 Cassirer also writes 'Every impression that man receives, every wish that stirs in him, every hope that lures him, every danger that threatens him can affect him thus religiously. Just let spontaneous feeling invest the object before him, or his own personal condition, or some display of power that surprises him with an air of holiness and the momentary god has been experienced and created' (p. 18).
4 Take for example Stekel, Jung, Silberer, Jones, Ferenczi.
5 [Cassirer, *Language and Myth*, p. 84.]
6 Cassirer writes: 'The image, too, achieves its purely representative, specifically "aesthetic" function only as the magic circle with which mythical consciousness surrounds it is broken, and it is recognized not as a mythico-magical form, but as a particular sort of formulation', p. 98.
7 [There is a play on the double meaning of 'entendre' here, both 'hear' and 'understand'.] In the 'Project', Freud writes, 'At first, the human organism is incapable of bringing about the specific action. It takes place by *extraneous help*, when the attention of an experienced person is drawn to the child's state by discharge along the path of internal change. In this way this path of discharge acquires a secondary function of the highest importance, that of *communication*, and the initial helplessness of human beings is the *primal source* of all *moral motives*'. Sigmund Freud, 'Project for a Scientific Psychology' in *The Standard Edition of the Complete Psychological Works of Sigmund Freud Vol I* trans. by James Strachey et al (London: The Hogarth Press, 1966), pp. 295–397, p. 318.
8 [Cassirer, *Language and Myth*, p. 88.]
9 [Cassirer, *Language and Myth*, p. 89.]
10 See John Forrester, *Language and the Origins of Psychoanalysis* (London: Macmillan, 1980), especially the chapters on 'Symbolism' and 'Philology'.
11 See the notion according to which memory and consciousness are mutually exclusive (Freud, Letter 52 to Fliess [See *The Standard Edition vol. I*, pp. 233–39], the 'Project for a Scientific Psychology' and chapter 7 of *The Interpretation of Dreams*.
12 See Laurence Kahn in 'L'Écran du mythe', *L'Écrit du temps* 4 (1983).
13 For a fuller discussion of this problem see my article 'La sollicitation à interpréter' [The Incitement to Interpret], *L'Écrit du temps* 4 (1983).
14 See 'The Site of the Stranger', *L'Écrit du temps* 2 (1983) [an earlier version of Chapter 1].

15 Jacques Lacan, 'The Function and Field of Speech and Language in Psycho-analysis' in *Écrits: A Selection*, trans. by Alan Sheridan (London: Tavistock, 1977), pp. 30–113.

16 See what Freud writes in 1914 when he retraces 'The History of the Psychoanalytic Movement'. [In Sigmund Freud, *The Standard Edition of the Complete Psychological Works of Sigmund Freud vol XII*, trans. by James Strachey et al (London: The Hogarth Press, 1958), pp. 267–78.]

17 *Corpus hippocraticum*, as cited by Jackie Pigeaud, *La Maladie de l'âme* (Paris: Belles-Lettres, 1981).

18 To be compared with Paul Klee's notes: 'Let action be the exception, not the rule. Action is the *aorist* tense; it must be confronted with a static situation. If I want to act light, the static situation must be laid on a dark base. If I want to act dark, we need a light base for our static situation. The effectiveness of the action is greater when its intensity is strong and the quantity of space occupied by it is small, but with slight situational intensity and great situational extension. Never give up the all-important extension of the static element! On a medium-toned static ground, however, a double action is possible, depending on whether one considers it from the point of view of lightness or that of darkness' (*The Diaries of Paul Klee* 1898–1918, trans. by Pierre B. Schneider, R.Y. Zachary and Max Knight (Berkeley, Los Angeles: University of California Press, 1973), p. 229).

19 Henri Maldiney, *Aîtres de la langue et demeures de la penséé* (Paris: Éditions L'Age d'Homme, 1975), p. 85.

20 That construction is the memory of infancy in speech which – encountering the patient's memory – says what has taken place.

21 See Pierre Fédida, *L'Absence* (Paris: Gallimard, 1978) and 'Le Cauchemar du moi' in *Nouvelle revue de psychanalyse* 24 (1981), pp. 165–86.

22 See Pierre Fédida, 'L'Oubli du rêve' in *Furor* 8 (1983), pp. 5–12.

23 The subject of a lecture I gave in Geneva, entitled 'En personne, le psychanalyste est un reste diurne' [In person, the psychoanalyst is a diurnal residue], (unpublished).

24 See *The Interpretation of Dreams*, 'Though the preceding considerations have reduced the importance of the part played by the day's residues in dreams, it is worthwhile devoting a little more attention to them. [...] And it is only possible to do so if we bear firmly in mind the part played by the unconscious wish and then seek for information from the psychology of the neuroses. We learn from the latter that an unconscious idea is as such quite incapable of entering the preconscious and that it can only exercise any effect there by establishing a connection with an idea which already belongs to the preconscious, by transferring (*überträgen*) its intensity on to it and by getting itself "covered" by it. [...] The unconscious prefers to weave its connections round preconscious impressions and ideas which are either indifferent and have thus had no attention paid to them, or have been rejected and have thus had attention promptly withdrawn from them' (Sigmund Freud, *The Interpretation of Dreams* in *The Standard Edition of the Complete Psychological Works of Sigmund Freud Vol. V*, trans. by James Strachey et al (London: The Hogarth Press, 1953), pp. 562–63. The preference accorded to indifferent elements arises, according to Freud, from the fact that they have the least to fear from censorship: 'It will be seen then that the day's residues, among which we may now class the indifferent impressions, not only *borrow* something from the Ucs. When they succeed in taking a share in the formation of a dream – namely the instinctual force which is at the disposal of the repressed wish – but that they also *offer* the unconscious something indispensable – namely the necessary point of attachment for a transference' (p. 564).

25 In this sense the conception of countertransference presented by Searles in his book *Countertransference and Related Subjects: Selected Papers* (New York: International Universities Press, 1979) is problematic.

26 Sandor Ferenczi, 'The Elasticity of Psychoanalytic Technique' (1928) and 'Confusion of Tongues between Adults and the Child' (1933) in *Final Contributions to the Problems and Methods of Psycho-Analysis*, trans. by Judith Dupont (London: Routledge, 1994 [1955]), pp. 87–101, pp. 156–67.

27 In Sigmund Freud, 'An Evidential Dream' in *The Standard Edition of the Complete Psychological Works of Sigmund Freud Vol XII*, trans. by James Strachey et al, pp. 267–77, pp. 273–74.

28 Freud, 'An Evidential Dream', p. 274.

29 Sandor Ferenczi, 'On the Revision of the Interpretation of Dreams' in *Final Contributions*, pp. 238–43, p. 239.

30 See my paper 'L'Effet de masse' in *Furor* 10 (1983), pp. 3–15.

31 This question is addressed at length later in this chapter.

32 The Heraclitean reference is never absent from Freud's thinking, whereas not so present in Ferenczi.

33 Ferenczi, 'On the Revision of the Interpretation of Dreams', p. 240.

34 Ferenczi, 'On the Revision of the Interpretation of Dreams', p. 242.

35 See Forrester, *Language and the Origins of Psychoanalysis*. I develop this point of view in more detail in my paper 'La sollicitation à interpréter' [The Incitement to Interpret], *L'Écrit du temps* 4 (1983).

36 Ferenczi, 'On the Revision of the Interpretation of Dreams', p. 238.

37 Ferenczi, 'On the Revision of the Interpretation of Dreams', p. 240.

38 Ferenczi, 'On the Revision of the Interpretation of Dreams', p. 239.

39 Maria Torok writes: 'Ferenczi thinks trauma is present each time something stops in the session: for Ferenczi *trauma* returns amidst the silence. This bears no relation to memory recall, on the contrary it corresponds to an impossibility of verbalisation' (Interview on Ferenczi in *Le Bloc Notes de la Psychanalyse* 2 (1982).

40 See 'L'Hypocondrie du rêve', in *Nouvelle revue de psychanalyse* 5 (1972). ['The Dream's Hypochondria'; Chapter 6 in this volume.]

41 Gilles Deleuze, *The Logic of Sense*, trans. Constantin V. Boudas, Mark Lester and Charles Stivale (New York: Columbia University Press, 1990), p. 149 [translation modified].

8   The Indistinct Breath of the Image

A dream, then, thinks (*denkt*) predominantly in visual images (*in visuellen Bildern*) – but not exclusively. It makes use (*arbeitet*) of auditory images (*Gehörsbildern*) as well, and, to a lesser extent, of impressions belonging to the other senses. Also, many things occur in dreams (just as they normally do in waking life) simply as thoughts or ideas – probably, in other words, in the form of residues of verbal representations. Nevertheless, only those elements of their content (*Inhaltselemente*) that behave like images are truly characteristic of dreams, whether they are like perceptions or memories (*Erinnerungsvorstellungen*).[1]

A dream hallucinates, Freud adds. It 'replaces' thoughts with hallucinations. In this sense – regarding the *hallucinatory* – there is no *essential* difference between 'visual' and 'acoustic' representations.

What can we *say* about images as they appear in *dreams*? In a way, just this: 'the elements of content (…) behave like images' and they are 'like' *perceptions* and *memories*. What *makes* the image – as far as it would be up to the dream to decide psychologically what the image is *fundamentally* – is this silent, almost autistic, behaviour of the image in front of itself. The image neither reflects nor thinks at all since it is the screen-mirror of a vision which, deprived of speech, is without a look. It's as if the image becomes, for a moment, a face with unseeing eyes. When *facing the unfamiliar*, a *mute response* sometimes makes the face autistic. How can a face thus be the mirror of no-one [*de personne*]?

Just as Dora simply replied '*The Madonna*' when asked 'what she liked so much' about the *Sistine Madonna*, we could also simply stop there, because when Dora says the name, nothing is named.[2] She only evokes the image in so far as she expresses the impotence of the word pronounced. The image of the virgin mother is as profoundly silent as Dora's *contemplative and dreamlike admiration, for two whole hours.* 'The Madonna' invokes the visual matter, both maternal and virginal, of a mirror-like *face* in which no one is reflected. Nothing is denominated by the name because it remains asleep in the acoustic space of the nocturnal dream. We then realise that such an '*image*' is inviolable or enclosed: it is a *fixed frontal*

DOI: 10.4324/9781032637600-9

plane, placed at an infinite distance. Freud puts the word 'image' in inverted commas in his text on Dora, highlighting it as a 'nodal point' (*Knotenpunkt*) in the mesh of dream thoughts.[3]

We could then say that what we call an *image* is, *momentarily*, the effect produced by language in its sudden deafness. To become aware of this is to recognise that both in aesthetic criticism and in psychoanalysis the image *halts language*, testing words to their limit. The voice may pronounce the word, but in reality the word makes language silent. The aesthetic view fears such auratic power in the image since it thwarts any grasp of the content. It is not directed at anything.

Images certainly derive their *plastic visual aspect* from sensory matter originating in the memory and destined to be part of a narrative. But if it is indeed a question of *aspect* here (in the Greek sense of the term), then it's the *nocturnal* face of the recesses of language. The image therefore includes a strange *technique* of reversal: produce a visible and bright plasticity at the darkest juncture, provide a shiny surface for the depths plummeted. Should an image then be called the dark visual ground of something that is *made to be seen*? In this sense the image *acts*: the manifest elements of content behave like images.

We can say that the image delves into the uncertain gap between perception and memory. Characteristically, Freud avoids contradicting commonly held beliefs in this area. Not only does the image *resemble* a memory (representation) or a perception but the dream narrative seems to call upon the same conscious memory that represents lived events. It's as if the image's infamous illusory power operates openly in front of our consciousness, with us ready to believe that the image is simply representing the seen and the lived. Isn't the dreamer's endopsychic belief in their dream all the more complete because the images behave as if they knowingly occupy a grey zone of veracity regarding our perceptions and memories? Images that appear to be clearly circumscribed entities function like psychological illusions, while for the dreamer other images – occasionally even in the same dream – seem to appear only in the guise of *ghostly appearances*. Perhaps these images, which are 'ghostly like indistinct breathing', belong to the same realm as the words of the dead.[4] Hence when speech is powerless to describe them and tell their story it nevertheless senses their strange presence without being able to make out their physical outline. Like *a ghostly form of writing that is impossible to read*, the speech that gives a form to these images has both a face and a voice, but it remembers with an anachronic sense of the past, withdrawn from a definitive sense of its own present self. The analyst knows that during a session these ghostly beings will disrupt the narration of a dream and disturb the representable: without an addressee, their only medium is the empty sound of the patient's breathing. Although the image's power to captivate language ends at this point, it can still tell how its *potential epic power* will affect the voice. Hence from the start the interlocutor isn't the recipient of a straightforward dream account. Would it be going too far to say that language therefore acts as its own and only interlocutor? Speech in therapy puts plastic images at a distance and separates them. At least silence, of the listening kind, can act as the material agent for the image's arrival and restore speech's enigma. This enigma is that of memory's illegibility.

But let's not get ahead of ourselves!

In the chapter from *The Interpretation of Dreams* about 'considerations of representability', Freud considers the plastic formation of the image as the advantage of a *substitution* carried out by the dream-work with respect to so-called abstract thoughts.[5] Such a substitution by no means implies that something considered 'abstract' is somehow devoid of imagination or image: propositions, ideas and concepts belong to an intellectual activity that is called abstract because of a process of reduction that ignores the phantasmatic element that in truth cannot be removed. Here 'substitution' would be better understood as *transposition* – such that the role of the imaginary in forming the concept is not at all neglected while the organising principle of the image itself is also recognised.

We completely misunderstand the notion of the figure – and even more so that of figurability – if we overlook the fully developed propositional logic of the image. 'A thing that is pictorial is', Freud says, 'from the point of view of a dream, a thing that is capable of being represented' [*Das Bildliche ist für den Traum darstellungsfähig*] and this transvaluation into a 'pictorial language' (*bildliche Sprache*) pushes speech to revive the existential and ancestral power of words – as poets do – in a common language where the potentiality of sense includes the power of the senses.[6] It's because language in general cannot be reduced to an isolated 'function' of any one language, that the image can never become a psychological product. One might go further: when the image is treated as a solipsistic product, this is because of the power of illusion that distracts from its phylogenetic resource and therefore from its hidden memory. It is inevitable that we should turn to poetry when we are trying to understand visuality. 'There is no need to be astonished at the part played by words in dream-formation.'[7] This dream formation (*Traumbildung*, here playing on the double meaning of image-making and individual development) is inconceivable outside language. 'Words,' Freud goes on, 'since they are the nodal points of numerous ideas, may be regarded as predestined to multiple meanings (*Vieldeutigkeit*)'.[8] And then he states a little further on: 'Yet, in spite of all this ambiguity, it is fair to say that the productions (*Darstellung*) of the dream-work, which, it must be remembered, are not made *with the intention of being understood*, present no greater difficulties to their translators (*Ubersetzer*) than do the ancient hieroglyphic scripts to those who seek to read them'.[9] Finally, if one holds that the 'visual content' is the 'core' of the 'manifest "dream picture"' (*manifesten Traumbild*) and that this visual content is also central to its 'sensory form' (*sinnliche Darstellbarkeit*), the dream-work's distancing of itself from the logical links between thoughts doesn't however signify that the manifest image, even as it appears to ignore these links, has cancelled them:[10] the image does indeed seem *agrammatical*, but isn't this exactly the image's inherent advantage, meaning that we should investigate its *aspect*, its *mode of presence* and its capacity to *resemble and differ*?[11] From the metapsychological point of view, the compression or *condensation* experienced by the material form of thoughts during the dream-work, the *Verdichtung* (condensation) responsible for this sensuous figurability that is a-logical and a-grammatical, is facilitated by the preference for 'the use of words the sound of which expresses different meanings'.[12] Hence it's not irrelevant to be aware that the plastic part of a dream image respects, even in its most clearly defined visual elements, phonological conventions that are a feature of root languages. Thus we might consider that the dream – in so far as it becomes *a theory of the image* (and of the imagination) here – determines the criteria for an *obscure reading of the image*.

Although there are problems with the term 'hermeticism',[13] it nonetheless applies when images appeal to our *sight* and yet our sight forms an obstacle to any *reading* of them. And this reading cannot be based on a writing in which meaning is materialised (for example, a sentence) since this writing provides the support for words which are made of speech rather than of text. To put it another way: when an image is called hermetic, just as hieroglyphs are, this isn't because of a hidden symbolism that it's a matter of unveiling and interpreting, but because its striking visual power makes a reading impossible. We talk about a reading being impossible when the characters of the written language are unfamiliar. But we can also say this when images are not semiological codes and are not functioning within a semantic context. As at the threshold of unutterable speech, images can thus seem structural theoretically (in the way dreams do) and present themselves only *through words as if they were invisible and enigmatic points of dissemination*. This is what Paul Klee has in mind when he speaks of weighing an image – 'the nowhere-existent something or somewhere-existent nothing' which can never be simply compared in weight but 'will remain forever unweighable and unmeasurable'.[14] Klee goes on:

> The pictorial symbol for this 'non-concept' is the point that is really not a point, the mathematical point. The nowhere-existent something or somewhere-existent nothing is a non-conceptual concept of freedom from opposition.[15]

The pictorial symbol of *chaos to which the image is reduced hermetically or rather within which it concentrates* and *condenses itself* (*verdichtet*) is this 'grey point', this originary point, 'cosmogenetic' in nature:

> The cosmogenetic moment is at hand. The establishment of a point in chaos, which, concentrated in principle, can only be grey, lends this

point a concentric character of the primordial. The order thus created radiates from it in all directions. When central importance is given to a point: this is the cosmogenetic moment.[16]

In its own way the dream knows that *the image is chaos* and that it is unreadable because it is the result of a projection onto a screen and not because of the medium, which can only be – even with painting – *verbal* and occupied with naming. The radiant tension of Klee's grey point, 'which can only be grey', which *doesn't know that it is grey* nor *a geometric point* either, and which is *fundamentally the centre* of the image, is as sonorous and musical as it is pictorial. This is why his definition of 'nowhere-existent something or somewhere-existent nothing' is more concerned with a process of germination *on the surface* of the medium of a manifestation that we call an image. Now, for this to happen (i.e. for us to avoid being blinded by an image's muteness), the *presentness* of the image – as the dream thinks of it as being – still needs to mean being definitely *present*: thus the indistinct breath of the word is silent rather than mute. Under these conditions, this definite presence of the image is at once very close to the celebrated sensory clarity and precision of the manifest dream content and far away in the obscure realm of condensation. As in the case of an ideogram, the *aspect* is the site of immanent temporalities silenced by the surface of the image. In Greek, verb tenses are subordinate to the nature of the temporal process that they designate and words (as in Homer) make images the primary site of action (phonic above all), of the specific distance of encounters, of the form of appearance of the interlocutors, and of the age that they occupy in the 'oneiric' space for speech and its memory. Klee's 'grey point' generates the process of the work of the image and could therefore be pictorially what language designates by the production (or 'creation') of the aspect. Like Pierre Boulez, let's not forget that the painted surface when considered as a *surface aspect* is, for Klee, a field of potential directions and as it were develops the following:

> From a black line a kind of very precise figure, as if it's been engraved, that has an unmistakeable form, whether animal or vege-table (...). Such forms are embedded in the painting and lead the viewer's gaze in one specific and intended direction.[17]

To which Boulez adds – implicitly referring to music:

> In paintings where the movement of the viewer's gaze is not deemed relevant, there can still be a kind of undefined ground that will mean that the gaze becomes mobile and that at the same time a morphology is discovered that then causes this movement to halt. It's the only example of this kind of mental pictorial imagination of which I am aware.[18]

Egypt and also Tunisia became important musico-graphical references for Klee at a moment when he was already developing this idea of restoring to the surface of a painting temporal language directions (*Sprachrichtungen*) which generate action aoristically.[19] Quoting Wagner's phrase ('*Der Raum wird hier zur Zeit*' – 'Here time becomes space'), Boulez shows how Klee takes his inspiration from musical writing:

> He then simply gives a purely visual transcription of the appearance of this writing (...). A musician can admire how the imagination of the painter has grasped the symbols of his compositions, whose visual seduction is all the more visible as they are no longer bypassed by their meaning: they are shown for their own sake.[20]

This de-signification and musical a-grammaticalisation of the note – itself inspired by hieroglyphs – is precisely image production in the aorist thanks to the *theoretical existence* of the surface aspect. As Jean Laude has argued, Klee's images are neither expressionist nor surrealist and so never re-present, even in a dream-like manner.[21] Chinese 'grass' [or 'cursive'] script is taken literally here:

> When I write the word wine with ink, the ink does not play the primary role but makes possible the permanent fixation of the concept wine. Thus ink helps us to obtain permanent wine. The word and the picture, that is, *word-making and form-building*, are one and the same.[22]

Central to my argument is how Klee enacts a kind of unexpected reversal in relation to Freud, which in the case of poetic and pictorial work constitutes an exception that proves the rule. As Klee wrote in his diary, 'Polyphonic painting is superior to music in that, here, the time element becomes a spatial element'.[23] Polyphonic spatialisation of the surface suits the eye that is incapable 'of seeing all the smallest details on the surface with equal intensity'.[24] Changing from looking to reading – since reading is like 'grazing' – means that the pictorial surface is treated as image theory in action, which is ultimately like a *decision* taken in the present moment.[25] To the extent that we could even parody Klee's well-known phrase by saying: Art 'does not reproduce' the visible but makes it *readable*.[26]

We will now dwell on some of the consequences of this theory of the image, which is even found in Paul Klee, and which is the result of *the work of the image when seen as a theoretical process*.

1. What is certain is that the word 'theory' itself does not refer to a theory that has been previously constructed and then 'applied'. Theory is the process itself, insofar as it generates 'conceptual' objects. In psychoanalysis, it is the process (the work) of *lifting* repression (or amnesia), of bringing to light and, we might add, of *formation* (one of the many senses of the word *Bildung*).[27] In this sense, then, the image cannot be described;

since its *visuality* is often so clear and intense, the image overshadows any as yet unwritten writing about it ('secret writing', as Novalis would say), and can only invite a re-working into writing that will not describe it, but will be one of its possible texts. Louis Marin's understanding of the semiology of the pictorial image shows that he has grasped this point very clearly.[28]

2. It is therefore possible to refer to *an image as a 'trompe-l'œil'* (which is true, although not because the error involved is 'Cartesian') on account of this distinction between the visible and the readable — as Surrealism showed, an image induces 'a swivelling in the eye' (Breton), even its pulsation (Duchamp) or its convulsion (Bataille). In reality, however, it is better to evoke the hermeticism of the image when the manifest image's clairvoyance (or sensory clarity) has induced obscurity in the letter or language (the unconscious?). Seeing images as essentially hermetic allows us to think of the obscurity encountered by the eye as only resolvable by speech. Images make words groan 'under an age-old load of false and distorted sincerity', wrote Paul Celan in *Edgar Jené and the Dream about the Dream*.[29] And Celan also writes the following in *The Meridian*:

> It is very common today to complain of the 'obscurity' of poetry. Allow me to quote, a bit abruptly – but do we not have a sudden opening here? – a phrase of Pascal's which I read in Leo Shestov: 'Ne nous reprochez pas le manque de clarté car nous en faisons profession!' [Do not reproach us for a lack of clarity because we profess that for ourselves!]. This obscurity, if it is not congenital, has been bestowed on poetry by strangeness and distance (perhaps of its own making) and for the sake of an encounter.[30]

And then a little further on, 'it is true, (...) the poem clearly shows a strong tendency towards silence' and 'it is lonely and *en route*'.[31] Images light up the poem, when condensation occurs on its surface through contact with the exterior, whilst the poem's obscurity is the strange distance it affords itself as the expansive and radiant field of the literally auto-erotic temporalities of its 'poietics'.[32] This strange distance is a kind of action *aiming* at an indistinct encounter with the medium of its Unknown. It is therefore not paradoxical to say that the obscurity of the *image's shadow* in relation to speech (in painting as well!) can only be, as it were, clarified by the silence of white background – no doubt this is like blank,[33] empty space in a spatial account of time – which then has the power of *dis-semination* like the *breath* in the depth of the image. 'Make the obscure obscurer,' says André du Bouchet. Make 'the remains of the obscure' more obscure. Then: 'a word translates the muteness which carries it off... the speaking air'.[34] White, light, silence: this is Celan's 'breathturn' – the 'speaking air' of the offcuts (Du Bouchet) of the image.[35] Every image will have to be *seen* at the threshold of *speech*; the sight of each image is this overcoming of the silence of the 'speaking air'.

3. The image's *surplus* in relation to the simplicity of its basic ingredients – interwoven with its breath – shouldn't however lead us back to the Platonist 'search for true being' discussed in the *Phaedo*.[36] Like a sophist, the image is varied and undulating – perhaps even with an animal or feminine essence – but doesn't retain anything. As Socrates puts it in the *Greater Hippias*, what can beautiful images know of beauty?[37] Hippias is a sophist who can only reply to this question by rejecting it with a shrug of the shoulders, since an image of beauty produces the effect of beauty, thus *defining* it because it will always affect us. Socrates repeats his question to show the sophist that he's falling into the trap of answering the question. An image resembles an essence and even tries to *imitate* it: but in fact it sits 'beside' the essence.[38] The *philosophical* quest to *define* the image ('what is an image?') is impossible – and perennially problematic – and so it is *untenable*. Still, while throughout *Theaetetus* we learn that the *sentient being* (the *quality*) of the image can neither be known nor explained, we can say that it *affects* us, communicating or transmitting the feeling that produced it originally. It is very noticeable that in order to talk about this *sentient quality* in the *image*, Plato turns to *white*, the colour white and its production from various mixtures: the colour white is not a 'distinct thing outside your eyes, or in your eyes either.'[39] If we try to think of its 'singular being', then we have to say that it is 'something which has come into being between them' and which is 'peculiar to each one' ('*metaxu ti hekastô idion gegonos*').[40] Here it would be understandable to make a link with the third genre – neither sensible nor intelligible – which Plato uses to introduce his notion of *chora* in *Timaeus*. He defines this primary site as coming from a hybrid being that appears 'dreamlike', and whose primary and primordial indistinctness makes it very difficult to encapsulate.[41] If the colour white is 'nothing distinct in itself', *just as* the image might be the intuition of the *kind* of colour involved, should the image still be set apart from the idea and its essence? Certainly, we still need to state that this *being is* indeed neither 'outside your eyes nor in your eyes either' – yet aren't we starting to *discern* that because *white* as *image* is not a 'distinct thing' in itself, it is 'something' that *appears* and is bound to *affect* us; or it's this *thing* that we can say nothing about, that is silent and imposes silence, and that Theaetetus is wrong to want to *talk about it*, since as soon as he *talks about the image* he uses formulas that attribute too much fixity to it or too much determinacy. Just like the colour white that is a mixed composition (although that is already claiming too much regarding the image) or rather just like *a blank*, no *statement* suits either the definition of the *image* or its *delimitation*. For making a statement here is to say that it is such and such, and what is more that it is not at all like something else. Thus the talk of the sophists is false, or in the manner of the image, much too superfluous (even verbose) claiming to know what an image is when by saying that white is *thus* we *designate* it and in a way render it too *stable* – which contravenes the demands of *language*. White

should provoke silence. When we talk about the image being white, we should *say* that it is both *so* and 'not even so' *(oud'houtoss)*.[42] If during such debate, the composite white is the background to the image, its exemplum – in other words in fact both this part and not even this part of something –, then what is called a *quality* applies to the *silence* of the *logos*. To claim to understand the image would mean, where relevant, making the logos become *obtuse* or *confused* or *white* or even *black* and *white* if it involves opposites. The perspective of understanding itself would be *affected* by this *talk* of near and far. Unlike the philosopher, the sophist cannot find the right distance nor the suitable *interpretative strategy*. His definition of the image is mainly at fault for allowing words to focus on the straightforward effect they want to have on the interlocutor. This constrains the image to think of the words used as part of itself: once we talk as if we know what the image is or *what it is made of* the attempt at definition becomes *stuck*, quite different from the genre of the image (moving, unstable, evanescent) and indicative of how speech has been affected. Along the way we realise that by disputing the sophist's account of how words can master images, the philosopher can sneak in his enquiry into the desire to save the image. The *aporia* of the question truly serves to warn us about flagrant collusion between speech and image when we make the mistake of ignorantly trying to *speak for* and *about* images. *White* remains the *background* to images – more accurately *the background to the silence of the indistinct*. Or again white is the silent indeterminacy of language that an image requires. *Leave the blank or the silence of the image undefined and indistinct*: is this not the only appropriate way for language to *protect* it and prevent speech from being at fault?

Yet the image is innocent. As in the case again of *Theaetetus*, it's not a question of blaming the image for the illusions it creates but rather of qualifying the image, as with *white*, as *inherently faulty*, meaning that falseness or causing falseness doesn't apply. We could say that it is an error for speech, which is supposedly acting like a *logos*, to make a connection between an affect due to the image and what should only be seen silently as an impression of a memory trace (as we would treat the appearance of light). Erroneous connections of this kind lead to hasty recognition, speech that rushes to talk about effects despite the potential for deception and that claims to know the essence of an image. The act of recollection at play here teaches the philosopher that images are evanescent, blurred, and dissolve once transmitted by the breath of speech. And although the wax tablet of memory preserved traces of the past as inscriptions, *Timaeus* reminds us that the image is a 'dreamlike'[43] genre and that the site, the hybrid space of *chora*, is not an enclosure:

> Earlier we distinguished two types of things, but now we have to disclose the existence of a third kind *(genos)*, different from the others. Our earlier discussion required no more than the two—the model, as

we suggested, and the copy (*mimema*) of the model (*paradeigmatos*), the first being intelligible and ever-consistent, the second visible and subject to creation (...). But now the argument seems to demand that our account should try to clarify this difficult and obscure kind of thing. / (...) What is its nature—what capacity or capacities does it have? We wouldn't be at all far from the mark if we thought of it as the receptacle (or nurse, if you like) of all creation.[44]

Take the example of someone who is modelling 'all the shapes there are' out of gold while never stopping 'remoulding each form and changing it into another'.[45] If you ask him 'what is it?', 'by far the safest reply is for him to say gold'.[46]

> He should never say 'it's a triangle' or any of the other shapes he's in the process of making, because that would imply that these shapes are what they are, when in fact they're changing even while they're being identified [...] By the same argument, the same *term* should always be used in speaking of the receptacle of all material bodies, because it is never anything other than what it is: it only ever acts as the receptacle for everything, and it never comes to resemble in any way whatsoever any of the things that enter in. Its nature is to act as the stuff from which everything is moulded—to be modified and altered by the things that enter it, with the result that it *appears* different at different times (...). Anyway, for the time being we should think of there being three kinds: the created world, the receptable of creation, and the source, in whose likeness the created world is born.[47]

Compared to *Theaetetus*, *Timaeus* seems momentarily to use the same vague terms to designate the *figures* (*schemata*) as to evoke the *image* (*eikon*). But it soon becomes clear that *the act of naming*, which has the power to determine the stability of the idea or model, looks for its material in what is changing. We could perhaps say here of the *image*, 'which neither is nor is not': 'to use the same term' for *that which* 'receives' and is at the same time 'the stuff from which everything is moulded' does not consist in letting it be absorbed by the term, nor even in limiting the term to that which bears imprints, but in saying that *naming* creates a *place* each time for a 'figure', no figure being thus definitively and therefore definitionally able to be identified with its physical medium.[48] And the material (sensory) sensitivity of the medium becomes such and such by the name giving rise to a figure. The *aspects* of the medium should even be held to be the only medium worthy of the name – imagining 'real' materiality only leads us to a comparison, *like* a mother, nurse, gold, impression-bearer. So, the material of the medium can only be of the order of the 'comparison' ('compare the receptacle to a mother'). And as for the material *noun* 'dividing up into figures' and producing the changing *aspects* of the material or *aspects* as the subjectile medium of figures, this noun, which in naming acts, has as its model only the being of that to which it is compared ('compare... the model to a father').[49] And Plato goes on:

> We should also bear in mind that in order for there to exist, as a product of the moulding stuff, something that bears the whole multifarious range of visible qualities, the moulding stuff itself, in which the product is formed and originates, absolutely must lack all those characteristics which it is to receive from elsewhere, otherwise it could not perform its function. After all, if it were similar to any of the things that enter it, it would be no good at receiving and copying contrary or utterly different qualities when *they* enter it, because it would leave traces of its own appearance as well. That is why, if it is to be the receptacle of *all* kinds, it must be *altogether* characterless... The same goes, then, for that which has to repeatedly accept, over its whole extent, all the copies of all the intelligible and eternally existing things: if it is to do this well, it should in itself be characterless. This explains, then, why in speaking of the mother or receptacle of every created thing, of all that is visible or otherwise perceptible, we shouldn't call it earth or air or fire or water, or any of their compounds or constituents. And so we won't go wrong if we think of it as an invisible, formless receptacle of everything, which is in some highly obscure fashion linked with the intelligible realm.[50]

The *visible*, the *becoming visible*, could therefore share something of the material that is its medium of coming into being. Its function is *to make something visible* but in terms of the *aspect* it belongs to the *invisible order*. However, when the image *becomes visible* this isn't because it emanates (rather than originates) through a process of this kind, any more than other kinds of appearance with their qualities of *aspect, presence* or *resemblance*. There is *no* discernible structure in this process of becoming visible, except to say that the act of naming moulds a form from the medium (material of the support). If only temporarily as a form, the figure is the name, or the name is the place of the figurable.[51] And this place of the figurable, thanks to the term that outlines it against an invisible backdrop, is a *place* because of its potential virtualities. The invisibility of the material of the medium could be considered like a negative (unrepresentable) without which the name or term couldn't be this place of figurable potential. This is where *Timaeus's* expression *'dreamlike'*, which enables us to perceive *that which creates a place*, is hugely significant. A dream is nothing, which is why it is the only strange and invisible material medium which is both able to conjure visible appearances that are images (retaining their sensory quality) and is only concretely real if compared with something else, since when it comes to speech words will have to name in order to outline or delineate that which can be called *figurable*.

4. To sum up: thinking about the image and its blank foundation, considering it to be monochrome and therefore full of potential, full of indistinct possibilities which the terms seem to glimpse through the act of naming, saying that the figurable is the space spread across the invisible medium whose modulation is only knowable through the changing aspects of the image: here aporia comes into play, provided that it remains as such while reappearing. After all, the Platonist hunt for images, which is a hunt for sophists who privilege images, could scarcely result in the philosophical seizure of images. To believe in the latter is to be carried away by the effect of the image's affect and the ultimate intelligibility of the visible in its entirety. It is, in other words, like the act of faith that mirrors proclaim forlornly, flatly and lifelessly despite their proffered angles and brightness. The sophist's discourse not only makes false connections between affect and elusive traces, it even tries to ascribe the (nonexistent) stability of images to memory, as if it was a printed repository of perfectly reflected things. Any essentialist view of the image, even if couched *avant la lettre* in semiological terms, begins with this iconological framework that privileges a positivist interpretation over a critical questioning of the purpose of images.

This is why, as stated in the *Critias*, it must be argued that what is recorded in writing must be recorded *elsewhere*, on stone, tablet or papyrus, in a country other than Greece.[52] The traced (*gramme*) comes before the written (*grammata*). These writings are simple Egyptian materials produced by the transliteration of the *phonetics* of speech into Greek: they are, according to Patrice Loraux, the 'ideographic-symbolic version of the inarticulate *phonetics* of the Barbarians'.[53] While these *grammata* are formed from the material of a braided line (*gramme*), this is only possible *if derived from the language schema* – see the power of the figure in barbarian phonic material, known as 'drawing a thing in the soul'. As indeterminate and, so to speak, inconsistent as the white background of the image is, the multiple *quality* of the raw material of speech has a phonic *air*, without which words would have no sense of their possible shape (in the *Odyssey*, words are sometimes traced in the air to the point of becoming things of the air) and which undoes or transforms them according to the force and tonality of the breath. W. von Humboldt referred to the *logos* as the 'internal form' (*innere Form*) of the unpronounceable things that are in the words of languages or their background images (*Grundbild*) - which are not strictly speaking 'images', since it is the motor actions of the breath that modulate and shape these images of unpronounceable speech.[54] Or, to use the words of René Daumal in *Les Pouvoirs de la parole*, the seed-words (*sphota*), whose 'images' are 'the blossoming of a flower, the development of a bud', are the breath-words of this white language of a *logos* before another language establishes the semiological functioning of its image-words.[55] As Gustave Guillaume points out, it was the Stoics who first understood the role of the consonant root of Semitic languages (in this case, *Syriac*) in order to state the existence of a *logos endiathetos* [internal logos], where such is the tension that meaning cannot be uttered, in opposition to the *logos prophorikos* [uttered logos], which corresponds to the meanings constituted in the words of communication. However widespread this research into the phonic material of the image-word may be, what interests us here is the determination of that logical moment when a *surface of white* qualifying the image as regards its background and the *air* out of which the language of the 'offcuts' (Du Bouchet) of any image is formed seem to intersect.

This moment is indeed logical, since it does not presuppose a cryptology of archaic depths. We can see the logic at work – in the same vein as the Platonic analysis of the image we have sketched here – once the *air of the image* becomes the sole interlocutory material of speech as the subjectile support of the image. That speech is the support at this moment clearly means that the inconsistency of the image makes a virtue of its *lack* of being. For this inconsistency could just as easily make the image, like the dream, the mirror of all perceptions (see Nicolas of Cusa), in effect the equivalent of *this* silence of the surface – painting canvas or sheet of paper – whose *tectonics* order language and give it, in the activity of enunciating signs (spaces, connections and written or painted objects) a *theoretical* efficacy (always in the processual sense that theory receives in this context). At the risk of repeating ourselves, let's remember that an image cannot be narrated or described, in the sense that only the word coming from *this process of surfacing from the depth of the image is capable* of this *figurability* in a writing of unsayable language. Even if it were to be conceived of in a mystical sense, the disadvantage of seeing the image as referring to the mirror of a vision is that of reintroducing a metaphorical function to the reflection. It is certainly understandable that painting has made extensive use of this[56] and that the mystical (see Nicholas of Cusa or Meister Eckhart) or philosophical (see Leibniz) analogy of the imagination with a catoptric mirror has been used for a visionary reading of signs that our minds are incapable of perceiving. And also that a whole baroque tradition (right up to Lacan's surrealism) then amplified this analogical-metaphorical regime of the mirror-dream supposed to constitute the 'extra-reality' (or 'super-real reality') of the mode of appearance of images (whether poetic or pictorial). But doesn't the fact that this is a metaphor always run the risk of sending us back to the excess value of the image, which then gives rise to an excess of description of an iconological nature, whereas the material reality of the surface of white and of the speaking air precisely preclude these features from the 'offcuts' of the image?

As Wittgenstein put it, 'I should like to say "What the picture tells me is itself." That is, it's telling me something consists in its own structure, in its own lines and colours'.[57] Every image has propositional meanings in a field of logical potentiality. For Wittgenstein, *that* is what the image is: propositional possibilities. And in the *Tractatus*, when reference is made to hieroglyphics ('writing… that reproduces (*abbildet*) the facts it describes'), it is in the sense that a *pictorial language* (*Bildersprache*) does not echo the dubious reputation of a language of images but instead constitutes the prototype of a propositional grammar of images:[58]

> … an essential characteristic of the theory of the propositional image set out in the *Tractatus* is that the only really indispensable figurative element in language is located in the configuration or arrangement of elements that don't themselves need to be figurative.[59]

A brief comparison of this propositional theory of the image with Peirce's theory of the icon (the diagrammatic structure of the image) would interestingly take us back to Peirce's emphasis on the *value of white*, since we are deploying this idea to rid the image of its representational narrative distraction. It also enables us to think semiotically about the diagrammatic logics of the figurative *schema* that sits as closely as possible to the surface in drawing. From this point of view, no doubt insufficient attention has been paid to the structure and diagrammatic operation of Freud's own schema. It is certainly not irrelevant, for example, that the schema of the psychic apparatus in chapter 7 of *The Interpretation of Dreams* emanates precisely from dream theory insofar as it produced – in an autoptic way, so to speak – logical propositions relating to the topic of regression. And the structure of Lacan's schema, right down to the drawing of the knots, is far from having a pedagogical explanatory function, but rather concerns the semiotic propositionality of language in the image. This, at any rate, is the condition for the validity of a graphic diagram that is no longer the theoretical backdrop to over-literally illustrative or persistently hyper-metaphorical images. It is as if we had to put forward this logical-semiotic idea that the *diagrammatic drawing of the schema* shows the theoretical activity of the image – producing, in Freud's case, a theory of dreams in harmony with a theory of memory and language – and that in this sense it enables the logical potentialities of the icon to be *readable*.

André du Bouchet is certainly one of the poets who has delved deeply into this conjunction of the white material support and the air – both where there is an image and so that the image is not immobilised and is not a casualty of the aforementioned blinding of words when they encounter the visual. The texts on Giacometti (*Sur le foyer des dessins d'Alberto Giacometti* [On the home of Alberto Giacometti's drawings], *Plus loin que le regard une figure* [A figure further away than our gaze], … *qui n'est pas tourné vers nous* [… which is not turned towards us]) locate the interlinked armature of whiteness, support, air, and figure in the drawings and sculptures. One could also remove the commas and say, 'the whiteness of the support of the air of the figure':

Breath over which signs never hold sway.

Free through the darkness of our figures.

... which is not turned ...

Soaring – with their ground, vertically. Taking their ground with them.

Where a figure, in the totality of its volume, is inscribed, withdrawn from our gaze the further it advances – in 'us' – air – paper – support – who discern of it only scattered rarefied features.

(...)

The whiteness in which a figure pivots and appears to reflect, when it is already there, from one side of its volume to the other, traversed.

Figures one after the other disappearing halfway up some indomitable foundation.

Halfway, again. The very summit – halfway.

Through every volume – facing 'us' – an empty space is formed, each time marking the extreme point of a journey that places it under the scrutiny of our gaze.

(...)

... which is not turned ...

The figure is returned to the plane of its base – which appears across the space until it reaches 'us'.

The part left to the air grows, like the traversed figure that returns, reaching 'us' and entering the paper that surrounds it. Air – nothing for the eye to see – where a body, in the volume of its mass, discovers itself – at ground level – immersed. Completed with all the sheet's depth, which is already crossing it. At the centre – and always in retreat, from the expanse without threshold that allows no inter-ference, even the volume of a mountain, however fleeting. But sta-tionary for a moment. Suspended on its abyss, when it reaches us – *our* abyss.

(...)

A volume – where our gaze interrupts itself (is interrupted).

The figure – on its white elevation – is stationary for a time, marginal to its support, which grows and, as if through it, sends us back to the very depth – half hidden from view – where 'we' have a foothold.

(...)

A figure, then, that unravels as it crosses the gap that separates us from it.

... which is not turned ...

The closer it gets to 'us', the closer it discovers itself – to this support – *nothing* – paper without a figure – once again in the light.

Drawing in the air. Cutting into paper.

Right down to the materiality of this medium, removed from the grasp of signs – and made manifest as soon as it 'reaches' us. An arid support, as if blind, or luminous, free – free of figures and signs – material (which concerns us, but only in part) and which, through it, highlights the unique movement that brought it to 'us'.

A figure of distance, which ceases – at a point already closest to 'us' – to occupy a visible space...

A place like no other that strikes at the representation of located things, and gives – through them – daylight... The seat of a figure that has been partially removed, and whose peak – where it interrupts itself – holds our gaze... Support – peak and support. Less rend than the submergence of this vestige – the summit... (that which precisely takes shape of a figure in place – with us – in the air – as close as possible to 'us' – except, again...) Of 'us', nothing... Nothing, in the air – of who has breathed. Apart from a word perhaps, but a word that accompanies another breath, goes with another breath.

Drawing in the air: a figure – on the way. Visible only on the way.[60]

Mountain is a *figure*. Or, more precisely, 'to draw in the air' is to cut out a figure as if it is a 'fraction' of space. The logical result of this process is that the mountain is therefore suspended in air.

Breath can enable an image to condense – to 'fix' the suspended image after it is has been 'condensed'; hence what we must now call an 'image' (mountain, glacier, path, earth, window or house...) is not a representa-tion, not even perhaps the presentation of a presence, but instead the state of the material produced by the breath of speech at the moment of the word being drawn or written in a part of the support's blank space – the blank sheet working to distil written speech. Still, it would be going too far to suggest that there is any kind of *relation* between poetry and paint-ing. *What* is painted on the canvas is (or isn't) language: if it is, then the silent language must *rise up* from the layers of time of the pictorial surface. And what breath holds and fixes for a moment, air undoes, not to destroy it and make it disappear but instead to place it at the distance occupied by figures. 'A figure is further away than the gaze'. This 'speaking air' receives in return the drawing that is already occupied by the blank that is, like heat, an emptied silence enrobing oblivion:[61]

> mountain: like space, returning as other in its fraction, iridescent, alone, for a moment will be without name.

Cézanne.

the same moment, every time

today

is not the same.   but going back, via the language of painting, to as mute as stone.

Cézanne.

> space, in its fraction, like the instant digs again – mountain: overhanging the streets of the relation, or of the bend of the road, of the remainder formless today,

as soon as that which consumes, will have let itself be apprehended beyond, as it articulates, the word of this language whose foundation, on all sides, will then never cease to tend towards the rupture of its summits: analogous, in the sky that it will locate, to the top of an inverted crucible.

And, further on:

on this block – similar to the block of air – also articulating, I stumble without naming it: mountain.
    death here – briefly – no more distinguishable from the living, than the airless from the air yet to be breathed.

this for the transparency of the block.

block, as I'd gone to him in the meantime, I didn't get out of the painting by going there. but on this cone, and outside the term in language, from the bottom upwards, as it culminates, from its crucible, I saw - Sainte-Victoire - capsize, redden the stone of the mountain.

right on this mountain, lower down the stone of the streets we have just walked through will have drawn up.

Therefore:

in celestial grey, grey figured by white.

And:

> on its removal, speech then as a tangent

In *Painting*, the text that this quotation is from, the support ('place of disappearance') is material, substance and matter – 'sky and earth matter' – that 'wanting memory' makes *signs* 'to memory again': certainly 'language... open onto its return... the substance that is painting'. '- the substance of painting: memory is the present's conscience'.[62] Might memory and its return through language be 'painting's ground'? And is the 'matter' of painting therefore this same mute matter of memory – the matter of words? And the plane that wouldn't exist without the mountain-air support is this developed point of time – the surface is the power of the point at which 'the substance of painting' unifies day as light and time. 'Speaking today: all speech being preceded by language, painting on the empty middle'. And the displacement of the trace beyond sight already involves – through to the words used in everyday language – the deliberate neglect of the point so that the plane has already changed position. Thus there is a shared support, whether of words or of painting.

'Mountain: simply language, hunting its own disappearance.' Perhaps it's enough to know that mountain equals the uprising of the support, its 'disturbance' if this is the 'distance between speech and gesture'. Opening, certainly, but above all 'future state' of the surface and the nascent planes of the image that the memory's material paint seemed to be unaware of. Unless we have a very serious case of the usual loss of precision in the meaning of words, the support has to exist and follow the admirable text 'Matter of the Interlocutor'.[63] 'The support's power of figuration' is linked to the *always temporal distance* involved in a meeting with – it goes without saying – the *other*. The support includes the matter of an image's invisibility, the resistance of an obstacle (time) and the existence of a community of men that speech both preserves and holds in check. Thus we need to say that the support's power of figuration is the support of the other – an essential alterity – as its formulation indicates – of language that has the right amount of distance at its disposal to avoid a figure disappearing into an image.

Cézanne is credited with the idea that we can tell how absent people are from the world by seeing what has happened to all the sensations that come at birth – beyond any representation in an image. This is achieved not by painting faces and bodies in an abstract way, but instead through *language* being immanent to the act of painting, whose gestures reconnect as it were with the silent memory of the earth – as Cézanne put it, 'memory painted by man, made concrete in what he sees.'[64] He is also supposed to have said this to Gasquet: 'We see all that man has seen in painting, all he wanted to see. We are the same man.'[65]

Rather than considering Cézanne's reported sayings, even if we improve their veracity by ensuring they match his letters and other observations, it's in the work, particularly in his later years, that we find this geology of memory through *reading* 'nature' (as a 'motif' or 'model'). This reading of nature doesn't originate in an intellectual theory but in what is *seen* 'beneath the veil of interpretation'. While private troubles may have led Cézanne to theorise his artistic practice, it is more accurate to note, as Lawrence Gowing does, the extreme care with which the artist used words and therefore what he stated when looking at nature.[66] *Interpreting* (or 'representing') is different from *making* ('rendering reality'). Interpretation conceived of as a method of reading is a combination of the eye and logic. The *optic* of the eye places sight as closely as possible to coloured sensations and volumes: this optic cannot be that of representation, once it is opposed to photographic vision.[67] Logic here is a logic of construction that emanates from this optic and supports it in turn. The reading that requires of sight that it stick to 'colouring sensations' and 'coloured marks' is an activity that models itself at the surface of its slightest 'points of contact, however transitory and tenuous', as if this reading of the surface brought the logic of an object's tectonic layers into existence. In other words, the surface needs to be architectural and in line with the memory of sensations. As Cézanne wrote in one of his last letters:

> Colour sensations, which make light in my painting, create abstractions that keep me from covering my canvas or defining the edges of objects where they delicately touch other objects, with the result that my image or picture is incomplete.[68]

With reference to earlier works by Cézanne when the artist was in his 40s, C. Greenberg writes:

> Cézanne sought (...) to convert the Impressionist method of registering variations of light into a way of indicating the variations in planar direction of solid surfaces. For traditional modelling in dark and light, he substituted modelling with the supposedly more natural differences of warm and cool.[69]

Thus it was that at this period, by exploiting the full value of 'prismatic colour as the exclusive determining factor of spatial position', with the line of contours becoming more contorted, that Cézanne seems to underline a 'plane system' anchoring volumes and treating them in a logical way once the sensations have been layered. A little later in his essay Greenberg adds:

> Once 'human interest' had been excluded, every visual sensation produced by the subject became equally important. Both the picture as picture, and space as space, became tighter and tauter—distended, in

a manner of speaking. One effect of this distention was to push the weight of the entire picture forward, squeezing its convexities and its concavities together and threatening to fuse the heterogenous content of the surface into a single image or form whose shape coincided with that of the canvas itself.[70]

As Meyer Schapiro also argues, Cézanne increases the rhythmic tension between the air and the surface as if the layers of squared touches of painting striated and fibered the planes of sight whilst the light's air reinforced the solidity of the things depicted.[71] The aerial logic (Cézanne's phrase) is therefore partly produced by this geology of the surface that the artist, obstinately determined to excavate the image to the point of exploding it, cannot contain: the figural – the schematic amalgam of the air's logic and geological memory - comes through *incompleteness*. We could say that this incompleteness of the *image* (or of the painting) has an *epic* quality, which leads Kandinsky to say regarding Cézanne:

> A man, a tree, an apple, are not *represented*, but used by Cézanne in building up a painterly thing called a 'picture', the inner sonority that is called an image.[72]

It is sometimes tempting to seek certain affiliations, if not direct links, between artistic practices that differ completely from each another and are of course even unknown to each other. Cézanne's discovery of a logic of interpretation linked to a practice based on this optic of reading things, should not lead us to make parallels with Freud's discoveries.[73] Not only were these systems not connected at the time, but mapping them onto each other today, even in a speculative way, isn't productive. Yet the beginning of the 20th Century saw a change in the *concept of sight*, following on from previous changes in the nature of the image. After the image's transformation, and moving beyond the lesson of photography, the aim was to escape the tautological definition of the image, while not threatening to make it disappear through an aesthetics of the figure, or a psychoanalytical account of the figurable.[74]

The seeming muteness or tautological 'autism' of the image, as we've seen, is not due to its silence, although it can be a contributing factor (as Paul Celan has demonstrated), but rather to the psychological sophism of acts of *definition*. The hallucinatory and hypnotic nature of the visual image, which can be reductively and simplistically reduced to the doubling effect of a powerful image, can be linked to a structural phenomenon of belief that among the moderns Kant was the first to want to comprehend in terms of its optical theory.[75] To reflect on the nature of the image, whether psychic or mental, leads us to the sophistry of decisions based on belief, inevitably part of this tautology and inclined to exacerbate an isolating and naïve attitude to visual phenomena. The only thing we can say about the image is that it *is* – neither true nor false – only and simply because it is and through what it produces. Already with Freud, and as we've sensed in Cézanne – and equally with Mallarmé and Valéry – if the metaphor of an optical apparatus was methodologically solicited in various ways, it was not with the aim of thereby deriving a *photo-logic* of memory or a technique for reproducing vision. After all, we know that the fictional use of this metaphor leads to the image being overcome by the image understood as a *diagrammatic scheme* (as with Peirce, Frege or Wittgenstein) and in line with the notion that an 'icon' or 'image' has a 'propositional' structure. At this level of image analysis, nevertheless, the logico-semiotic reading of images sits comfortably with the view that they are theoretically like dreams – meaning we are talking less about a theory of the image than about one of memory and language. Molzahn's injunction, 'Forget about reading! Look!', can now pass as the motto of the future 'primitive eye' pulling off the paradox of a veritable communicative 'tautism' (Sfez).[76]

What of this tautology of the image? Interrogating the image in this way is particularly productive as it allows you to be the sophist and show precisely the theoretical underpinnings of the status of the image, as well as the way the meaning of image shifts at the same time as the meaning of *'autos'* (self) and *'taut-autos'* (same-self). Thus we might note that one contemporary use of the prefix 'self' (self-organisation, self-referential, self-poietic, etc.) overlooks Freud's distinction between autoeroticism (*Autoerotismus*) and self-preservation (*Selbsterhaltung*). The slippage from the Greek *autos* to *self* (*selbst* or *soi*), or rather the logical reduction of 'autos', removes the potential identificatory schemata and the bases for otherness that are included in autos and eros when combined (autoeroticism).[77] This is because the paradigm of autoeroticism – from which symptom, dream and transference are developed – of course concerns the status of the image directly. As noted, the aporia of the image sometimes results in a reproduction that is a psychic or cultural tautology and at other times is intrinsically determined by the dream and transference when understood in the Freudian sense of autoeroticism. The equivocal nature of the image largely stems from the constitutive ideological regime of aporia. As Georges Didi-Huberman has shown so clearly, iconology frames itself in the same way.[78]

'[D]reams behave like [the] neurotic symptoms', 'let us say, [of] a hysteric', Freud notes in *The Interpretation of Dreams*.[79] But thinking about the hysteria of a symptom enables us to see that 'suffering from reminiscences' is like being literally trapped in an image and that the suggestion of liberation under hypnosis in fact reinforces the capture.[80] All the evidence, including the observations made at La Salpêtrière, points to the image's photo-logic when seen in an excessive state. The Freudian advance in this area is the development of a theory of memory (concentric layers, stratified organisation around a kernel or a blind spot in the image). It is very striking that this theory of memory (see 'Letter 52' to Fliess) is epistemologically isomorphic with hysterical images, as if the latter were its prototype.[81] It is no less remarkable that the theory of memory developed from the present *belief* in the image – based on its muteness – subsumes the theory of language.

The dream becomes the theory of the image. Rather than the image's autism, here we are talking about a phenomenological *solipsism* that could be described as both *Präsens* – i.e. the 'temporal form' of the image of a wish that is presenting itself as accomplished – and the *removal* of the interlocutor. The image's *present presence (Präsens)* is like the state of *passive* being, completely and trustingly drawn into what is seen in the images of the night's dream. Such a present presence is indeed the equivalent of a hallucinatory snapshot as long as, however, we remember than unlike an image formed in an optical apparatus (whose model arrives just after, as per regression), this immediacy of the sensorial dream image is that of affect making up the specific sleeping and dreaming being's *solus ipse*. We could add that it is part of the affective destiny of this locus ipse to be in every sense of the word a *focus* – both an actual enclosure of time (as in Paul Celan's elegant expression 'timestead' [*Zeitgehöft*]) and a secret preserve of potent memory hidden from the image by its own passion. Freud's continual insistence that the dream is the only 'psychic product' that is incomprehensible to the dreamer ascribes the absolute enclosure of existential solipsism to the dream. And so the purely and simply psychic (or iconological) regime of the image as a phenomenon of belief would *hypothetically* be that of a veritable *eco-nomy* of the *disappearance of the interlocutor*. A manner perhaps of considering the terror that arises when somebody (*personne/Jemand*) shifts into nobody (*personne/Niemand*), in other words the nothingness of somebody-nobody occurring via the ascetically negative crystalline purity of an imageless word. In the vertiginous spiral culminating in this degree of autism, the silence of the image has seemingly been converted into manifest muteness.

Whether as a result of this erroneous interpretation or of the image's innate misfortune – to be nothing but then become itself during its enigmatic combination of forgotten memories and dream-like aphasia –, the issue of the tautology of the image's autistic definition is decided. If, as Bleuler said, autism is autoeroticism with the eros, then we now have the means to reflect on the disappearance of the interlocutor. Disappearance is manifest in the image in a plastic way (in its visuality), since what is forgotten is any allusion to having been able to see and to what was seen. Seen or touched: the Heraclitean dream of the image signifies here that the seeing involved in this kind of image in its inner hearth ('lighting a fire') is tantamount to 'touching death'. Thus, *fundamentally* the image is the mask of the memory of language, but it also robs that memory of any vision of faces. Which faces? Doubtless those of the *named* disappeared. Always the same and unrecognisable like any individual no matter which *visual*

features (aspects) are given to them by the dream, since the face seen by
the image is *fundamentally* that of the dead who cannot be remembered.
Mirrors are helpless to recover these faces! Tragic Narcissus knows this all
too well. Yet since speech comes through the act of naming, name-acts will
be able to deliver some faces, even if as fragments. And we should add
that if mourning is the work of dreams, then this process of mourning
concerns what cannot be forgotten. This is because *the faceless dead person
who is in the depth of the image* – if forgotten in name by those alive (such is
our usual justification for life) – is the very face that the dying man tries to
connect with to take possession of their death, all the while hoping that
the living will have the grace to allow his face to live on in them during
the time of mourning's memory.

However, haste is the fear of missing one's goal, and so we have gone
too quickly and will need to take a few steps backwards in order to reach
our conclusion.

It is not only a definition of the image that would be tautological, but
the image that is made tautological by the thought that tries to define it.
David Hume had anticipated this point perfectly by noting that memory
has the faculty to 'paint its objects in more distinct colours' than our ima-
ginations; in the imagination, 'the perception is faint and languid, and
cannot without difficulty be preserv'd by the mind steddy and uniform for
any considerable time'.[82] Memory therefore usually preserves 'the original
form, in which its objects were presented' and the imagination seems able
to forego challenging this capacity of memory to contribute to human
understanding strict order and arrangement in the association of ideas.[83]
But if 'an idea of the memory, by losing its force and vivacity' can
degenerate to such a degree as to be 'taken for an idea of the imagination'
or equally, on the other hand, if an image comes to acquire such force and
vivacity as 'to pass for an idea of the memory and counterfeit its effects on
belief and judgment', then – as attested by someone who pretends, simu-
lates or lies with complete conviction at his invention – images can produce and reproduce themselves in a disordered manner, leading judgment
to doubt the appearance that is imposed on our minds by the illusion that
ideas can be understood in a clear and distinct way.[84] This means that if
the image comes to alter our understanding of why its own definition is
alienated, then memory has been superseded. Charcot, a close reader of
Hume, recognised how hysteria could be like an illness undermining
physical imitation with its capacity as well for never-ending and chaotic
image-reproduction to the point where the image, iconologically, can bear
the emblematic power of the memory of suffering and of the simple gesture of its sign (the notion of 'suffering attitude'). Charles S. Peirce's later
critique of Hume may be summarised thus: the imagination of a colour
isn't more or less lively than that which the memory of it can restore to us,
it is simply endowed with a more or less clear consciousness, such that
we'll *recognise* it or not. Still, we mustn't consider as *pictures* – for example

images from dreams – images that have gained in precision from the stories that we tell about them; it is more appropriate to keep the word *image* for connoted sensations such as those produced by speech. Hence Peirce rejects the idea of a perspectival image – and indeed of a retinal image – since they lead us back to equivocations around the image:

> I will now go so far as to say that even in real perception we have no images. That the image is not perceptible on the nerves of the retina is absolutely certain, if, as physiologists tell us, these nerves, pointed like needles, tend towards the light and are separated from each other by spaces considerably larger than the minimum visible. This is revealed by our inability to perceive that there is a large blind spot towards the middle of the retina. Thus, if we have an image before us when we see, it is an image constructed by the mind at the suggestion of previous sensations (…). If we have such a visual or other image, we must have in our minds the representation of a surface which is only a part of all the surfaces we see, and we must see that each part, however small, is of such and such a colour. If we look at a speckled surface, at a certain distance, it would seem that we do not see whether it is speckled or not; but if we have an image before us, it must appear to us as either speckled or not.[85]

It is noteworthy that at this period (1868) Peirce is loosely following Humean empiricism but wants to extricate the image – both picture and image – from the illusions of its subjective psychology, based primarily on a fake reference to visual perception. In his view, this is how to avoid the impasse of the tautology of definition. It is of course by no means accidental that when it comes to tautology, philosophers and psychologists up until Freud think of the dream image as the most clearly illusory example of a visual image based on perception.[86] As Georges Didi-Huberman has noted, the most convincing semiotic distinction is between index and icon, according to Peirce's scheme. Didi-Huberman is analysing the fresco *Noli me tangere* from the San Marco convent in Florence, where the small red flowers of the field are indexical signs (stains, pure physical coloured traces, emerging from the shadow *between* the flower and the stigmata, creating the sense of a *link*) and iconic signs (the 'little red blotches would therefore be *icons* for flowers in a meadow').[87] For Peirce, the purest model of the icon is the geometric diagram:

> In the middle part of our reasonings we largely forget that abstractness, and the diagram is for us the very thing. So, in contemplating a painting, there is a moment when we lose the consciousness that it is not the thing, the distinction of the real and the copy disappears, and *it is for the moment a pure dream*, – not any particular existence, and yet not general. At that moment we are contemplating an icon.[88]

While photographs are commonly thought to resemble the objects that they represent, they in fact belong to Peirce's 'second class of signs, those by physical connection'.[89] The semiotic typology therefore has the advantage of freeing us from the aporia of the image's authority.

The interest expressed by psychoanalysis and anthropology at the end of the 19th and beginning of the 20th Centuries in 'primitive writing' – ideogrammatical writing, modelled in particular on Egyptian hieroglyphs – continued to aim to bring together the pictoriality of this writing and a phonic and sonorous source, as it were gestural, for the visual image. It is well known that in psychoanalysis this inevitably resulted in errant archetypal symbolism in the hands of Jung to the detriment of a *symbolic order*. But at the same time wasn't there the risk of denying the hypnotic and suggestive character of the image while retaining the fundamental structure of language as the only certainty – that of the unconscious?

The challenge that we come to at the provisional end of this enquiry is as follows: the image remains a realm of ambiguity, while its *theoretical* foundation – the palimpsestual dream being its paradigm – is the enigmatic interlocutor (not the addressee) of the reminiscent present of an anachronic past.[90] The 'here in two' [*ici en deux*] in the analytical situation signifies that every image establishes the temporal places of transferences. That is, as long as the analyst doesn't seek to position themselves at this point and expect to be the addressee of their *imago*.

The breath of the image is indistinct as long as it is held back by the impotence of its own narrative. The 'here in two' of the image: its affective and sensorial strength participates in speech-giving sleep. In a way this sleep, which is like hypnotic sleep, is the domain of language – at the threshold of unpronounceable words where figures are formed.

In the *Odyssey*, the air is the breath of the song as much as the sea. Images are formed, transformed and dissolve. In this context speech recovers the surface of a readable memory, once the images have seen and then forgotten.

Translated by Patrick ffrench and Nigel Saint

Notes

1 Sigmund Freud, *The Interpretation of Dreams* in *The Standard Edition of the Complete Psychological Works of Sigmund Freud Volume IV*, trans. by James Strachey et al (London: The Hogarth Press, 1953). [Fédida's reference is to the German: S. Freud, *Die Traumdeutung*, GW, II–III, p. 52. Strachey et al's translation has been adapted here to reflect Fédida's lexical decisions and emphases. Fédida keeps 'Traum' in the singular, unlike Strachey et al, while the major alteration concerns 'ähnlicher sind als': whereas Freud wrote, 'd. h. des Wahrnehmungen ähnlicher sind als den Erinnerungsvorstellungen', translated by Strachey et al as 'which are more like perceptions, that is, than they are like mnemic presentations', Fédida has turned the comparative comment made by Freud into a statement of

equivalence ('whether they are like perceptions or memories' – soit donc ceux qui sont semblables aux perceptions ainsi qu'aux représentations de souvenir).]

2 [Fédida refers to and cites here from Sigmund Freud, 'Fragments of an Analysis of a Case of Hysteria' in *The Standard Edition of the Complete Psychological Works of Sigmund Freud Volume VII*, trans. by James Strachey et al (London: The Hogarth Press, 1953), pp. 7–122, p. 96.]

3 [Freud, 'Fragments of an Analysis of a Case of Hysteria', p. 96.]

4 [Fédida puts the words 'fantomatiques comme un souffle indistinct' (ghostly like the sound of indistinct breathing) in quotation marks, as if to indicate a quotation, but does not give the source. We tend to think that he is using the quotation marks for emphasis, to highlight these words which feature in the title of his essay. He may have in mind the English phrase 'indistinct souffle' where the French word is used to mean a vascular or cardiac murmur; *souffle* also means blowing or breath; a *souffleur* is a theatre prompter or glass blower.]

5 [See Sigmund Freud, 'Considerations of Representability' in *The Interpretation of Dreams* in *The Standard Edition of the Complete Psychological Works of Sigmund Freud Volume V*, trans. by James Strachey et al (London: The Hogarth Press, 1953), pp. 339–49.]

6 [Freud, 'Considerations of Representability', p. 339–40.]

7 [Freud, 'Considerations of Representability', p. 340.]

8 [Freud, 'Considerations of Representability'. Translation modified.]

9 [Freud, 'Considerations of Representability', p. 341.]

10 [Fédida's references and citations here switch to Freud's *Jokes and their Relation to the Unconscious* in *The Standard Edition of the Complete Psychological Works of Sigmund Freud Volume VIII*, trans. by James Strachey et al (London: The Hogarth Press, 1960), pp. 162–63. We should note that Strachey et al's rendering 'sensory form' is somewhat more prosaic than the French 'figurabilité sensible', in which the reference to the question of figural representability or 'figurability' is emphasised.]

11 On this topic, see J.-F. Champollion: 'The images of gods and goddesses that cover all the various kinds of Egyptian monument are accompanied by hieroglyphic captions that always begin with three or four similar characters, which can be likened to the Coptic formula ⲦⲀⲓ ⲦⲈ ⲐⲈ or ⲦⲀⲓ ⲐⲎ, meaning this is the *aspect*, or *manner*, or *presence*, or *resemblance*. The preposition "of" always comes after this formula, expressed either by a *horizontal* or *broken* line, or by the lituus (military trumpet) with its curved top, which are always pronounced in the same way; and the preposition is immediately followed by the proper name of the god or goddess' (*Précis du système hiéroglyphique des anciens Égyptiens* (Paris: Treuttel and Würtz, 1824), p. 84).

As Jean Louis Schefer says in his truly remarkable article, 'The Image: Invested Meaning' (*Communications* 15 (1970), pp. 210–21), Champollion's manoeuvre 'consists of organising the different economic levels of the hieroglyphic system (phonemes/symbols/images) both as a specifically differential economy and as a basic system for deciphering (Greek/Coptic/Egyptian)' (p. 214).

See also Ludwig Binswanger, *Dream and Existence*, trans. by Keith Hoeller (New Jersey: Humanities Press, 1993), with the fine preface by Michel Foucault. This work deals with the whole question of the *stylistics* of the image, in relation to semantics and from the perspective of existential thinking about the dream.

12 [Freud, *Jokes and their Relation to the Unconscious*, p. 163.]

13 Sieghild Bogumil (University of Bochum) has pointed out these drawbacks in an unpublished paper on 'The Rational Order of the Discourse of the Unconscious'.

14 Paul Klee, *Das Bildnerische Denken* (Basel and Stuttgart: Schwabe, 1964), p. 3 [P. Klee, *Notebooks, Volume 1. The Thinking Eye*, trans. Ralph Manheim (London:

Percy Lund, Humphries & Co, 1961), p. 3. Subsequent references to *Das Bild-nerische Denken*, although not indicated explicitly by Fédida, will be made to this English translation, abbreviated to *The Thinking Eye*].

15 Klee, *The Thinking Eye*, p. 3.

16 Klee, *The Thinking Eye*, p. 4.

17 Pierre Boulez, *Le Pays fertile: Paul Klee*, edited with an introduction by Paule Thévenin (Paris: Gallimard, 1989), p. 166.

18 Boulez, *Le Pays fertile: Paul Klee*, pp. 166–68.

19 In his diary Klee noted the following: 'Let action be the exception, not the rule. Action is in the *aorist* tense (*Handlung ist aoristich*); it must be contrasted with a static situation. If I want to act light, the static situation must be laid on a dark base. If I want to act dark, we need a light base for our static situation. The effectiveness of the action is greater when its intensity is strong and the quan-tity of space occupied by it is small, but with slight situational intensity and great situational extension' (*The Diaries of Paul Klee, 1898–1918*, edited with an introduction by Felix Klee and translated by Pierre B. Schneider, R.Y. Zachary and Max Knight (Berkeley: University of California Press, 1968), p. 229). In a sense the 'aorist action' and 'static situation' would allow us to think of the image as a dynamic tension existing in an aorist tense of action.

20 Boulez, *Le Pays fertile: Paul Klee*, p. 101. [The correct formulation for Wagner's phrase is 'Zum Raum wird hier die Zeit'.]

21 Jean Laude, 'Paul Klee: "lettres", "écritures", "signes"', in *Ecritures: systèmes idéographiques et pratiques expressives*, ed. Anne-Marie Christin and Pierre Amiet (Paris: Le Sycomore, 1982), pp. 349–402. This is a remarkable study of text-image relations in Paul Klee.

22 Paul Klee, 'Philosophie de la création' in *Théorie de l'art moderne* (Paris: Denoël, 1964), p. 57–62, p. 58. [Klee, *The Thinking Eye*, p. 17. Fédida's emphasis. The French text quoted by Fédida pulls together some extracts from Klee, *Das Bildnerische Denken*, first referenced above, n. 14.]

23 [Klee, *The Diaries of Paul Klee, 1898–1918*, p. 374.]

24 [Klee, *The Thinking Eye*, p. 358 (translation modified).]

25 [Klee, *The Thinking Eye*, p. 359.]

26 [Klee, *The Thinking Eye*, p. 76.]

27 [Fédida's second mention of *Bildung*'s polysemy (see p. 160). It also means individual development, education and training.]

28 Louis Marin's essay, 'Stating a Mysterious Figure', in R. Bogue (ed.) *Mimesis in Contemporary Theory: An Interdisciplinary Approach Vol. II: Mimesis, Semiosis and Power* (Philadelphia: Benjamins Pub. Co, 1991), pp. 45–64 [originally published in French in *La Part de l'œil* 3, 1987, pp. 117–33], begins with St Bernardine of Siena's sermon 'On the Holy Name of Jesus Christ' and then aims 'to conceive of the articulation-points between word and image and allow painting to speak'. The 'figurability of the in-between' (in Fra Angelico's Annunciation altar-piece in Cortona), in other words of an encounter between the Angel and the Virgin Mary, makes the panel/wall between the figures an interval between the words being spoken and heard. Marin notes: '*Mystery of figur-ability*: by its very *vacuity*, as a vacuum emptied of any figure, painting would *show the invisible* condition of possibility of figures, as a space of painting, a space of light where the uncircumscribable appears within the place of repre-sented bodies' (p. 49). Throughout this text, Marin demonstrates my hypothesis that the writing of the image proceeds from the (invisible) uncovering of the figurable and thus from the theoretical process of which the image is 'capable'. In other work, Louis Marin has clearly marked this distinction between writing and describing (see for example his work on Poussin). This leads me to argue that – risking a deliberate but I believe worthwhile shorthand – from a critical

perspective regarding the art object, the implementation of the theoretical depends on the power of the writing/figurability of the image.

29 [Paul Celan, 'Edgar Jené and the Dream about the Dream' in *Collected Prose*, trans. by Rosmarie Waldrop (Manchester: Carcanet Press, 1986), pp. 3–10. In the original French, Fédida adds the name of the publication where his text about Jené appeared: *Die Pestsaüle*, an Austrian journal.]

30 [Paul Celan, 'The Meridian' in *Collected Prose*, pp. 37–55, p. 46. Fédida cites the poet André du Bouchet's translation of Celan and will engage at length with Du Bouchet's work later in this essay. The original sentence from Pascal is formulated a little differently: 'Qu'on ne nous reproche donc plus le manque de clarté, puisque nous en faisons profession' [We should not be accused of a lack of clarity any longer, therefore, since that is what we lay claim to] (Blaise Pascal, *Pensées*, ed. Alain Cantillon, 'Les Prophéties / Les Figures', Pensée A716 (Paris: Thierry Marchaisse, 2023), p. 332; Blaise Pascal, *Pensées and other writings*, trans. by Honor Levi, introduction and notes by Anthony Levi, 'XIX. Foundations of Religion and Answer to Objections', Pensée 260 (Oxford: Oxford University Press, 1995), p. 78.)]

31 [Celan, 'The Meridian' in *Collected Prose*, pp. 48–49.]

32 See Pierre Fédida, 'Auto-érotisme et autisme. Conditions d'efficacité d'un paradigme en psychopathologie', *Revue internationale de psychopathologie* 2 (1990), pp. 395–414 [reprinted in *Crise et contre-transfert* (Paris: PUF, 1992), pp. 267–86] and 'Topique des instances et topologie des réseaux: A propos du concept du soi', *Revue internationale de psychopathologie* 3 (1991), pp. 191–202.

33 [Fédida is using the different senses of the French word *blanc*, particularly that it can mean both 'white' and 'blank' in English. According to Louis Marin, Fédida had in mind 'textual, vocal and visual' connections between these two senses of the word (*une voix blanche* is a flat voice; *une écriture blanche* is colourless writing): see Louis Marin, 'The Concept of Figurability, or the Encounter between Art History and Psychoanalysis' (1990), an interview with Odile Asselineau and Marie-Jeanne Guedj, in *On Representation*, ed. Daniel Arasse et al, trans. by Catherine Porter (Stanford: Stanford University Press, 2001, pp. 554–63, p. 63.]

34 [Fédida doesn't give references for these quotations. 'Speaking air' ('air parlant') is from André du Bouchet, 'Hercules Segers', *L'Incohérence* (Paris: Gallimard, 2024 [1979]), pp. 55–99, p. 96.]

35 ['Breathturn' alludes to Paul Celan's 1967 collection *Atemwende*, as translated by Pierre Joris. We have translated 'défets' as 'offcuts', since while 'défets' could be translated as 'defects', this sense of the word is archaic in French. Fédida no doubt has in mind Du Bouchet's use of the word as a title for one of his collections (*Défets*, Paris: Clivages, 1981), where, given Du Bouchet's attention to typography and to the space and materiality of the page, it signifies something more like an offcut.]

36 [See Plato, *Phaedo*, trans. by David Gallop (Oxford: Oxford University Press, 1993).]

37 [See Plato, *Cratylus. Parmenides. Greater Hippias. Lesser Hippias*, trans. by Harold North Fowler (Cambridge, MA: Harvard University Press, 1926), Loeb Classical Library 167.]

38 An essay by Monique Canto, 'Le faux semblant et ses œuvres' [Pretence and its Works], has led me to the Platonic search for a *super-logos* that draws together all the *logos* that speak about images. The search for such a *logos* with a sure hold on the *image* is the search for a fundamental *iconology* where the notion of the *icon* would still be problematic. See also Victor Goldschmidt, *Les Dialogues de Platon* (Paris: PUF, 1947).

39 [See Plato, *Theaetetus*, trans. by John McDowell, with an introduction and notes by Lesley Brown (Oxford: Oxford University Press, 1973), 153e, p. 20.]

40 [Plato, *Theaetetus*, 154a–b.]

41 [Plato, *Timaeus*, in *Timaeus* and *Critias*, trans. by R. Waterfield, introduction and notes by A. Gregory (Oxford: Oxford University Press, 2008), 52b, p. 45.] See my essay 'Théorie des lieux'. [In *Le Site de l'étranger: La situation psychanalytique*, pp. 267–98.]

42 [Plato, *Theaetetus*, p. 65, 183a–b.]

43 [Plato, *Timaeus*, 52b, p. 45.]

44 Plato, *Timaeus*, 48e–49a, p. 40. [Waterfield notes that it is uncertain how the receptacle acts like a nurse or nurturer (pp. 139–40). We have indicated an ellipsis towards the end of this quotation, where Waterfield adds a linking phrase not in the French translation of *Timaeus* cited by Fédida.]

45 [Plato, *Timaeus*, 50b, p. 42.]

46 [Plato, *Timaeus*, 50b, p. 42.]

47 [Plato, *Timaeus*, 50b–50d, p. 42.]

48 [This paragraph contains quotations from Plato, *Timaeus*, 50b–51b.]

49 ['Subjectile', a combination of 'subject' and 'projectile', is a word borrowed from Antonin Artaud by Jacques Derrida in his discussion of Artaud's drawings, 'To Unsense the Subjectile' in *The Secret Art of Antonin Artaud*, trans. by Mary Ann Caws (Cambridge and London: The MIT Press, 1998), p. 77. In this translation of a volume originally published in 1986, Derrida notes that he has since become aware of earlier uses of 'subjectile' by the painter Pierre Bonnard in 1921, among others (p. 64).]

50 Plato, *Timaeus*, 50d–51b, pp. 42–43.

51 Georges Didi-Huberman, *Fra Angelico: Dissemblance and Figuration*, trans. by Jane Marie Todd (Chicago: University of Chicago Press, 1995).

52 [See Plato, *Critias* in *Timaeus* and *Critias*.]

53 Patrice Loraux, 'L'Art platonicien d'avoir l'air d'écrire' in *Les Savoirs de l'écriture en Grèce ancienne*, ed. Marcel Detienne with Giorgio Camassa (Villeneuved'Ascq: Presses Universitaires de Lille, 1988), p. 446.

54 [See Wilhem von Humboldt, *On Language: On the Diversity of Human Language Construction and its Influence on the Mental Development of the Human Species*, ed. by Michael Losonsky and translated by Peter Heath (Cambridge: Cambridge University Press, 2008).]

55 [Fédida is citing René Daumal, 'Pour approcher l'art poétique hindoue' in *Les Pouvoirs de la parole: Essais et Notes 1935–1943*, ed. Claude Rugafiori (Paris: Gallimard, 1972). A version in English is included in *Rasa or Knowledge of the Self: Essays on Indian Aesthetics and Selected Sanskrit Studies* (New York: New Directions, 1992).]

56 In the introduction to her 1986 translation of Nicholas of Cusa's *On the Vision of God* (N. de Cues, *Le tableau ou la vision de Dieu* (Paris: Le Cerf, 1986)), Agnès Minazzoli quotes Nicholas: 'If a painter were to make two images, one of which, dead, would in fact seem to resemble him more, while the other, less resembling, would be alive, that is to say, such that, stimulated by its object to move, it could render itself ever more conformable to it, no one hesitates to say that the second would be more perfect in that it would imitate more closely the art of the painter' (p. 17). See also A. Minazzoli, *La Première ombre: Réflexion sur le miroir et la pensée* (Paris: Minuit, 1990).

57 Quoted by Jacques Bouveresse in his very important essay 'Théorie de l'image dans la philosophie de Wittgenstein' in *Macula* 5–6 (1979), pp. 150–64. [The English translation can be found in Ludwig Wittgenstein, *Philosophical Investigations*, trans. by G.E.M. Anscombe (Oxford: Basil Blackwell, 1958), p. 142, $523.]

58 [Fédida quotes from Bouveresse, 'Théorie de l'image dans la philosophie de Wittgenstein'. The English translation of the relevant proposition in Wittgenstein can be found in the *Tractatus Logico-Philosophicus*, trans. by D.F. Pears and B.F. McGuinness (London and New York: Routledge, 1961), p. 24, $4.016: 'In order to understand the essential nature of a proposition, we should consider hieroglyphic script, which depicts the facts that it describes.']

59 Bouveresse, 'Théorie de l'image dans la philosophie de Wittgenstein', p. 154.

60 [Fédida refers to and cites from André du Bouchet, *Qui n'est pas tourné vers nous* (Paris: Mercure de France, 1972), p. 37 onwards.]

61 [Fédida echoes the title of Du Bouchet's collection *Dans la chaleur vacante* in his use of the words 'chaleur' [heat] and 'vacant' [emptied] at the end of this sentence. The volume has been translated into English: André du Bouchet, *Where Heat Looms*, trans. by David Mus (Los Angeles: Sun and Moon Classics, 2000).]

62 André du Bouchet, *Peinture* (Paris: Fata Morgana, 1983).

63 André du Bouchet, 'Matière d'interlocuteur', *La Part de l'œil 3* (1997), pp. 65-89.

64 Joachim Gasquet, '"What He Told Me …": Excerpt from *Cézanne*' in Michael Doran (ed.), *Conversations with Cézanne*, trans. by Julie Lawrence Cochran, introduced by Richard Shiff and with an essay by Sir Lawrence Gowing (Berkeley, CA: University of California Press, 2001), p. 126. This critical edition is seminal since it examines and arranges all the sayings that may be ascribed to Cézanne with a reasonable degree of certainty. Certain of the formulas noted by Gasquet as being Cézanne's are not considered to be reliable. The philosophers [Maurice] Merleau-Ponty and [Henri] Maldiney, among others, have relied on these suspect sayings. I would like to thank Jean Clay, who is a Cézanne specialist, for casting a critical eye over the use I myself have made in the past of these doubtful sayings. [The original French volume was published in 1978 by Macula: *Conversations avec Cézanne*, édition critique présentée par P-M. Doran.]

65 [Gasquet, '"What He Told Me …": Excerpt from *Cézanne*', p. 126.]

66 Laurence Gowing, 'Cézanne: The Logic of Organized Sensations', in Doran (ed.), *Conversations with Cézanne*, pp. 180–214. Gowing's extremely careful and precise study avoids hasty generalisations. His theoretical enquiry into Cézanne's technique and vision of painting is especially valuable as it is based on a chronological arrangement of the works. [Gowing's essay was published in French in the same year as *Conversations avec Cézanne*: 'Le Système de la couleur chez Cézanne' in *Macula* 3/4 (1978), pp. 84–101. It first appeared in the exhibition catalogue *Cézanne: The Late Work* (New York: Museum of Modern Art, 1977), pp. 55–71.]

67 See Rosalind Krauss, *Le Photographique, pour une théorie des écarts* [The Photographic: For a Theory of Divergences] (Paris: Macula, 1990). Rosalind Krauss's thorough investigation into the links between painting and photography particularly underlines the optical decentring that followed the radical work of Seurat and Cézanne, whereby the canvas is thought of as a retinal projection whose surface can construct external reality. [This collection of essays by Krauss on questions relating to photographic representation has not been published in English as a stand-alone volume.]

68 [Paul Cézanne, 'Letters to Emile Bernard, July 1904 to September 1906' in Doran (ed.), *Conversations with Cézanne*, p. 48 (23 October 1905).]

69 Clement Greenberg, 'Cézanne' in *Art and Culture: Critical Essays* (Boston: Beacon Press, 1965), p. 52. [Fédida omits '– and Impressionist –' before 'differences of warm and cool'.]

70 [Greenberg, 'Cézanne' in *Art and Culture*, p. 54.]

71 Meyer Schapiro, *Cézanne* (New York: Harry N. Abrams, Inc., 1960). See also Schapiro's essay 'On some problems in the semiotics of visual art: field and

vehicle in Image-Signs' in *Semiotica* 1: 3 (1969), pp. 223–42, translated into French by Jean-Claude Lebensztejn and published in the review *Critique* (315–316) in 1973. This essay discusses the non-mimetic elements of the iconic sign and their role in the making of signs.

72 Wassily Kandinsky, *Concerning the Spiritual in Art, and painting in particular*, trans. by Michael Sadleir, with re-translation by Francis Golffing, Michael Harrison and Ferdinand Ostertag (New York: George Wittenborn, Inc., 1947), p. 36. [Fédida cites the French translation by Charles Estienne, *Du spirituel dans l'art et dans la peinture en particulier* (Paris: Ed. de Beaune, 1953), p. 92, which also includes the phrase 'la sonorité intérieure que l'on nomme image' (the inner sonority that is called an image).]

73 This section is very loosely based on a paper presented in October 1990 at the Musée d'Orsay (Paris) on 'Cézanne: concave/convex, the fibres of sight and the logic of air', part of a series of talks and debates on 'When the point of view changes: Art and Psychoanalysis'.

74 Krauss, *Le Photographique, pour une théorie des écarts*.

75 Immanuel Kant, *Dreams of a Spirit-Seer – Illustrated by Dreams of Metaphysics*, trans. by E.F. Goerwitz (London: Swan Sonnenschein & Co., 1900). Reference may also be made to Jacques Rozenberg's work on Kant's optical theory.

76 Molzahn is quoted in Krauss, *Le Photographique, pour une théorie des écarts*, p. 200. ['Tautism' is a neologism coined by the French political scientist Lucien Sfez conjoining the terms autism and tautology.]

77 Fédida, 'Auto-érotisme et autisme. Conditions d'efficacité d'un paradigme en psychopathologie', and Fédida, 'Topique des instances et topologie des réseaux: A propos du concept du soi'.

78 Georges Didi-Huberman, *Confronting Images*, trans. by John Goodman (University Park, PA: Pennsylvania State University Press, 2005).

79 [Fédida refers to Freud, *The Interpretation of Dreams*, p. 522.]

80 [Fédida alludes to Josef Breuer and Sigmund Freud, *Studies in Hysteria* in *The Standard Edition of the Complete Psychological Works of Sigmund Freud Volume II*, trans. by James Strachey et al (London: The Hogarth Press, 1955), p. 7: 'Hysterics suffer mainly from reminiscences'.]

81 [See Sigmund Freud, 'Letter 52' in 'Extracts from the Fliess Papers' in *The Standard Edition of the Complete Psychological Works of Sigmund Freud Volume I*, trans. by James Strachey et al (London: The Hogarth Press, 1966), pp. 233–39.]

82 [Fédida cites from a French translation of David Hume, *Treatise on Human Nature*, Volume 1, ed. A.M. Lindsay (London: Dent, 1911), p. 18.]

83 [Hume, *Treatise on Human Nature*, p. 18.]

84 [Fédida cites and paraphrases liberally from Hume, *Treatise on Human Nature*, pp. 88–89.]

85 Charles Sanders Peirce, 'Questions Concerning Certain Faculties Claimed for Man' in *Journal of Speculative Philosophy* 2 (1868). [Fédida quotes from the translation into French by Berthe Fouchier-Axelsen and Clara Foz in *Textes fondamentaux de sémiotique* (Paris: Klinksieck, 1987), p. 95. Since the translation into French cited by Fédida differs considerably from the original English we have translated directly from the French translation, rather than reverting to the original.]

86 See the many discussions by Husserl of this important issue. In terms of the dream image specifically, see the neglected study by Detlev von Uslar, *Der Traum als Welt* [The Dream as a World] (Pfüllingen: Gunther Neske, 1964), especially the chapter on 'Die Aporie des Traums als Welt' [The aporia of the dream as a world].

87 Didi-Huberman, *Fra Angelico*, p. 20.

88 [Charles Sanders Peirce, 'On the Algebra of Logic: A Contribution to the Philosophy of Notation' in *American Journal of Mathematics* 7: 2 (January 1885), pp. 180–96, p. 181.] Peirce also states: 'I call a sign which stands for something merely because it resembles it, an *icon*' ('On the Algebra of Logic: A Contribution to the Philosophy of Notation', p. 181).

89 [Charles Sanders Peirce, 'What is a Sign?' in *The Essential Peirce: Selected Philosophical Writings 2: 1893–1913*, ed. Peirce Edition Project, ed. Nathan Houser (Bloomington: Indiana University Press, 1998), pp. 4–10, p. 6.]

90 Pierre Fédida, 'Passé anachronique et présent réminiscent: Épos et puissance mémoriale du langage' in *L'Écrit du temps* 10 (1985), pp. 23–45. Cf. the articles on the topic of 'Memory and Recollection: the point of view of hysteria' ('Mémoire et Réminiscence: du point de vue de l'hystérie') in *Revue internationale de psychopathologie* 4 (1991).

Bibliography

Original Sources of Essays Translated in this Volume

'Le Site de l'étranger' [The Site of the Stranger] in *Le Site de l'étranger* (Paris: Presses universitaires de France, 1995), pp. 53–69.

'L'Interlocuteur' [The Interlocutor] in *Le Site de l'étranger* (Paris: Presses universitaires de France, 1995), pp. 121–186.

'La Régression' [Regression] in *Le Site de l'étranger* (Paris: Presses universitaires de France, 1995), pp. 221–244. Originally in *Les Évolutions. Phylogenèse de l'évolution* (Paris: Presses universitaires de France, 1993), pp. 45–66.

'Par où commence le corps humain?' [Where does the Human Body Begin?] in *Par où commence le corps humain* (Paris: Presses universitaires de France, 2000), pp. 29–43. Originally in *Le Fait de l'analyse* 5 (1998).

'Du primitif' [On the Primitive] in *Par où commence le corps humain* (Paris: Presses universitaires de France, 2000), pp. 45–60. Originally in *L'Inactuel* 2 (1999).

'L'Hypochondrie du rêve' [The Dream's Hypochondria] in *Nouvelle revue de psychanalyse* 5 'L'Espace du rêve' (1972), pp. 225–238. Reprinted with some small changes in *Corps du vide et espace de séance* (Paris: Jean-Pierre Delarge, 1977), pp. 51–65.

'Restes diurnes. Restes de vie' [Day's Residues, Life's Residues] in *Crise et contre-transfert* (Paris: Presses universitaires de France, 1992), pp. 45–66. Originally in Pierre Fédida and Jean Guyotat (eds.), *Événement et psychopathologie* (Villeurbanne: SIMEP, 1985), pp. 168–181.

'Le Souffle indistinct de l'image' [The Indistinct Breath of the Image] in *Le Site de l'étranger* (Paris: Presses universitaires de France, 1995) pp. 187–220. Originally in *La Part de l'œil* 9 (1993), pp. 29–50.

Books by Pierre Fédida

Le Concept et la violence (Paris: Union générale d'éditions, 1977). Republished by MJW Fédition, 2012.

Corps du vide et espace de séance (Paris: Jean-Pierre Delarge, 1977). Republished by MJW Fédition, 2012.

L'Absence (Paris: Gallimard, 1978).

Crise et contre-transfert (Paris: Presses universitaires de France, 1992).

Le Site de l'étranger (Paris: Presses universitaires de France, 1995).

Par où commence le corps humain: retour sur la régression (Paris: Presses universitaires de France, 2000).

Des Bienfaits de la dépression: Éloge de la psychothérapie (Paris: Odile Jacob, 2001).

Collected Works by Pierre Fédida

Ouvrir la parole: textes choisis par Riccardo Galiani (Paris: MJW Fédition, 2014). Original French texts of the Italian *Aprire la parola: Scritti 1963–2002*, ed. Ricardo Galliani (Rome: Borla, 2012).

Œuvres complètes Vol. 1 1963–1975 (Paris: MJW Fédition, 2018).

Œuvres complètes Vol. 2 1975–1976 (Paris: MJW Fédition, 2019).

Œuvres complètes Vol. 3 1977–1982 (Paris: MJW Fédition, 2020).

Œuvres complètes Vol. 4 1982–1984 (Paris: MJW Fédition, 2020).

Œuvres complètes Vol. 5 1983–1985 (Paris: MJW Fédition, 2020).

Œuvres complètes Vol. 6 1986–1990 (Vanves: MJW Fédition, 2021).

Œuvres complètes Vol. 7 1991–1993 (Vanves: MJW Fédition, 2021).

Œuvres complètes Vol. 8 1994–1995 (Vanves: MJW Fédition, 2022).

Œuvres complètes Vol. 9 1990–1993 (Vanves: MJW Fédition, 2023).

Œuvres complètes Vol. 10 1995–1996 (Vanves: MJW Fédition, 2024).

Œuvres complètes Vol. 11 1996–1998 (Vanves: MJW Fédition, 2024).

Selected Collective Volumes by Pierre Fédida

Dictionnaire abrégé, comparatif et critique des notions principales de la psychanalyse (Paris: Larousse, 1974).

Communication et représentation: Nouvelles sémiologies et psychopathologie, ed. by Pierre Fédida (Paris: Presses universitaires de France, 1986).

Phénoménologie, psychiatrie, psychanalyse, ed. by Pierre Fédida and Mareike Wolf-Fédida (Paris: GREUPP, 1986).

Généalogie et transmission, ed. by Pierre Fédida and Jean Guyotat (Paris: GREUPP, 1986).

Actualités transgénérationnelles en psychopathologie, ed. by Pierre Fédida and Jean Guyotat (Paris: GREUPP, 1986).

Les Évolutions: phylogenèse de l'individuation (Paris: Presses universitaires de France, Colloques de la Revue internationale de psychopathologie, 1994).

Actualité des modèles freudiens, ed. by Pierre Fédida and Daniel Widlöcher (Paris: Presses universitaires de France, Colloques de la Revue internationale de psychopathologie, 1995).

L'Embryon humain est-il humain?, by Pierre Fédida et al (Paris: Presses universitaires de France, Forum Diderot, 1998).

La Fin de la vie, qui en décide?, ed. by Pierre Fédida and Dominique Lecourt (Paris: Presses universitaires de France, 1998).

Le Cas en controverse, ed. by Pierre Fédida and François Villa (Paris: Presses universitaires de France, 1999).

La Depression est-elle passée de mode?, ed. by Dominique Lecourt and Pierre Fédida (Paris: Presses universitaires de France, Forum Diderot, 2000).

L'Humain est-il expérimentable?, ed. by Pierre Fédida (Paris: Presses universitaires de France, Forum Diderot, 2000).

Qu'est-ce qui guérit dans la psychanalyse?, ed. by Pierre Fédida and Dominique Clerc-Maugendre (Paris: Presses universitaires de France, Forum Diderot, 2001).

Humain/déshumain (Paris: Presses universitaires de France, 2007).

Psychiatrie et existence, ed. by Pierre Fédida and Jacques Schotte (Paris: Jerôme Millon, 2007).

Essays and Articles by Pierre Fédida in English

'Depressive Doing and Acting: A Phenomenological Contribution to the Psychoanalytical Theory of Depression' in *Analecta Husserliana VII. The Human Being in Action: The Irreducible Element in Man Vol II: Investigations at the Intersection of Philosophy and Psychiatry*, ed. by Anna-Teresa Tymieniecka (Dordrecht, Holland; Boston, USA: D. Reidel Publishing Company, 1978), pp. 81–92.

'The Movement of the Informe', trans. by Michael Stone-Richards, in *Qui Parle* 10:1 (Fall/ Winter 1996), pp. 17–28.

'Constructing Place: The Supervision of a Psychoanalytic Cure. Psychoanalysis and Psychotherapy', trans. by Anne-Marie Smith, *The Bulletin of the European Psychoanalytical Federation* 56 (2002), pp. 17–28.

'The Body of Emptiness', trans. by Anne-Marie Smith, in *Pages/Paysages, Embodied, Figures in a Landscape* 9 (Birkhäuser, Autumn 2002) pp. 78–83.

'The Relic and the Work of Mourning', trans. by Michael Stone-Richards in *Journal of Visual Culture* 2:1 (2003), pp. 62–68.

'Anxiety in the Eyes', trans. by Patrick ffrench and Nigel Saint, in *Psychoanalysis and History* 25:1 (April 2023), pp. 83–94.

Critical Writing on Pierre Fédida

In English

ffrench, Patrick and Nigel Saint, '"Anxiety in the Eyes" Translators' Introduction' in *Psychoanalysis and History* 25:1 (April 2023), pp. 79–82.

Saint, Nigel, 'Dream Images, Psychoanalysis and Atrocity: Pierre Fédida and Georges Didi-Huberman' in *Dreams and Atrocity: The Oneiric in Representations of Trauma*, ed. by Emily-Rose Baker and Diane Otosaka (Manchester: Manchester University Press, 2023), pp. 19–38.

Smith, Anne-Marie, 'In Memoriam: Pierre Fedida, or That Singular Insistence on the Dream' in *Paragraph* 27:3 (November 2004), pp. 113–120.

Smith-Di Biasio, Anne-Marie, 'Emerging Phantom-Like from Some Other Reality: Thinking Back and the Apparition of the Feminine' in *Paragraph* 32:2 (July 2009), pp. 214–225.

Soreanu, Raluca and Dany Nobus, 'Responses to "Anxiety in the Eyes"' in *Psychoanalysis and History* 25:1 (April 2023), pp. 95–100.

Stone-Richards, Michael and Ming Tiampo, 'To Introduce Pierre Fédida' in *Qui parle* 10:1 (Fall/Winter 1996), pp. 43–48.

Stone-Richards, Michael, 'Pierre Fédida 1934–2002: a mémoire' in *Journal of Visual Culture* 2:1 (2003), pp. 69–72.

Stone-Richards, Michael, 'Depression and the logic of separation: situating Pierre Fédida's "La Relique et le travail du deuil"' in *Journal of Visual Culture* 2:1 (2003), pp. 51–61.

In French

Brun, Danièle, 'Sur l'écriture de Pierre Fédida' in *Carnet/Psy* 77 (2003), pp. 42–43.
Brun, Danièle, 'Sur l'écriture de Pierre Fédida' in 'Hommage à Pierre Fédida: le déchirement de la parole' in *Recherches en Psychanalyse* 3:1 (2005), pp. 141–144.
Cyssau, Catherine, *Au lieu du geste* (Paris: Presses universitaires de France, 1998).
Cyssau, Catherine, 'Un parcours de transmission' in *Recherches en Psychanalyse* 3:1 (2005), pp. 167–171.
David-Ménard, Monique (ed.), *Autour de Pierre Fédida: regards, savoirs, pratiques* (Paris: PUF, 2007).
Deleuze, Gilles, 'The Complaint and the Body' in *Two Regimes of Madness: Texts and Interviews 1975–1995*, ed. by David Lapoujade, trans. by Ames Hodges and Mike Taormina (New York: Semiotexte, 2006), pp. 164–165.
Didi-Huberman, Georges, *Gestes d'air et de pierre: corps, parole, souffle, image* (Paris: Minuit, 2005).
Gori, Roland, 'A Pierre Fédida, mon ami' in *Carnet/Psy* 77 (2003), pp. 40–42.
Guyotat, Jean, 'Transmission, Filiation' in *Recherches en Psychanalyse* 3:1 (2005), pp. 115–119.
James, Laurent, 'Approche de la temporalité dans l'œuvre de Pierre Fédida' in *Les Lettres de la SPF* 41:1 (2019), pp. 181–190.
Laufer, Laurie, *L'Énigme du deuil* (Paris: PUF, 2006).
Mijolla-Mellor, Sophie, 'Pierre Fédida à l'université' in *Carnet/Psy* 77 (2003), pp. 38–40.
Mijolla-Mellor, Sophie, 'Pierre Fédida à l'université','L'informe selon Pierre Fédida' in *Recherches en Psychanalyse* 3:1 (2005), pp. 163–166.
Schneider, Monique, 'De l'absence au vivant' in *Recherches en Psychanalyse* 3:1 (2005), pp. 131–140.
Smith-Di Biasio, Anne-Marie, 'Hommage à Pierre Fédida' in Maurice Corcos (ed.), *Adolescence, Arts et littératures* 26:2 and in *L'Esprit du Temps* 64 (2008), pp. 339–345.
Smith-Di Biasio, Anne-Marie, 'Pierre Fédida, lecteur de Walter Benjamin' in Claire Joubert (ed.) *Le Texte étranger: travaux 2006–2008, Travaux et documents* 43 (2009), pp. 83–91.
Smith-Di Biasio, Anne-Marie, 'Dormir, rêver peut-être': 'Time Passes' ou le monde fantôme de l'écriture au prisme de Charles Mauron et du 'souffle indistinct de l'image' de Pierre Fédida' in *Virginia Woolf, lectures françaises, Travaux de littérature* (Geneva: Droz, 2025).
Widlöcher, Daniel, 'Pierre Fédida, le psychanalyste' in *Carnet/Psy*, 77 (2003), pp. 37–38.
Wolf-Fédida, Mareike, *Psychopathologie fondamentale suivie de L'Abécédaire de Pierre Fédida* (Vanves: MJW Fédition, 2008).

Index

For Product Safety Concerns and Information please contact our EU
representative GPSR@taylorandfrancis.com
Taylor & Francis Verlag GmbH, Kaufingerstraße 24, 80331 München, Germany

www.ingramcontent.com/pod-product-compliance
Lightning Source LLC
Chambersburg PA
CBHW070328270326
41926CB00017B/3802

9 781032 637587